Executive continuity:
How to build and retain an effective management team

Executive continuity:

How to build and retain an effective management team

WALTER R. MAHLER
President, Mahler Associates, Inc.

and

WILLIAM F. WRIGHTNOUR
formerly, Vice President of Personnel,
Uniroyal, Inc.

 1973

DOW JONES-IRWIN, INC.   Homewood, Illinois   60430

To a continuity of four generations
stretching almost a century—
from Roger to great grandfather Mahler
W. R. M.

In appreciation of
my wife's encouragement
and support
W. F. W.

First Printing, October 1973

ISBN 0-87094-062-7
Library of Congress Catalog Card No. 73–82313
Printed in the United States of America

Preface

Over the last two decades leaders of business organizations have recognized that a good "farm system" is as critical to their organizations as it is to baseball. This recognition has led to the development of many new methods and procedures. However, the new methods and procedures are often a snare and a delusion. They do not lead to the result management expected—namely, a continuity of effective executives.

Since the process is an ongoing one, it takes some time for this disparity to become recognized.

This book is dedicated to those who recognize the disparity between methods and results. The title might suggest this is a "how to" book—a "cook book." This it is not. We prefer to believe we are writing to "chefs," those planning to become "chefs" and those utilizing "chefs."

The authors are deeply concerned about how to get executive continuity decade after decade in the major institutions of society. This is a result of great consequence to society in general and to each institution. In this book we will advocate a "systems approach." This is a convenient phrase implying that numerous things have to be done, in an integrated manner, to achieve an outcome which is complex.

Chief executives have executive continuity as a significant responsibility. It cannot really be delegated. This book should aid chief executives in thinking through to an appropriate philosophy for the entire organization.

We see a vital role for a staff individual or group to play. Those individuals with a staff responsibility will find the book of real assistance in designing a new overall approach or in improving upon an established program. Those in staff positions should also benefit from the specific suggestions presented and the illustrations provided by several large enterprises.

The authors are deeply indebted to the many executives who, over a period of years, worked with us on and permitted us to conduct experiments.

We are particularly indebted to George Vila, Chairman of Uniroyal, to Roy Johnson and his organization at General Electric, to Bill Daume and his staff at Monsanto, for the opportunity to develop and test our approach.

We wish to acknowledge the generosity of Exxon, DuPont, General Electric, and Uniroyal in permitting us to include illustrations of their proven methodology.

September 1973   WALTER R. MAHLER
                                                        WILLIAM F. WRIGHTNOUR

Contents

ministrative routines and results. Summary. An in-company study. Study applications. The impact of structure on future needs. The impact of the business cycle on future needs. The executive of the future for your organization: *1. Descriptive study of current executives. 2. Comparison of your executives with prevailing patterns. 3. Predicting the type of executive required in the future. 4. Preparation of position specifications.* Age and mobility analysis. Replacement planning: *Weaknesses of traditional methods. Characteristics of an effective process.* Summary.

A definition of "good" data. Why is objective data so important? Most organizations have inadequate data. Major sources of information. Analysis of sources. The accomplishment analysis program: *Purpose. Historical development. Process. Requirements.* Summary.

Four critical career crossroads: *Crossroad # 1—shift to a functional manager. Crossroad # 2—shift to managing a business. Crossroad # 3—shift to managing several businesses. Crossroad # 4—shift to institutional leadership.* Crossroad data in selected companies. Implications of crossroads data. Factors influencing growth of managers: *Early opportunities. Variety of models. Timely assignments. Experience with adversity. Multifunction experience. Coaching. Educational experiences.* Personal factors pertaining to growth. College recruiting and accelerated development: *A special recruit is needed. The recruiting spigot cannot be turned on and off. A change in orientation is needed.* Career planning and accelerated development. Initial work experience and accelerated development. Early identification is a necessity. Summary.

Coaching practices of company presidents. Does formal coaching make a difference? *Conclusion.* The Pygmalion effect in executive coaching. Suggestions for improving the coaching practices of executives. Summary.

Prevailing patterns of advanced management programs: *University-sponsored programs. Andrews study. In-company.* Potential pitfalls. Requirements that might be met by educational program. Trends in executive education. Summary.

Major factors: *Depth of management. Sound knowledge of candidates. Basic policies and procedures. Direct involvement of top management. A skillful staff contribution.* Selection procedures:

Position specifications. Candidate sources. Candidate screening. Slate preparation and approval. Candidate availability. Selection interviews and decision. Selection follow-up. The selection process at the top. Removals. International placement. Summary.

1

Introduction

Executive continuity—what is it and why should it be of concern to a chief executive? Executive continuity, like a relay race, has to do with passing on responsibility. To continue the analogy, each leg of the race must be run to best competition and the transfer of responsibility must be swift and sure. Effective executive continuity insures that each executive position is filled with a competent executive at all times. Effective executive continuity implies that each enterprise has its own farm system; the enterprise, therefore, rarely has to go outside to fill its top positions.

Each enterprise has a limited number of jobs considered to be critical. Openings periodically occur in these jobs. In some instances the openings are predictable, like a retirement. In others, they occur abruptly, due to such factors as a sudden death or an unexpected resignation. Executive continuity insures that a qualified individual is ready to step into any opening that occurs in any of the critical positions.

We use the term executive to refer to the individuals occupying critical positions. Such positions would include the top officers of the organization. They would also include positions near the top of the organization. More often than not the individuals in these critical positions would be generalists. The term *generalist* implies direct supervision of an overall organization. In a business organization the generalist would supervise managers of major functions such as marketing and manufacturing. The generalist might well supervise a level of general managers. These positions are usually given a group title.

A SOURCE OF CONCERN TO TOP MANAGEMENT

Executive continuity is a significant source of concern to top executives. Two recent studies of top management provide documentation of this concern. Professor Paul Holden of Stanford University recently repeated a study of top management in large manufacturing organizations after an interval of 25 years. One major area of study was the selection and development of executive personnel. Holden makes the following broad generalization:*

> The chief executive officers of the fifteen large companies visited expressed primary concern over their company's short-term and long-term plans and programs for the selection and development of executive personnel. Although the degree of top-executive involvement varied considerably in the fifteen companies studied, it was crystal clear at every company that this activity merited a top priority position in terms of the president's time and attention. One president expressed this by saying: "The selection and development of managerial and executive talent will be our number one problem during the next ten years." Another chief executive officer said: "People are the basis of our success. The only way to make everyone in the corporation take a strong interest in the development of people is for me to lead the way in becoming personally involved in the selection and development of the young men who are destined to become the future leaders of the corporation."
>
> There was general recognition of the increasing need to accelerate the flow of top quality executives to meet the new managerial challenges of an expanding economy and to cope with significantly more complex problems caused by technological and social changes. Frequent mention was made of the constant shortage of imaginative, flexible, and broad-gauged managerial personnel with a capability in general management.[1]

Professor George Steiner of the University of California at Los Angeles conducted a study of strategic factors related to business success. He asked 250 business executives to rate the importance of 71 factors to the success of the company in the future. The five strategic factors rated the most important for future success of the companies surveyed, in order of importance, were:

1. Attracting high quality top management.
2. Developing future managers for domestic operations.
3. Motivating a sufficient managerial drive for profits.
4. Assuring better judgment, creativity, and imagination in decision-making at top management levels.
5. Perceiving new needs and opportunities for profit.[2]

It is noteworthy that the top three factors have to do with executive continuity.

---

*From *Top Management* by Holden, Pederson, and Germane. Copyright 1968, McGraw-Hill Book Company. Used with permission of McGraw-Hill Book Company.

REASONS FOR CONCERN ABOUT EXECUTIVE CONTINUITY

An immediate and rather personal reason has to do with the chief executive's future financial situation. Will his successor manage in such a way that the value of his stock will be sustained or enhanced? Will he feel like buying or selling company stock upon leaving and turning the reins over to the new, younger team?

Obviously there are more basic reasons for the chief executive's concern about executive continuity than his personal situation. A company is an ongoing enterprise. Its continued success has a big impact on stockholders, on current personnel, on customers, on suppliers, on retirees, on taxing agencies and, often, on governmental relations, particularly in global enterprises. There are, therefore, both basic and personal reasons for the chief executive's concern about executive continuity. There is another important reason. If the chief executive is not concerned, no one else in the organization is likely to be. Stated more bluntly, executive continuity is one responsibility chief executive officers find they cannot delegate.

Chief executives have always taken a very keen interest in cash flow. They are beginning to take the same interest in *people flow*, another apt term for executive continuity.

THE CRITICAL NATURE OF EXECUTIVE CONTINUITY EFFORTS

The importance of executive continuity has been well stated by management consultant, author, and educator Peter Drucker.

> Let me say that I believe there are few things which are so important, not only to the individual business but to the country, as a sound executive development program to meet the problem of, where do tomorrow's executives come from? Now when you talk to management people about executive development and why they are interested in it, they rightly and understandably begin with the needs of their own company. Frankly I don't think that is the starting point. I think there is one aspect of the concern for tomorrow's management which we, in management, tend to forget, but which may very well be as important as the contribution to our own business and to American management in general.
>
> The question of tomorrow's management is, above all, a concern of our society. Let me put it bluntly—we have reached a point where we simply will not be able to tolerate as a country, as a Society, as a government, the danger that anyone of our major companies will decline or collapse because it has not made adequate provisions for management succession.
>
> Unless we in management anticipate this responsibility and can prove to society that we can take care of this problem, we are bound to get government regulation. This is one of the areas in which an industrial

society will be left to private enterprise only if private enterprise can convince the public that it is doing a job and is recognizing its responsibility.[3]

Drucker's comments were made in 1953. They were made long before society had to come to the rescue of a railroad and an airplane builder. Drucker went on to caution that the great surge of interest in executive development may not be built on a sound, solid base for real development. He worried about the stress on technique, on method and leaving the task to newly created staff groups.

Drucker's concerns of two decades ago were well justified. One large organization that got started with the entire paraphernalia of executive development in the late 1940s was the Uniroyal organization. A decade later the chief executive officer faced the unpleasant conclusion that he was in no better position to appoint competent executives to key positions than he had been ten years earlier. He commissioned H. Gordon Smith, a recently retired executive vice president, to find out why. An intensive study of both Uniroyal and other major companies led this executive to the following conclusions:

Over the last ten to fifteen years, the term "executive development" has been quite largely misused in business generally and in our own organization. Consciously or unconsciously, "executive development" has come to mean the procedures or tools set up in organizations, either with the belief that providing these tools would assure good executives or because it has become the custom or fashion of organizations which consider themselves progressive to set up such tools. Thus, organizations have established:
--a plan of annual recruitment from universities and engineering schools;
--formal training courses within their own organizations;
--annual appraisals of the work and future potential of individuals considered eligible for future promotion;
--organization replacement charts;
--the use of psychological tests as part of employment procedures and/or in consideration for promotions;
--provided job descriptions, or adopted various other procedures.
These organizations assume that they have established "management development" within their organizations. They have proceeded on the assumption, which sometimes proved grossly misleading, that these procedures would more or less automatically develop good executives. In our own organization, we have also used the tools of sending apparently promising men for several weeks refresher training at various business schools and other educational institutions, and obtained lists of men annually who are considered most promising prospects for top executive posts.

Many of these are good tools and they have sometimes helped us obtain good results. Too often, however, it has seemed that the good has been principally in the lower levels of business organizations and the need for qualified men for the most important higher executive positions has not been satisfactorily met.

In too many cases in the past, both in other organizations and in ours, there has not been a consistent, clear distinction between the methods and procedures which are the tools of executive development and the actual production of qualified executives. These methods and procedures can well be likened to power tools. Carefully and skillfully used in situations which call for the use of these tools, they can help produce a better product more quickly than can be done without them. Carelessly or ignorantly used, they can ruin the product and may seriously injure the user.

All of us concerned with this responsibility need continually to remind ourselves, "Our job is to develop competent men who will manage our business successfully." Nothing short of the actual experience of getting successful management from men whom we have helped develop can be called effective executive development.[4]

The attitude of top management toward the importance of executive development is well revealed by a comment made by Crawford H. Greenwalt, former President of DuPont, in a speech to security analysts:

This is a question not only of return realized on money but I think even more importantly the return realized on the managerial talent which has to be allocated to these various developments. It is frequently true that a dying business or a pedestrian business requires a higher degree of managerial talent to keep it alive than a young, healthy growing business. I think that so far as management talent is concerned you never really have enough. You always like to have a whole stable full of bright, able people and you're always struggling to find them. It's much harder to find really good, competent management than it is to find a hundred million dollars.[5]

The National Industrial Conference Board took a look at top executive positions in a report entitled *The Chief Executive and His Job*. Many of their findings pertain to executive continuity. Four Conference Board conclusions were:

1. Generalized, the answer to the overall question; "To whom is the chief executive accountable, and for what?" is: The chief executive is ultimately accountable principally to the owners, but also to the employees, to the customers, to the community, and to himself for:
   --Growth in assets, sales, and profits.
   --Character (reputation, esteem, status) of the company.

––Perpetuation, as evidenced by the company's capacity to sustain its momentum, and most particularly by the internal management capability developed by the chief executive. The effect of any chief executive's decisions are not limited to his particular period in office. The decisions and actions that emerge as having the most vital after-effects, in the eyes of most chief executives responding to the Conference Board study, are those related to the management personnel he has selected and developed, particularly his successor.

2. The 200 chief executives involved in the study went on to identify eight more important duties or responsibilities. Among the eight were two which had to do with executive continuity:

––Organization and key executive selection and development. Next to establishing objectives and policies, the job of organizing and selecting key executives is most frequently mentioned by the chief executive.

––Development and designation of a successor. While generally conceded to be a board responsibility, most chief executives have a large say in designating who the board will consider.

3. Executives were asked to identify their real problems—those aspects of the business that are consistently most perplexing. By far the most perplexing problem is said to be people, particularly people who will manage the business. Three out of five chief executives single out people problems as their major concern.

4. When talking about their main job satisfactions, the two top ranked sources of satisfaction were:

––Satisfaction of knowing he has proved himself capable of heading a business.

––The satisfaction of having encouraged the personal growth of other individuals.[6]

In summary, executive continuity is an ever present challenge for top officers of organizations, both large and small. The last two decades have seen a great increase in techniques and methods. But are competent executives available when needed? Often not. This is the critical challenge to which we address ourselves in this book. How can an organization be assured that executive continuity is really achieved. How can the chief executive be assured that key positions are filled with competent men in the future—not only tomorrow, but next year and 5, 10, and 25 years from now.

A SYSTEMS APPROACH IS NECESSARY

We firmly believe that the critical challenge of executive continuity can be successfully accomplished. It can be accomplished but it takes a comprehensive approach. We call it a systems approach. Consider the term *systems approach*. What is its meaning? Is it really required to achieve executive continuity? The genesis of the current usage of the term is generally conceded to complex military efforts. The Early Warning System, for example, was a complex radar network setup to detect the approach of enemy missiles and destroy them. The system was installed long before the general populace knew it existed. Since the system has never actually been used, there is still conjecture as to its ability to do what was expected. Not so the landing on the moon. Moon landings involve a complex systems approach. It has proven itself with most of the world watching.

A genuine system involves:

1. A mission or central objective.
2. Numerous parts, called components or subsystems. Duplicate or redundant components are provided where potential failure is critical.
3. Feedback mechanism.
4. Interaction among components based on feedback. The components are programmed to act, react, and interact to achieve the central objective.
5. Once installed, the system must be maintained and improved.
6. The systems approach also requires system designers and operators.

This description may not do justice to the full complexity of a weapon system or a moon-landing, but it is sufficient to determine if the systems approach is relevant to the challenge of executive continuity. Earlier we used the term people flow. This term implies that executive continuity can be thought of as a "pipeline" stretching from recruitment into the organization to retirement from it. Numerous actions have to be taken regularly on a year after year basis to achieve the people flow desired.

The systems approach is a necessity for several reasons:

--Achievement of executive continuity objectives is really a complex undertaking.

--Simple attempts of the past have proven to be relatively fruitless.

--Successful applications of the systems approach to technological and social problems now provides models.

--Finally, the basic objective of executive continuity is becoming critical to the continued success of the enterprise. The chief executive, in the future, will want to be confident that the farm system is working. Numerous activities will be undertaken in a comprehensive and integrated manner to do this. In effect, a systems approach will be used.

Further evidence that the approach to executive continuity will become more systematic is provided by Paul Holden in his previously

mentioned study of top management. He had this to say about planning
for selection and development of executives:

> When the original study, *Top Management Organization Control,* was
> made twenty-five years ago, formal executive selection and development
> programs, including replacement charts, backup schedules, personal in-
> ventory records, and scheduled individual personal development plans
> were almost non-existent. Considerable progress has been made on this
> front, particularly during the past ten years. One of the areas that has
> shown great improvement is that of corporate manpower planning at the
> managerial and executive levels. The identification and planned develop-
> ment of key personnel has become a vital part of the total long-range
> planning activity in all the fifteen corporations included in the present
> study. Replacement charts, backup lists, and individual development
> plans for each executive position are the rule rather than the exception
> today.
>
> Among the companies visited, however, there was considerable varia-
> tion in the degree of centralized planning and control of executive selec-
> tion and development activities. Some of the participating companies
> possessed highly structured, formal programs with strong centralized
> functional guidance and coordination. Others selected, evaluated, and
> developed their executive and managerial personnel largely on a decen-
> tralized basis with active participation by line management and with a
> minimum of coordination and control by the corporate functional staff.
>
> Four of the fifteen companies use top-level committees in the adminis-
> tration of their executive selection and development programs; two of
> these companies have established special committees, whereas the other
> two utilize their regular executive committees to perform this function.
> The remaining eleven companies rely upon line management with the
> assistance of corporate or divisional staff personnel. All fifteen companies
> have a functional corporate staff executive to provide service and overall
> coordination.[7]

Holden found that in spite of the wide divergence in methodology
and structure in planning executive development programs, there was
a consensus among the executives visited that certain significant
changes had taken place during the past few years in administering
these programs within their corporations. The improved changes and
future trends most frequently mentioned included:
1. Increased personal involvement and commitment by top management.
2. More effective integration at the executive level of manpower planning and corporate long-range plans and operations.
3. Greater use of an improved professional corporate staff service,
   which includes a more sophisticated information system for use in
   manpower planning.

4. Improved selection and early identification of young men with top management potential.
5. A more realistic approach to executive appraisal encompassing separate evaluations on past performance and on long-term future potential.
6. Increased emphasis upon development programs geared to the personal needs of each individual and including considerable personal involvement by top management.

MAJOR REQUIREMENTS FOR A SYSTEMS APPROACH

An attempt to identify the major requirements in a comprehensive executive continuity system cannot avoid a certain arbitrariness. We suggest that there are ten major requirements. It might be asked if there are other major ones. Possibly, but the ten recommended ones have proven themselves in a variety of organizations. Some skeptic may well question if all ten are necessary. No, they are not. Considerable progress toward the executive continuity objectives can be made with sustained action on three or four of the requirements. However, experience with numerous companies suggests that the organization which implements more of the requirements increases its likelihood of achieving successful results.

The ten major requirements are:

1. Top management action.
2. An effective staff contribution specifically for executive personnel.
3. Identification of the kind and number of executives needed in the future.
4. Objective, descriptive information about candidates for executive positions.
5. Accelerated development of high-potential candidates.
6. Increased effectiveness in coaching executive personnel.
7. Specialized educational programs.
8. An organization-wide approach to selection and placement.
9. Integration of personnel programs and management processes with the continuity system.
10. Design of a system to meet the unique needs of each organization.

AVOIDING PITFALLS

This book is designed to help the reader avoid two pitfalls. One is the mechanistic approach to the challenge of executive continuity. Such an approach leads to a complex web of policies, pronouncements, procedures, and programs. However, the critical result, namely, a "flow" of qualified candidates never appears. The other pitfall is to take an academic or theoretical approach. Task forces are established, studies are conducted, research studies are commissioned, professors are consulted. Activity and effort are high. But the high expectations are likely to be unfulfilled. Again, the flow of qualified candidates does not appear.

The balance of this book is divided into two parts. The first part consists of ten chapters, each one devoted to one of the basic requirements for the systems approach. Each chapter concentrates upon identifying the best prevailing practices to insure that the academic pitfall is avoided. In addition, where possible we introduce data of the results presently being obtained in business and industrial organizations. This data suggests we will have to go beyond prevailing practices to insure successful results. The opportunity and need for interaction among the ten requirements is frequently identified. This should assist in avoiding the mechanistic pitfall.

The second part of the book consists of methods, procedures, and policy statements from numerous organizations. We put this material in the Appendix. Including an example of a method, a procedure, or a policy does not necessarily mean an endorsement. However, examples are helpful in planning implementation action. Implementation does require well conceived and executed procedures and methods.

References cited in the text are listed, by chapter, following the Appendix.

The reader who is in an organization with a formal executive continuity effort will find it helpful to compare his or her own program with the ten basic requirements. There will be occasions of confirmation. Other comparisons will suggest needed additions or changes. Some comparisons may provide justifiable pride when you find yourself out ahead of our recommendations. We would like to hear about such developments in the art of achieving executive continuity.

The reader who does not have a formal program might plan to read the first nine requirements as a basic orientation. The tenth requirement provides suggestions on designing one's own systems approach. Once the system is designed, the methods and procedures presented in the Appendix will, we hope, prove helpful.

2

Top management action

The importance of top management action justifies the designation of this requirement as the first one. Without top management's initial interest and support a continuity effort usually does not get started. More importantly, without sustained interest of and action by top management, year after year, such a program does not continue to operate effectively.

It is important to establish a tradition that one of top management's prime responsibilities is executive continuity. It is not sufficient for a chief executive to recognize or even be enthusiastic about an effort such as this. It must become a habitual part of the top management role to carry out certain actions on a regular basis decade after decade; this attitude must become institutionalized.

Paul Holden's study of top management reported several findings which are pertinent here. He says:*

--It was crystal clear in each of the 15 large manufacturing companies visited that the selection and development of executive personnel was a responsibility which merited top priority on the part of presidents.

--Compared with a similar study done 25 years earlier, there was a significant trend for increased personal involvement and commitment by top management.[1]

---

* From *Top Management* by Holden, Pederson, and Germane. Copyright 1968, McGraw-Hill Book Company. Used with permission of McGraw-Hill Book Company.

Let us consider several examples of organizations where attention to executive continuity has been institutionalized. For more than twenty-five years Exxon has had a committee on Compensation and Executive Development. The very top executives make up the committee. Once a year, the head of each of Exxon's operating groups and functional departments are called before the committee to forecast movements within his managerial realm over the next five years and to recommend promotions for the top spots. This top committee concerns itself with the top 250 jobs in the company. A recent business publication has this to say about Exxon's program:

> Most big companies, of course, have executive development programs. But probably at no other company is executive development so vital and integral a part of company operations—or is so much top management muscle exerted to make it work—as at Exxon. J. Kenneth Jamieson, Exxon's 59-year old Chairman, estimates that as much as a fifth of his time may be taken up with executive development matters. Jamieson believes, moreover, that executive development has been a major contributor to Exxon's glittering record. "It's not just oil in the ground," he says, "you've got to have the management talent to produce and sell it. The reason our system works isn't just because there is pressure from the top, but because there is cooperation from below. It is a cycling process that has to start at the grass roots level and work its way upward, because we have to depend on management at the lower levels to bring talent to our attention."[2]

A good example of top management interest is to be found in Henry Ford II. When he took over control of the Ford Motor Company it was readily apparent to him that his most critical problem was lack of a management group. As Peter Drucker has well said, Henry Ford's primary ambition was to prove that he could run the Ford Motor Company without any managers.[3] Consequently, both in public statements and in day to day actions, Henry Ford II has given the problem of executive continuity topmost priority.

Another interesting illustration of the recognition of the importance of this entire objective is to be found in the tradition at the top of General Motors. Alfred P. Sloan recognized early the importance of executive talent. It is interesting to note that in his book *My Years with General Motors* he does not mention one of the most important policies of the entire company—that policy is to pay extremely handsome salaries to top executives.[4] This process permits the attraction and retention of capable talent. It also provides some rather unusual motivation when an individual's bonus can equal, double, or triple his base salary. The top management of General Motors has established a tradition that executive continuity is a most important responsibility.

John W. McGovern, former president of Uniroyal, identified the critical importance of executive continuity in a memorandum to his division and department managers. To quote from a part of the memo:

> While there has been some variation in progress with this plan in the many departments of the Company, there has been substantial progress in the Company as a whole in:
> 1. Organized planning for placements.
> 2. Job descriptions for key management positions.
> 3. Appraisals of the performance of individuals.
> 4. Better and more complete personnel files.
> 5. Planned use of job rotation, special assignments, and promotion for development of individuals.
> The progress we have made, however, has not been equal to our needs. There have been too many cases where we have needed men for important managerial jobs and have not had men who were known to be qualified to fill these jobs. There have been too many cases where men who had good records in their previous, more specialized jobs, failed to measure up to the needs of the jobs into which they were promoted. We still need to learn (1) to what extent our lack of success has been due to failure to bring into our organization men of exceptional latent capacity for management work, (2) to what extent it has been due to failure to use the best methods for building up the management ability of good men by giving them the opportunity to learn by doing in addition to formal and informal training off the job, and (3) to what extent we have failed to select the right men from among the many capable people we now have in the organization.[5]

Unilever is another organization that stresses the importance of top management's giving attention to executive continuity. With more than 100 businesses scattered over the entire world, this organization early recognized that the problem of continuity would be a frequently recurring one and one with which only top management could really deal effectively.

Discussion with executives in a large number of enterprises over a period of years, leads the authors to conclude that this kind of attitude on the part of top management is somewhat atypical. The following are much more typical of the type of top management actions generally taken:

--Top management verbalizes high concern about a problem of executive continuity. This is not followed by any action.

--Top management encourages and supports the establishment of a management school or the extensive use of outside courses. But it does little or nothing else.

--Many top managers avoid doing anything personally about the development of their own immediate subordinates. They shy away from having any dialogues with a subordinate about his performance or about his managerial effectiveness.

--Top managers quite often accept replacement plans as presented.

It would be safe to say top managers' behavior is characterized by the verbalization of concern about executive continuity. This concern becomes acute when a decision has to be made. Often this is about the extent of the deliberate action taken by most top executives. This first and most important requirement is not met in many organizations. Much can be accomplished by deliberate effort on the other requirements, but optimum results require top management interest and action on a regular and sustained basis.

WHY THE LIMITED ACTION OF TOP MANAGEMENT?

One of the most important reasons why executive action is usually so limited is that it often takes a traumatic experience to demonstrate to the current executives the importance of developing future executives. This is particularly true of organizations that have a sales volume of $1 billion or less. Such companies usually have 15 to 20 key executive positions. A president has to appoint several key executives during his five or ten years tenure, but this seldom happens more often than once a year. In some instances two and three years may go by without the need to appoint a key executive. If most of these appointments work out without any really dramatic exception, current top managers convince themselves that this is a problem of limited magnitude. Dramatic exceptions are quite often treated as an isolated incident.

A second important reason for the lack of action on the part of top management is the lack of a competent staff. Management may be concerned, but it does not have enough confidence in a current staff executive to ask him to spearhead an executive continuity effort.

A third reason why top management does not take appropriate action is the lack of a tradition that this is a top management responsibility. There is not likely to be any question in the minds of future presidents of Exxon that one of their primary responsibilities is executive continuity. This philosophy has carried over for successive generations of top leaders. But for most organizations this tradition has not been established and until it is, the likelihood that there will be sustained top management action is problematical.

A fourth reason for limited action is that many top managers do not have a concept of identification, development, and selection of key executives *as a process.* They do not see this as a very complex, occasionally time-consuming, series of actions that need to be taken on a continuous basis year after year. Most managers' concept of the process has been built out of their own experience. No wonder it seems to them to be a haphazard or accidental process. Along with this goes the rather smug assumption that the past practice was sufficient to generate the current talented leadership, so what can be so wrong with the current practices?

A final reason is psychological. Retirement terrifies many chief executives, who avoid thinking of that dreaded day. Executive continuity efforts force such thinking. Some chief executives avoid the formalities of the continuity effort because it requires them to think of an unpleasant future event—their own retirement.

ACTION ALTERNATIVES FOR TOP MANAGEMENT

It is of critical importance that the entire management group of an organization knows that the top officers are vitally concerned about executive continuity. The exact tactics to be used will vary considerably with the unique characteristics of each enterprise. Here are nine action alternatives.

Talk with other executives

A helpful initial step is for the chief executive of an organization to talk with some of the top management of organizations mentioned in this chapter about their attitudes and actions concerning an executive continuity program. There are others who also are worth considering. This type of discussion is likely to be much more helpful than listening to any amount of orations by consultants or professors.

In such a discussion, the chief executive might seek to determine how many of the ten requirements for a comprehensive system mentioned in the previous chapter are being utilized by the company being visited. This input can be compared with the number of alternatives for top executive action which are in effect in one's own organization.

Conduct a study of current conditions

A second action alternative is to conduct a study of the current situation within the organization. There are numerous kinds of studies which might be requested. One that is worth conducting is to analyze past experiences with regard to successful and unsuccessful appointments of general managers; in some instances it is possible to come up with rough estimates of the cost of having appointed individuals who subsequently failed. In addition, it is helpful to study the number of talented managers lost to other companies and the primary reasons for this. A third type of study is sometimes called a *coaching practices survey*. It gives some indication of the extent to which future executives are receiving the benefit of coaching from their superiors.

A fourth type of study explores the conditions that are having an important positive and negative impact upon achieving executive continuity. A basis for deciding which studies to commission can be gained from examples which will be presented in subsequent chapters.

Assign staff responsibility

A third important action alternative is the assignment of staff responsibility to a competent, respected staff executive. This is not the spot to use for taking care of a problem executive. It is also important that the executive report to the chief executive or have ready access to him. It is also necessary to clarify the responsibilities and power of the new staff position. A final word of caution. The chief executive cannot shift his responsibility to the newly appointed staff executive. This is a responsibility that cannot be shifted without an adverse impact on the executive continuity effort.

Design an executive continuity system

A fourth important action alternative is to request that an initial executive continuity system be designed and installed. In the previous chapter ten requirements for a system were identified. Each requirement will be explored more fully in the chapters to follow.

Establish a climate favorable to executive continuity

The climate established by top management can either help or hinder when it comes to attracting, developing, and retaining high-potential personnel. Top management develops a reputation, an image, whether it wants to or not. A climate that contributes to executive continuity would have the following characteristics:
  --Responsibility is delegated.
  --Individuals are trusted.
  --Individuals are given challenging opportunities to test themselves.
  --Rewards go to those who produce.
  --Individuals are treated with dignity and respect.
  --Both individual performance and team performance are stressed.
  --A consultative approach to problem-solving and planning is
    used.
Earlier we suggested that a study of current conditions be conducted. Instead of guessing at the positive or negative nature of the existing climate, study it to find out whether there are opportunities for improving it.

Undertake a pilot study

A sixth action alternative is to have a pilot study conducted in a major division. Undertaking a comprehensive executive continuity effort involves both risks and investment of time and money. Often a pilot study will permit testing before a system is extended to the entire organization. It is possible to identify major elements that other companies are using in their continuity efforts. However, those which are most appropriate for a given company can only be determined by an actual test. A pilot test of the initial design, leading to subsequent modifications is a very commendable alternative.

Conduct an annual manpower review

An annual top executive manpower review has demonstrated its value in several large business organizations. Examples of company programs and suggestions for conduct of such reviews are provided in Appendix A. General Electric, IBM, Johnson & Johnson, Exxon, and Uniroyal all have been making regular use of such reviews.

The Exxon organization has used such a review process, which they call the Management Development Review, for more than 25 years. The review is conducted by the Compensation and Executive Development Committee composed of the chairman, the president and the senior vice presidents (a total of nine). Once a year the head of each of the major regional and operating components is called before the committee.

Through its top review process, the committee concentrates on approximately the top 250 jobs in the company. In addition, Management Development Reviews are conducted by similar groups in each affiliate company.

The review process contributes in several ways. A variety of management processes, such as budget preparation and monthly reporting, insure that everyone recognizes top management has a strong interest in cash flow and other financial results. A formal executive manpower review makes it apparent that top management is concerned about "people flow" at the executive level.

The review process usually requires that the "visiting" executive share his thinking on such subjects as the following:

--Future plans for the structure of the organization.
--Evaluation of individuals in critical positions.
--Actions planned for individuals in critical positions.
--Individuals judged to have potential.
--Recommended actions for those with potential.
--Results of accelerated development effort.
--Results of college recruiting effort.

The first year such reviews are conducted, the results obtained are often disappointing. However, as the annual process is repeated the quality of the thinking, evaluating, planning, and follow-through begins to improve noticeably. The annual executive manpower review is a sound step for top executives to undertake.

Establish guideline policies

An eighth action alternative for the chief executive is to establish policies that reflect his genuine concern about executive continuity. For example, a rather strong policy statement might be made encouraging cross-functional and cross-divisional movement of personnel. In most organizations there is a very heavy egocentricity built around functions and around operating divisions. It takes numerous actions, only one of which is the pronouncement of a policy, to begin to break down the barriers that exist. Many opportunities will arise for establishing meaningful policy statements pertaining to executive continuity. In subsequent chapters we identify many of these opportunities. It is important not only that the policies be enunciated; it is equally important that top management be sure that the policies are understood and appropriately implemented. In some instances discipline will be required to get the necessary compliance.

Set up an educational program

An educational effort is one vital component in an overall systems approach to executive continuity. However, it is important that top management not rely on formal educational efforts to do the entire continuity job. Overreliance on any one particular method can be quite disastrous. Moreover, it is quite unlikely both that education is a most important requirement and that it needs to be done first. Properly combined with other requirements the educational process can make a very worthwhile contribution. But top management should not lull themselves into a false sense of security because they have authorized a management school or regularly send their top executives to a university program.

THE BOARD OF DIRECTORS' ROLE

After years of studying the actions and inactions of corporate directors, Myles Mace of the Harvard Business School concluded there was a considerable gap between what professors and business executives have stated board of directors should do and what they in fact do. His article, "The President and the Board of Directors,"[6] in the *Harvard Business Review* describes the workings of the board system in publicly held companies of relatively large size. The directors, although ostensibly the ones who appoint chief executives, in most instances confirm the successor recommended by the retiring officer. Even if a director or group of directors becomes convinced that a chief executive is unsatisfactory, only rarely is he asked to resign.

A board may not be in a position to do other than accept the succession plan as recommended. However, we would argue that a board can insist that an executive continuity system be designed, installed, and directed so as to produce several qualified candidates for the chief executive position. A choice from several qualified candidates leaves both the board and the chief executive officer in a good position. A recent trend in this direction has been reported by Robert Estes, senior vice president, general counsel, and secretary of General Electric Company.[7]

Estes reports that five committees of the board have been established by the General Electric Company. One has to do with management development and compensation. Regular meetings of the committee provide a basis for acquiring much greater knowledge, greater involvement, and greater contribution to management development and compensation issues.

An interesting example of top management involvement is provided by large industrial organizations in Japan. Let us consider how they do it.

THE JAPANESE PATTERN OF TOP MANAGEMENT INVOLVEMENT

Peter Drucker commends the "godfather" concept of the Japanese. This system enables young managerial and professional people to become the special concern of senior men. Highlights of the godfather concept as described by Drucker include the following:

--Young men enter a company directly from the university. Until the age of 45 they are promoted and paid by seniority.

--Superiors do not chose subordinates. The personnel function does this. It is unthinkable that a young man ask for a transfer or decide to go to another company.

--Upon reaching age 45, the "Day of Reckoning" arrives. A very small group of candidates are picked to become company directors or top managers. They can stay in management long past any retirement age known in the West.

--Those not selected stay on only until age 55. A select group who do not get into top management do get assigned to top management of subsidiaries.

--This critical selection decision is based upon the godfather recommendations. Godfathers are highly respected members of upper middle management.

--During the first ten years or so of a young man's career the godfather is expected to be in close touch with his godchildren. He may have 100 such godchildren at any one time. He is expected to know the young man, see him fairly regularly, be available for advice and counsel. He discusses his godchildren with top management and the personnel staff.

Drucker goes on to observe that it is precisely because Japanese managers have "lifetime employment" and, as a rule, can be neither fired nor moved, and because advancement for the first 25 years of a man's life is through seniority alone, that the Japanese have made the care and feeding of their young people the first responsibility of management.

Although relationships are far less formal in the West, Drucker says we still need, just as much as the Japanese do, the senior manager who serves as a human contact, a listener, a guide for the young people during their first ten years. Our management books say the first-line supervisor can fill this role. This is simply nonsense says Drucker. The absence of a genuine contact is an important reason for the heavy turnover among these people. They need a human relationship that is job-focused and work-focused, a mentor who is concerned about them, a mentor who is not a personnel specialist but an experienced, respected, and successful manager.[8]

SUMMARY

The first and most critical requirement of any executive continuity system is top management interest and action decade after decade. Data on trends suggest that there is a significant trend for more personal involvement and commitment by top management. Nevertheless, in the authors' opinion, this first requirement is not met in many organizations. There are a variety of reasons for this. These obstacles must be overcome by action. Nine alternatives for top management action were suggested. They are:

--Talk with other executives.

--Conduct a study of current conditions.

--Assign staff responsibility.

--Design an executive continuity system.

--Establish a climate favorable to executive continuity.

--Undertake a pilot study.

--Conduct an annual manpower review.

---Establish guideline policies.

---Set up an educational program, but do not rely too heavily on it.

A challenge to our traditional way of thinking was provided by Drucker's explanation of the approach to executive continuity taken in Japan.

3

An effective staff contribution

An effective staff contribution is a most critical requirement. It is second in importance only to the top management requirement discussed in the previous chapter. This recommendation requires an investment, an investment in personnel. It will help in gauging the potential returns to be gained from this investment if the staff contribution is first described. The rationale for considering this requirement so important will then be presented, followed by consideration of staff qualifications, organizational alternatives, major areas of work, and potential pitfalls.

What is an effective staff contribution?

The basic responsibilities include:
1. Designing an overall program. This involves designing a systems approach and establishing the timetable for the implementation of this approach.
2. Securing sound data. It is especially important that good descriptive information about all candidates for executive positions be secured.
3. Stimulating the anticipatory actions and planning on the part of operating managers that are needed to implement the systems approach.
4. Facilitating a corporate-wide approach to the selection decisions pertaining to key executives.
5. Implementing programs requiring a comprehensive or a corporate-wide approach such as college recruiting, accelerated develop-

ment, manpower inventory, manpower planning, and executive compensation.

6. Conducting organizational studies, participating in organizational planning processes.

Theodore LeVino of the General Electric organization has identified several roles to be fulfilled:

> The manpower planner may be asked to fulfill one of several different roles in his component. He may be the Chief Placement Officer in charge of candidate searches and outplacement cases. He may be the inside Talent Scout charged with discovering and assessing high potentials. He may be sort of a component Ombudsman—a third party counselor or confidant. He may be an internal Management Consultant on organization and management process problems. Or he may be some combination of these. When he is all or most, he approaches what Douglas McGregor first labeled—and recent management literature calls—the Change Agent.[1]

Examples of documents describing responsibilities and objectives of the top staff contribution are provided in Appendix B.

Why is it a critical requirement?

It was argued in chapter one that a systems approach was absolutely necessary. This basic argument requires a staff contribution. A design contribution is needed initially. Executive management must look to a specialized group to design an appropriate systems approach. Implementation of the design will require changing old habits and developing new habits at all levels of the enterprise. A change in habits is going to meet with resistance. A gadfly or catalyst staff contribution is needed if the organization is really going to change.

Large enterprises which have become serious about executive continuity have recognized the importance of such staff contributions. One of the most venerable staff contributions would be that of the Exxon organization. The Exxon Company has had the same basic organizational arrangement for executive continuity for more than 25 years. As mentioned in the previous chapter, a formal committee was established. It is called the Compensation and Executive Development Committee (COED). Membership includes the very top executives of the company. The chief executive is chairman. The secretary of this committee is a staff man. He is not an officer of the company, but he, in effect, reports to the chief executive.

Among the major responsibilities of the top staff group are the following:

--Maintain all records concerning executive personnel above a certain level.

--Participate in the annual Executive Development Reviews conducted by the COED with each company head.

--Secure evaluative information upon high level candidates.

--Develope and administrate compensation practices for high level personnel.

--Follow-up on development planning.

--Assist in making developmental transfers.

In addition to the COED of the parent company, each affiliate of Exxon has a similar committee. A staff executive is assigned to perform functions similar to the secretary of the COED.

The DuPont Company also has a special group, entitled Organization Planning, to concentrate upon executive continuity work. This group is part of the personnel division. One of the division manager's primary responsibilities is working with corporate and department managements on succession planning. The responsibilities of this function include:

1. Maintain a central inventory of all personnel above a certain salary level.
2. Analyze and chart promotability forecasts.
3. Provide general managers of operating departments and staff departments with an annual critique.
4. Provide candidate lists for key positions.

The General Electric Company set up a special group at corporate level and within major operating groups in the mid-1960s to concentrate on executive manpower management.

General Motors, in the early 1970s, appointed a Harvard professor to head up a group specializing in executive and managerial personnel. Prior to this a small group operated within the traditional corporate personnel and labor relations group.

Qualifications of the top staff man

Establishing the position of a top staff man to concentrate on the implementation of a systems approach is an important step. Equally important is the selection of a well-qualified man. Let us consider some of the characteristics to be sought in this "water walker." The major qualifications are as follows:

1. He should have an ability to understand and evaluate executive ability and performance.
2. He needs to have a keen understanding of people, their motives, and their interests and their values.
3. He needs an ability to establish and sustain effective working relationships with all levels of management.
4. He must have the courage of his convictions.

5. He needs a knowledge of managing as a process.
6. He needs an intimate knowledge of the organization.
7. He needs sound grounding in organization planning.
8. He needs a knowledge of the major personnel functions, such as compensation, personnel development, and personnel placement.

It is unlikely that an individual is going to possess all of these virtues. In a large organization this can be overcome by selecting supporting staff to complement the top staff man.

Organizational alternatives

There are two basic alternatives worthy of consideration. One is to set up a special staff group to concentrate on this entire problem at the executive level. The second is to ask the current personnel organization to rise to the challenge of taking on this new range of responsibilities. There are advantages and disadvantages to each alternative. First let us consider some of the advantages of a special staff. The main advantage is that the special staff individual can concentrate exclusively on this program. A second advantage is that this individual can report directly to the top man in the organization. In addition, it is possible to select the individual to fill this spot since it is a new position. Another advantage is that there are few precedents and traditions for the new group.

There are also certain disadvantages to the establishment of a special staff. One of these is that an effective systems approach requires setting up a farm system that begins with the initial hiring of college graduates. When a special group is set up separate from the regular personnel group, this leads to a rather interesting problem as to the division of labor that takes place in operating components. The special group inevitably has problems of integrating with the regular group, particularly at lower levels of the enterprise.

A second disadvantage is that the setting up of a special group does increase the possibility that it will become a "kingmaker" group. This does not have to happen, but it is a potential danger.

Another disadvantage is the likelihood that there will be rivalry and competition between the new staff group and the regular staff group.

The advantages of asking the regular personnel group to take on this increased responsibility for high level personnel administration are several. One of the first advantages is that this change does raise the status of the regular group, in effect it makes them a more important group. It gives them an opportunity to have cognizance over all human resources, including the high risk individuals represented at the general management and top management levels. A second benefit is that this arrangement does facilitate the coordination of the numerous personnel functions from college recruiting right on up the line. In effect, one personnel organization is charged with the responsibility for personnel administration at all levels of the organization, hence coordination is easier to obtain. Another advantage is that this avoids setting up a special group with whom conflict and duplication is almost inevitable.

There are several disadvantages. One of the most likely disadvantages, although this is not necessarily the case in all instances, is that the current personnel group lacks the capability to do the new job. In some cases it is possible for a personnel group to rise to the challenge, but in many instances this is difficult and in some instances it has proven to be impossible. Another potential disadvantage is the prevailing image of the personnel group in a company. If this is at all negative, then this negative image does carry over as a liability in getting the cooperation that is necessary in the new program. A third disadvantage is that the top individual to be assigned to this program will likely report to the vice president of personnel or vice president of administration, and not the president or chief executive officer. This does prove to be a disadvantage in most instances. This is particularly true if the vice president of personnel chooses to concentrate exclusively on getting the labor relations job done, and this is often the case.

First and foremost, it is our position that the systems approach does require an effective staff contribution. This staff contribution can be achieved in either one of the two ways which we have just discussed. An examination of the situation at several large companies reveals some organizations doing it one way and some doing it the other way.

Ideally we believe that there should be a top man in personnel reporting directly to either the president or the chairman. This top personnel man should be sufficiently broad-gauged and creative to undertake the responsibilities for the total personnel job, including the process of identification, development, and selection of executives—or, to put it in terms we have been using in this book, responsibility for the design and implementation of a systems approach to executive continuity. In this ideal organization there would likely be an individual with the title of Director of Executive Development reporting directly to the top personnel man. This same individual would have responsibility for such major functions as organization planning, in addition to a traditional responsibility for executive selection, development, compensation, and communications. The problem of selection certainly is intimately involved with the entire process of organization planning. As will be noted in a subsequent chapter, the executive continuity system has to be integrated with organization structure. Therefore, it is of considerable help to have the organization planning function also report to the top personnel man.

However, in most organizations, even the largest ones, this ideal organization is likely to be a long time coming. Practically, the alternative to be selected should be that which can be established most readily. One then needs to keep the ideal organization as a long-term objective towards which to evolve.

Major areas of work

The following major areas of work must be considered in assigning staff responsibilities:

1. Design, installation, and administration of executive continuity programs such as an annual manpower review, executive appraisals, cross-functional transfers, and manpower planning at executive level.
2. Executive compensation policies and administration.
3. Corporate-wide selection processes for executive positions.
4. Data gathering and processing for executive personnel and personnel with executive potential.
5. Educational courses, internal and external, for executive personnel.
6. Planning organizational structural changes.
7. Recruiting of college graduates and/or experienced personnel.

Pitfalls to avoid

There are several roles which could be described as pitfalls to be avoided. One is the kingmaker role. In this type of role the staff group is seen as being responsible for selections and appointments. Two cautions are in order here; the first caution is to avoid exercising the potential power inherent in this new position. The second precaution is to avoid any appearance of taking on the kingmaker's role. We will have some suggestions to make in subsequent chapters as to whether specific actions should be avoided, particularly in the selection process but also in the manpower planning and the replacement planning processes.

The second type of role pitfall is that of becoming a "mechanic." Individuals in this role quite often become preoccupied with the mechanics, the processes, the procedures, mistaking these for accomplishments. They often end up with some very impressive books, usually in fancy colors, but the results, namely, developing executives does not take place. The organization fails to have qualified executives from whom a choice can be make when making appointments. In effect, such a staff often jeopardizes the organization, for the assumption is made that the executive continuity program is successful because the mechanics have been carried out.

Another interesting pitfall is the professorial or academic role. Individuals playing this role rely heavily on the study of desired executive qualities, the utilization of behavioral research, and the educational approach to development. The ability to design and install an effective executive continuity system requires a pragmatist who can get an organization to change.

Making a staff contribution in the absence of affirmative action by top management

In some organizations a systems approach is initiated by a request on the part of top management that such a program be established, and the appointment of a staff man or group to lead the way. However, there are many organizations where the established personnel group does have an opportunity to make an important contribution even when top management hasn't asked for a complete systems approach. In this case an alert staff group can begin to achieve many of the desired conditions mentioned in this requirement by taking a variety of actions.

One action is to initiate a pilot study in a major component of the enterprise. A component can be selected where the general manager is cooperative. As often as not, the cooperative general manager also has potential to move higher. If he has had a meaningful experience with the initial pilot study he is quite likely to ask that this same process be applied on a larger scale when he gets promoted. In any case, the pilot study provides a rather concrete example for top management. Often this concrete example is easier for the top managers to comprehend, accept, and appreciate than is a theoretical description of an ideal approach.

Another worthwhile approach for an established personnel organization is to identify with the most important concern that top management has with regard to this entire problem of executive continuity. Usually this will be found to be one of the major requirements identified in the systems approach. In many cases top management does have a strong concern. Therefore if a staff group designs an effective approach by which to take care of this concern they have in effect established a beachhead. Once one of the requirements has been accomplished successfully, it is quite often possible to ride piggyback on this accomplishment and slowly build in additional requirements that have been identified in this systems approach.

Another possible approach is for the staff group to take the initiative in presenting a design for an overall program. In this case it is wise to have the overall systems approach in mind, but it is not necessary to have the initial program be nearly as comprehensive. Stress on four or five actions usually constitutes a sufficient initial effort to be worth undertaking. This avoids the frequent difficulty of building up resistance because the approach is thought to be too comprehensive, too all-inclusive, or too academic and theoretical.

Still another important action to be taken, particularly by an established staff group, is an aggressive effort to upgrade the capabilities of their own staff. For example, some organizations find it extremely helpful to provide their top staff people with training in intensive, or depth, interviewing. Other organizations have deemed it advisable to train their top staff people in the Accomplishment Analysis process described in a later chapter. An alert, aggressive staff group can begin to develop the skills and talent that they anticipate will be necessary in the implementation of the systems approach. Certainly it is safe to conclude that the design and implementation of the systems approach to executive continuity is not an assignment for amateurs. The stakes are great, the risks are high, the consequences are critical. Hence staff men had better be professional in their abilities before undertaking efforts such as this.

SUMMARY

The requirement we consider to be second in importance to top management action is an effective staff contribution. A comprehensive systems approach just cannot get off the ground without a significant staff contribution. This contribution is needed to insure that a sustained effort is maintained decade after decade. It takes an unusually well rounded individual to be the top staff man. This rarified atmosphere dooms the amateur. Two basic organizational alternatives are worthy of consideration. In most instances, setting up a special group reporting to the chief executive has been the initial step. In a few instances, an established personnel group is capable of taking on the new challenge of an executive continuity effort. In effect, it requires doing effective personnel work at the executive level.

Major areas of work include design, installation, and administration of system components. In addition, the group often has responsibility for executive compensation and organization planning. Pitfalls to be avoided include that of being considered as kingmakers and becoming immersed in the mechanics of the system.

An aggressive staff group can make significant strides in the absence of affirmative action by top management.

Let us now turn to one of the requirements a staff group will be directly concerned about, namely, anticipating future needs. This, in effect, is the definition of the outcomes expected of the system in the future.

4

Anticipating future needs

This chapter deals with another very important requirement of the overall system. Stress has been placed earlier on the importance of establishing precise objectives for the systems approach. Stating that one wants a continuity of competent executives is fine as far as it goes. But it doesn't go far enough. A people flow of competent executives is needed for 5 years hence, for 10 years hence, for 20 years hence. It is likely that the type of executive who headed companies 25 years ago would have difficulty being successful today. However, it seems to be less obvious, or at least to be of less concern, that the type of executive who will be successful 25 years from now will, in all likelihood, be quite different from executives of today.

Anticipating future needs is the first step in coming to grips with the magnitude of the job for which the system is to be designed. Each organization will need to make judgments on both the number and, even more importantly, the type of executive needed in the future. Even though the precision with which it is possible to determine the number of executives that will be needed in the next 5, 10, or 20 years is not as great as one would like, nevertheless an effort needs to be made to get a reasonable estimate. This reasonable estimate can then be progressively modified as additional data and experience become available. Quite a few organizations have given attention to the problem of estimating future needs in terms of numbers. Not many organizations have given attention to the problem of the *type* of executive which will be needed in the future. This problem is a most complex one. Arriving at a reasonable estimate is frustrating. Again, it is necessary to arrive at some assumptions, for these assumptions are needed to guide decision making all along the people flow system from recruitment to retirement.

Three studies will first be reviewed to assist in the process of arriving at assumptions about the type of executive needed in the future. The first study is a report by an executive recruiting firm on characteristics of current presidents of large business organizations. The second study has to do with the motivational aspects of position requirements. The third study reports on an effort of a group of top managers in Uniroyal to think through the kind of executive required in the future.

Attention then will be directed to methodology for estimating future needs, studying current executives, and identifying the kind of executive needed in the future. Special attention will then be given to replacement planning.

STUDY OF COMPANY PRESIDENTS

Heidrick and Struggles, an executive recruiting firm, conducts a survey at five-year intervals of the presidents of the 500 largest industrial companies and the 50 largest firms in merchandising, transportation, life insurance, finance, and utility organizations as ranked by *Fortune Magazine*.[1] A response of 65 to 70 percent is secured, making the data quite representative of the entire population. A portion of the results more pertinent to continuity issue have been selected. Results for the surveys of 1962, 1967 and 1972 are summarized below. The comments are the author's and not Heidrick and Struggles.

Present age. The trend over the three survey periods is for presidents to be younger. This results from the growing size and complexity

	All companies		
Age	1962	1967	1972
Under 50	22%	23%	25%
50–59	43	51	57
60 and over	35	26	16
Medium age	56	55	53

of America's largest business organizations, and the frequent division of responsibilities at the top between a chairman and a president, as well as the trend to earlier executive retirements.

Age when presidency was assumed. Interestingly, there has not been much shift in age when presidency is assumed over the three survey periods. About half the time the presidents assume their position before the age of 50.

	All companies		
Age	1962	1967	1972
Under 50	51%	49%	52%
50 – 59	41	45	43
60 and over	8	6	5

Years as president. There is a definite trend toward brevity of service. "Old war horses" seem to be fading away.

Years president	All companies		
	1962	1967	1972
Five or fewer	55%	62%	72%
6 to 10	25	25	19
11 or more	20	12	9

Level of education. The level of education of presidents in 1972 was considerably higher that of presidents ten years earlier. The level did not change much in the last five year period. There is still one chance out of six that a president will not have a college degree.

	All companies		
Education	1962	1967	1972
Less than college	26%	17%	16%
College degree	49	47	46
Graduate degree	25	36	38

Undergraduate major. Engineering and science are the predominant majors for presidents in organizations in general. This is especially so in industrial and utility organizations. Since 1967, there seems to have been an increased number of presidents with a liberal arts major.

Route to the top. General administration has become the primary route to the top. In 1962 manufacturing was the primary route. Marketing has always been one of the more important routes. As one might expect, the route most frequently travelled is quite different for industrial, utilities, merchandising, transportation, and finance institutions.

| | All companies | |
Previous experience	1967	1972
General administration	25%	28%
Marketing	21	23
Finance	15	17
Manufacturing	11	6
Legal	9	10
Technical	6	10
Personnel	3	1
International	2	1
Other	4	4

Number of other companies worked for. The number of presidents devoting their careers to a single employer has dropped dramatically over the past decade. The number of highly mobile individuals becoming president has remained virtually unchanged during this span. Mobility appears to be inversely related to size of organization.

| Other companies | All companies | | |
worked for	1962	1967	1972
None	41%	35%	31%
One	23	27	25
Two	16	18	22
Three	9	11	11
Four or more	11	9	11

Summary. The Heidrick and Struggles studies are of interest for several reasons. They illustrate a type of study of executives that might well be repeated at regular intervals within a large enterprise to detect trends. The profile of current company presidents does provide one additional input in arriving at requirements to be met by the executive of the future. The profiles also permit comparison of a current company situation with the prevailing pattern.

STUDY OF MOTIVATIONAL REQUIREMENTS

Behavioral scientists have been studying both effective and ineffective executive behavior for many years. It is possible that some of their studies might make the problem of identifying the kind of executive needed in the future a bit more susceptible to solution. If their conclusions about the relationship of motivational factors to position requirements were to hold true both for today and the foreseeable future, it would make the task before us more manageable. It is too early to know how enduring their results are, but the position requirement-motivational theory proposed by John B. Miner of the University of Maryland is provocative.[2] This theory assumes that there are certain position requirements that operate across a great many managerial positions in business and industry. This seems like a defensible assumption. It is further assumed that the extent to which an executive anticipates positive or negative emotional experiences as he faces the various requirements of his managerial position represents a major determinant of his behavior in that position. If he believes behaving in accordance with role requirements will be unpleasant he is likely to avoid the role requirements. If he experiences a high degree of congruence between his anticipated sources of satisfaction and the position requirements, he can be expected to exhibit behavior which is consistent with the position requirements.

The theory on prediction of executive success is that those individuals who repeatedly associate positive rather than negative emotions with position requirements pertinent to management positions will tend to meet existing organization criteria of effectiveness. Those in whom negative emotional reactions predominate will likely be considered relative ineffective. This does not mean that motivational factors are the only ones which operate to determine an executive's performance level. Job and industry knowledge, past experience, and physical factors, among other things, are certainly important.

Competitive behavior

There is, at least insofar as peers are concerned, a strong competitive element built into managerial work. A manager must compete for the available rewards, both for himself and for his group. Managers must characteristically strive to win for themselves and their groups, and accept such challenges as other managers at comparable level may offer. On occasion the challenge may come from below, even from among one's own subordinates. In order to meet this position requirement a man should be favorably disposed toward engaging in competition. He should, ideally, enjoy rivalry of this kind and be motivated to seek it whenever possible. If he is unwilling to fight for position, status, advancement, and his ideas, he is unlikely to succeed. Any generalized tendency to associate unpleasant emotion, such as anxiety and depression, with performance in competitive situations will almost inevitably result in behavior which falls short of position demands.

Exercising power

Another position requirement with motivational implications is that managers must exercise power over their subordinates and direct their behavior in a manner consistent with organizational, and presumably their own, objectives. They must tell others what to do when this becomes necessary, and enforce their words through appropriate use of positive and negative sanctions. Managers who find such behavior difficult, who do not wish to impose their wishes on others or believe it is wrong to do so, would not be expected to meet this particular position requirement. On the other hand, a favorable attitude toward activities of this kind, perhaps even an enjoyment of power, should contribute to the successful performance as a manager. In the typical hierarchical situation subordinates are expected to perform in a manner which will be conducive to the attainment of organizational goals. The person placed in a position of authority over them would therefore, ideally, desire to behave in ways calculated to help subordinates' objectives.

Independent posture

The managerial job tends to require a person to behave in ways differing in a number of respects from the behavior of others in the same face-to-face group. A manager must, in this sense, stand out from his group and assume a position of independence. One cannot use the actions of the people with whom one is most frequently associated, one's subordinates, as a guide for his own behavior as a manager. Rather he must deviate from the immediate group and do things which will inevitably invite attention, discussion, and perhaps criticism from those reporting to him. The managerial position requires that an individual assume a position of considerable independence insofar as the motives and emotions of other people are concerned. When this prospect is viewed as unattractive, when the idea of standing out from the group, of behaving in a different manner, and of being independent elicits feelings of unpleasantness, then behavior appropriate to the position will occur much less often than would otherwise be the case. It is the man who enjoys being the center of attention and who prefers to deviate to some degree from those around him who is most likely to meet the demands of his position in this area. Such a person will presumably wish to gain visibility and will have many of the characteristics of a good actor. Certainly, a manager is frequently "on stage," and the appropriate motivation should make him more effective in his work.

Administrative routines and results

A manager is faced with the process of getting the work out and keeping on top of administrative demands. The things that have to be done must actually be done. They range from constructing budgets to serving on committees, to talking on the telephone, to filling out employee ratings forms and making salary change recommendations. There are administrative requirements of this kind in all managerial work, although the specific activities will vary from one situation to another. To meet these requirements a manager must at least be willing to face this type of routine, and, ideally, he will gain some satisfaction from it. If, on the other hand, such behavior is consistently viewed with apprehension or loathing the man's chances of success would appear to be less. A desire to avoid or put off the more or less standard administrative duties of the managerial job can only result in considerable deviation from role prescriptions, and thus in less effective performance.

Summary

As we reviewed the above position requirements from a motivational emphasis we found them helpful in explaining effective and ineffective executives. They don't explain everything but in numerous cases they do help explain what happened and why. The approach needs to be explored more intensively. It certainly is a superior alternative to the traditional concern about traits which has preoccupied executives and behavioral scientists for years.

AN IN-COMPANY STUDY

The Uniroyal organization wanted to think through what kind of an executive would be needed in the future. The top three levels of the organization studied a selected list of readings, consisting of abstracts from a great many sources covering a wide range of subjects pertaining to the future. Each executive then identified the more important characteristics that he foresaw for large manufacturing organizations ten years in the future. In light of this, he identified the type of executive that would be necessary at that time. Listed below are the major characteristics of large manufacturing organizations identified by these managers. This list represents the consensus reached by members of this group. The characteristics are not listed in the order of their importance.

1. Business will be operating on a global basis. Manufacturing plants will be scattered around the world. Components will be made in the most economical territory and assembled near the point of sale.
2. Production will be highly automated.
3. The decision making process will depend heavily upon mathematical models of companies, industries, nations, and the world.
4. Governmental influence, involvement, and heavy impact upon management decisions will be more important in the future. This is

particularly true in many foreign countries. It will become increasingly true also in the United States.

5. Industrial organizations are coming closer to hiring an employee for life. This is particularly the case in many foreign countries now; it becomes an increasing trend in the United States as well.

6. Labor costs will continue to increase steadily. Scarce labor, particularly managerial and highly talented specialists, will command premium rates.

7. Unions are likely to become more and more involved in management questions such as subcontracting, pricing, and offshore production. They also will become more involved in politics. Involvement of government in negotiations and disputes will continue to increase.

8. Novel ways of compensating employees at all levels will be developed.

9. The trend toward the shorter work week will continue, except for the higher level executives where the most predictable consequence is a continued existence of a long work week.

10. The rapid obsolescence of products sometimes referred to as a short life cycle will characterize the large manufacturing organization of the future. In some instances we will begin to see the obsolescence of entire businesses and industries.

11. Manufacturing organizations of the conglomerate or multiple type will continue to increase steadily. The organization of the future will be a much larger one in terms of assets and employees.

12. More and more buinesses will be integrated from raw material to customer sales, in industry after industry.

13. There will be many more specialists found at all levels of the organization.

14. Large capital "reservoirs" will take a much more active interest in the management of enterprises. Foundations and pension funds, as well as banks, will begin to get more actively involved in the review of management plans of companies they are "supporting."

15. The continued stress on a more systematic approach to management, sometimes called professionalization of management, will continue in the United States and begin to evolve and spread throughout all other countries.

16. The manufacturing organization of the future will need a large number of highly skilled technicians. It will need a smaller number of operators. This is already true in process industries; it will become more so in assembly type organizations.

17. More attention will be given to genuine employee participation and involvement at all levels of the enterprise.

Based upon the preceding analyses of the dominant characteristics of a large manufacturing organization ten years hence, the same top management group then grappled with the problem of the kind of top executive that will be needed ten years from now. Here are their conclusions:

Knowledge. The executive will need a knowledge of world business conditions and a knowledge of governmental affairs both in United States and worldwide. He will need a knowledge of organization planning and the intricacies of changing an organization in a dynamic worldwide operation. He will need to be able to master a knowledge of new markets, new products, and new developments; and particularly he will need to have a knowledge of the entire sequence of events from the germination of new ideas to their conversion into products and subsequently into sales.

Experience. The executive of the future will need certain types of experiences. He will need to have a depth of experience in several functions, one of which must be in the area of marketing. He will need to have an intimate exposure to top level problems early in his career. He should have had experience both as a line manager and as a staff manager. He should have had experience in several types of businesses and he should have had experience in a series of high-risk-type jobs.

Abilities. The executive of the future will need to have the ability to manage highly technical groups. He will need to be able to make effective use of numerous specialists. He will need to be able to master the art of delegating and controlling large organizations, and he will need to view problems broadly, avoiding a parochial attitude. He must be able to anticipate the future and make firm decisions about the allocation of resources, and adhere to these basic decisions. He must be able to view complex problems from the three points of view simultaneously: financial, technical, and human. He will need to have the ability to plan and carry out changes in the organization in an effective manner; to be able to calculate risks and then take the calculated risk; to be able to secure effective teamwork in a complex organization; and to be able to use the new tools of management, such as data processing, information systems, automation, new incentive methods, and mathematical models.

It is not suggested that the conclusions of this management group necessarily have universal application. However, the process does illustrate one way to anticipate and describe the kind of top executive that will be needed in the future. It becomes quite apparent, as the above conclusions about characteristics of future executives are considered, that very few current executives come close to meeting these requirements. It also becomes apparent that a very deliberate effort will have to be made starting quite early in the career of high-potential personnel if many of these requirements are going to be achieved.

STUDY APPLICATIONS

We mentioned early that it is necessary that top management arrive at some convictions about the type of executive that will be needed in the future. Preliminary studies can be done by a staff group. However, the convictions must be firmly held by top management. This requires deliberation and discussion. The three studies just reviewed can assist in this process. A comparison can be made between one's own executives and the pattern of company presidents presented by the Heidrick and Struggles surveys. Such a comparison may well lead to a conviction that one or more changes would be desirable.

The behavioral study also has interesting implications. An organization can make a list of their successful and unsuccessful executives. Each executive could be assessed upon the variables suggested by the behavioral scientists. If results tend to confirm the importance of the motivational aspects of position requirements, then this would lead to a process of gathering data on these motivational variables early in the career of managerial personnel. A method for doing just this will be discussed in the next chapter.

The Uniroyal study of the kind of executive needed in the future should not be accepted at face value. It would help for top management to think through their own assumptions about the future and then decide upon the kind of knowledge, experience, and abilities deemed essential in future executives.

One conviction the authors share is that the successful executive of the future will, of necessity, have to be quite different from today's executive. In Chapter 1 we noted that Drucker had a basic concern that companies would develop elaborate mechanisms and in the process fail to develop executives. The above conviction provides a specific test for an organization. *Are you now developing executives who will be the quite different executives needed in the future?* Anything but a strong, affirmative answer may well mean that the pitfall of form over substance is likely to occur.

Another conviction the authors share is that it is much more important to give attention to the type of executive required in the future than it is to be concerned about the number to be required.

In a subsequent chapter we will come to grips with the challenge of planning for accelerated development and then implementing these plans as a means of developing managers who do meet the requirements of the future. Attention will now be given to methodology for determining future needs and the type of executive needed in the future. Let us first take up the problem of estimating future needs.

THE IMPACT OF STRUCTURE ON FUTURE NEEDS

It is interesting to consider the impact of organizational structure on the type of executive needed. Consider large oil companies, for example. Most of them have established a headquarters entity and major subdivisions, usually by geography. Within a major subdivision the primary structure is a process one, including such areas as exploration, production, and distribution. However, each subsidiary has a top group which is usually an inside board. Each member is strong in one or more specialties. The nature of the process type industry leads to a combination of top manager leadership, aided by strong committee support, directing major process groups.

How many broad-gauged generalists are needed in such an organization? Each major geographic subdivision and the corporation itself require such an executive. Must the executive be experienced in more than one major process? It might be of some value. However, a full-time, internal board exists, made up of at least one man with a strength in every major process. This structure certainly affects the number and type of generalists a large oil company needs.

What type of executives are needed in such companies? Certainly a strong leader is needed for the chief executive role in the corporation and in each major geographic subdivision. However, if he has an inside board made up of a talented group of specialists, then he doesn't have to be strong in each major function. He does have to be capable at integrating diverse individuals into an effective team.

Capable men in each process specialty, such as exploration, are needed at two levels, the policy level and the operating level. This analysis leads to the conclusion that a multibillion dollar oil company needs a small number of top leaders. The leaders do not need to have a personal mastery of each basic process (exploration, production, and distribution). They have to be skillful integrators. In addition, a flow of competent managers of process specialties is needed. They need to be developed in sufficient depth to staff policy positions as inside board members and top operating positions in operating subdivisions.

Consider a large manufacturing organization made up of autonomous business entities, each with its own major functions of research, engineering, manufacturing, marketing, finance, and personnel. Typical organizations like this would be General Electic, Johnson & Johnson, IT&T, U.S. Industries. Many others could be mentioned. The large manufacturing organization usually consists of a hierarchy of generalist positions as shown in Figure 4–1.

Let us assume an organization has about 100 general managers of a business. They will likely need 15 to 20 group vice-presidents, and 3 to 4 executive vice-presidents. The number needed in the office of the chief executive will likely vary from one to four. The obvious point is that a large number of generalists are needed. Less obvious is the likelihood that the nature of the generalists needed will vary at successive levels.

There is another interesting type of organization. It is often found in the computer and electronic industry. The organization may do business on a multi-billion dollar scale, yet it is set up functionally. A

FIGURE 4–1

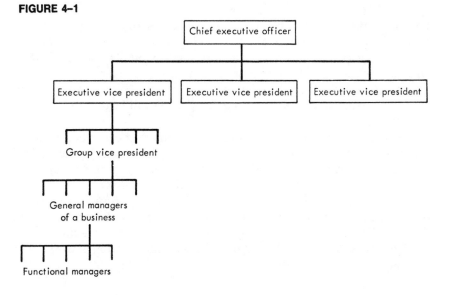

top management group, in effect, directs a large research and development group, a large manufacturing group, a large field service group, and a large marketing and selling force. Here again, the number of generalists needed is extremely small. The top group, somewhat like the oil company, is made up of a top leader and several other key executives with complementary backgrounds. In addition, the generalist, beginning with the general manager of a business, should be a broad-gauged generalist, capable of directing each major function and making trade-offs across functions. The type of generalist needed in a multi-business manufacturing organization could, we believe, be quite different from the kind required in a large oil company. The multi-business organization will likely find it quite advantageous to transfer individuals from one function to another and do so early in the individuals' careers.

Organizations, such as major oil companies, and computer companies must develop a flow of top leaders and a hierarchy of competence within each major functional group. In all likelihood, little need exists to move individuals from one function to another. However, moving from one facet to another facet within a given function would be critical.

Consider a fourth type of organization—a large bank which provides services. Dominant activities have to do with investments, loans, and operations. Each activity operates quite autonomously. Each represents a lifetime career. The top officers, usually numbering one to four, must be capable of directing each major activity and integrating them when necessary. But, historically, an executive climbs all the way to the top in one activity. In addition, at each level he has an option of managing or doing personal work. The operations side would be an exception. This unique nature of the structure in large banks makes for interesting complexities in deciding how many of what type of executives will be needed. A somewhat similar situation exists within large insurance organizations.

We would, therefore, caution organizations on borrowing ideas on executive continuity methods from other organizations, particularly if they are quite different in structure. We will be suggesting numerous activities in subsequent chapters. They will not necessarily be relevant to all organizations. Therefore, we urge thinking through the type of executives needed on the part of each organization. A firm fix on the outcome desired will permit designing an appropriate executive continuity system. It also permits adjusting the administration of the system to insure achieving the desired outcomes.

THE IMPACT OF THE BUSINESS CYCLE ON FUTURE NEEDS

The life cycle of a business is a well understood phenomena. The cycle is usually divided into a series of stages. Figure 4–2 represents one illustration of a business life cycle. Five stages are depicted. Stage 1 is

FIGURE 4–2
Business life cycle

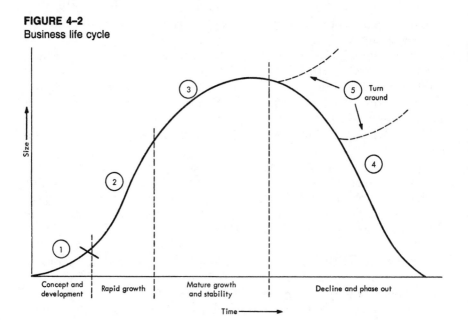

the embryonic state of concept and development. Stage 2 represents the initial growth. Growth brings with it increased size and complexity. Stage 3 is the mature growth, the stable period. Stage 4 brings in the decline and possible phasing out of a business. Stage 5 calls for a turn-around, a change in direction to maintain the size or to grow.

Increasingly, large enterprises consist of a variety of businesses in each of the basic stages. The interesting challenge is to relate the entire process of corporate-wide selection to the dynamics introduced by businesses in varying stages of their life cycle.

The executive who is extremely good at the tasks in Stage 1 may make the transition into and through Stage 2. Our studies suggest they seldom perform well in Stage 3. It is common to find executives who can manage well in only one or possibly two stages.

Earlier in the chapter we stressed the need to look at the type of manager needed in the future. Organizations consisting of businesses that move through the above business cycle will need to develop managers capable of managing in each of the basic stages. If our assumption is correct, it will be possible to develop managers who are capable of managing in one and possibly two stages. The art of timing will be required to achieve a sustained match between a manager and a changing business.

THE EXECUTIVE OF THE FUTURE FOR YOUR ORGANIZATION

Some individuals might very well question whether it is possible to define or describe the type or kind of executive that will be needed in the future. These individuals might very well argue that we have a difficult time describing the type of executive which is required at the present time. The truth of the matter is that very few organizations have given serious attention to the problem of what kind of executive is needed to occupy current positions. However, as difficult as this problem is, several approaches can produce helpful assumptions and implications for action.

1. Descriptive study of current executives

One very worthwhile approach is to do a descriptive analysis of current executives. This starts with readily available data, such as the average age, the average amount of education, the more frequent type of education, the average age upon becoming a general manager. It is also possible to determine the average age when executives reached critical stages in their career. (An example of such a study is given in chapter six.) These and other similar types of data can provide a very interesting and useful description of the current general manager.

While the initial study a company might make is of considerable interest, it is also quite helpful to repeat studies at periodic intervals. The repetition of studies quite often shows some interesting changes in the nature of the executive population that take place somewhat unbeknown to everyone involved.

2. Comparison of your executives with prevailing patterns

It is of interest to compare candidates for a position, such as president, with available studies such as the Heidrick and Struggles' study reported upon earlier in this chapter. These studies quite often reveal trends, such as those reported on by Heidrick and Struggles:
--Slightly younger age
--Significantly higher educational level
--Generalist experience becoming the predominant route to the top
Variances between one's current situation and such trends are certainly suggestive of needed action.

3. Predicting the type of executive required in the future

The two-step process used by the Uniroyal organization for thinking about the type of executive required in the future was reported upon earlier in this study. A meaningful project might involve having one's own executives complete the same two-step study process. The main requirements are:
--Advanced readings to stimulate realistic thinking about the future.
--Independent judgments on future characteristics of large enterprises.
--Independent judgments on kind of executive required in the future.
--Discussion time to permit arriving at a consensus representing the best thinking of the group.

4. Preparation of position specifications

Another step in coming to grips with the problem of the kind of future executives that will be needed is to struggle with the problem of preparing position specifications for executive positions. It is of little consequence to get this assignment accomplished by a staff group. It is much more important that the eventual decision makers on appointments to executive positions invest time in discussion of the specifications that they deem to be necessary. Examples of several such documents are included in Appendix C.

Once a position specification has been prepared and fully discussed and accepted by the top management of an organization, it can serve a variety of useful purposes. A serious criticism of most replacement planning is that little or no effort is devoted to the task of identifying what it takes to qualify as an executive and then asking managers to identify those individuals who now qualify or who they predict will likely qualify in the future. This will be discussed more fully later in this chapter.

Preparation of current position specifications will be helpful in preparing individual development plans. An analysis of the individuals deemed to have potential against the requirements will likely reveal certain variances against which improvement plans can be prepared.

The specifications also will come in handy in having career discussions with an individual; these career discussions may be for the purpose of advising him that he has not been selected, or they may be for the purpose of advising him of current limitations with suggestions on needed improvements. Another benefit is considering the modifications that will have to be made in the specifications for executives five or ten years hence.

Here is an example of the inter-relationship that becomes built up among the components of the systems approach. A value of a given technique cannot be measured in terms of its contribution to one specific purpose, it must be considered in terms of its contribution to the entire system.

AGE AND MOBILITY ANALYSIS

One of the best indications of whether your continuity program is working is the age differential among the various levels of management. A fairly wide age differential is obviously to be desired. This, in essence, shows that the required people flow is occurring without gaps or log jams. There are several ways of preparing age differential studies.

Figure 4–3 pictures the situations for all current officers in a medium size company. In a span of four years following the current year, five of the company's top seven officers will be retired. Loss of too many key men in a short period of time often creates a serious problem for a company. One interesting additional analysis which might be made is to project the age differential for the above executives and their likely replacements five years hence. The age of replacement is charted. As often as not the die is cast for another loss of a major portion of the company's officers some five or more years down the road.

In manpower planning and in preparing specifications there is a tendency to expect candidates to fall within a fairly limited age bracket. The inevitable result is that executives within each level of management will be in a narrow age range.

FIGURE 4–3
Years to retirement

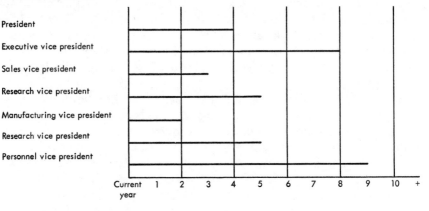

FIGURE 4–4
Average age at key management levels

Level	Average age
Office of the president	58.5
Group vice presidents	55.4
Divisional presidents	53.0
Divisional vice presidents	50.0

Figure 4–4 pictures the situation for a large divisionalized company. The number of executives is so large we need to use averages. The narrow difference in average age for the successive levels of this large company foreshadows several problems. There will be limited mobility which may contribute to restiveness on the part of good men. There will be periodic vacuums in management when an entire group grows old together and retires together.

An astute observer of executive performance has suggested that the average executive's most dynamic years fall between the ages of 40 and 60. Certainly from both physiological and motivational consideration this seems like a defensible assumption. Figure 4–5 illustrates the situation in a very large manufacturing company.

This organization prides itself on having group vice presidents and division general managers in their peak productive years. With the exception of their non-operating divisions, the above pattern looks good. They also expect a man to be about 60 before being appointed to one of the three top-level executive positions.

The question of how long an individual should remain in a given

FIGURE 4–5
Peak production analysis

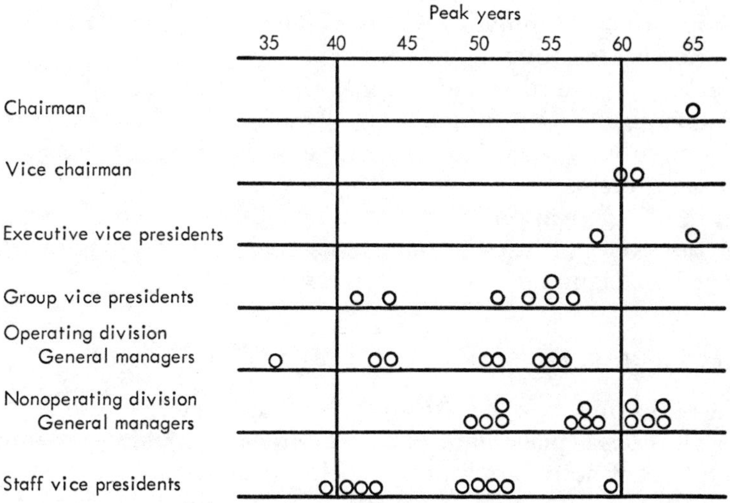

Peak years

	35	40	45	50	55	60	65

Chairman

Vice chairman

Executive vice presidents

Group vice presidents

Operating division
General managers

Nonoperating division
General managers

Staff vice presidents

position is beginning to get serious consideration. One student of executive behavior suggests it should not be any longer than seven years. It may not be possible to be quite this arbitrary. However, all the evidence points to the strong likelihood of adverse consequences arising from increased longevity. The negative consequences show up in business decisions, business results, and overall morale of the organization.

Figure 4–6 reflects a longevity analysis for a medium size company. The age analysis and mobility charts we have been talking about certainly do not solve any problems. They do warn of situations that will develop in the future unless corrective action is taken early enough to avoid the problem.

Such charts serve to dramatize the pipeline, the people flow impera-

FIGURE 4–6
Position longevity analysis

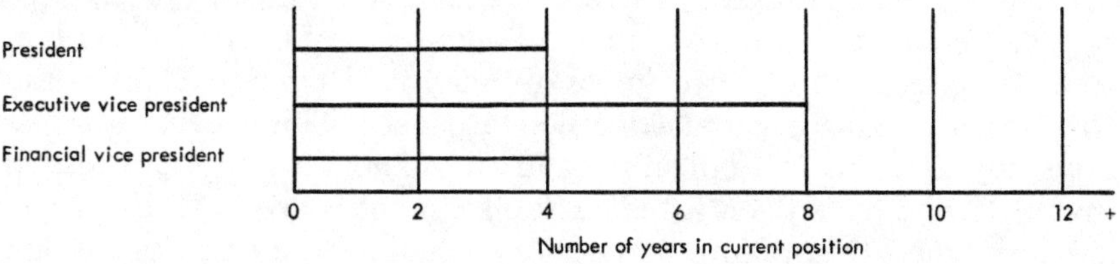

President

Executive vice president

Financial vice president

0	2	4	6	8	10	12	+

Number of years in current position

tives, of the executive continuity challenge. In subsequent chapters we will discuss a variety of appropriate actions. Among them are:

--Appointing an individual who is quite a bit older or quite a bit younger than the incumbent.

--Making lateral moves across major divisions or groups.

--Judicious early retirements.

--Use of a line executive on a special assignment or task force for several years.

Let us now give attention to a well established, one might say traditional, device that is used in most large organizations, namely, that of replacement planning.

REPLACEMENT PLANNING

One of the most popular executive continuity methods used by many organizations is replacement planning. An early booklet pertaining to executive continuity, published in 1948, recommended the use of replacement planning. Many organizations have felt they were well on their way to securing executive continuity once they had undertaken replacement planning. However, in organization after organization replacement planning has proven to be less productive than was expected. The main reasons can be accounted for by weaknesses of traditional methods of replacement planning.

Weaknesses of traditional methods

The traditional approach of replacement planning is characterized by several very critical weaknesses. More often than not, a manager is asked to indicate who he will appoint if called upon to do so. This is sometimes referred to as the "truck accident" question. If an executive was run over by a truck, whom would you put in his place? Notice that the executive has not had to identify an individual who is qualified. This is a critical weakness.

Another critical weakness is that many plans do not call for any subsequent action. No individual development plans are prepared or implemented, consequently little or no improvement takes place other than that which would have occurred in the normal course of events. The process, in effect, keeps a record or tally on current talent, but it does not develop or improve in a deliberate manner upon this talent. Another indication of a weakness of many replacement plans is that they are ignored when actual decisions are made. This is a very interesting study to make. Periodically, contrast the appointment of those individuals who have been listed on replacement charts with those who are subsequently appointed. Many organizations are surprised to find a very low relationship. A weakness of the entire replacement planning process is that it becomes a mere routine in which managers submit a required report once a year. Another critical weakness is that top management often assumes that they have real depth of management when all the spaces are filled in on the replacement charts. Another way of saying it is that they sometimes believe the colors on the charts. In our experience, half the names on replacement charts should not be there. But which half is the question.

The identification of these weaknesses is not done with the intention of eliminating the process; it is a very valuable component of the overall system. Most of these weaknesses reflect an ineffective or inappropriate use of a tool. The challenge actually is to overcome the above noted weaknesses and get the maximum mileage from the planning and programming which goes into a replacement planning process. Let us now take a positive view of the replacement planning process.

Characteristics of an effective process

There are several characteristics of an effective replacement planning process. The more a given organization's replacement planning process meets these criteria the better. Many organizations ask for nominations of individuals for replacements for a specific position. When looking for replacements for future executives it is a limitation that can and should be avoided. Therefore, the first characteristic of a replacement planning process for future executives is that executives be asked to identify individuals under their supervision who they believe to be, either currently qualified, or potentially qualified for a given executive level. Notice that we are not asking them to be identified as a replacement or backup for a specific position. Later when we start talking about company-wide selection moves, it will become apparent that quite often a position will be filled by an individual from some other division or from some other component of the enterprise. If there has been a rather heavy emphasis on getting an understudy ready or a backup man ready, then the arrival of a "foreigner" is a rather big shock to the individuals who do the replacement planning, as well as to the rest of the organization. The replacement planning process should call for a statement justifying the evaluation of the individual as now qualified or having potential to qualify. In addition, a specific plan of action should be required. This plan should ask for the next two desirable position moves for this individual plus other special action such as course attendance, exposure to special task forces, and so on. The replacement plan should also call for the identification of individuals of about age 30 who are deemed to have high potential.

Another characteristic or criterion of a sound replacement planning process is that the process is repeated each year. Another characteristic is that organizations do their planning at successive levels so that it is possible to get independent judgments from at least two levels.

One organization which has long implemented most of the above suggestions is the DuPont Company. The organization is a typical multi-divisional one. Let us consider how the process works for an operating division. Each vice president and general manager of an operating division prepares a Promotability Forecast annually. Four categories of potential have been established.

1. Middle management employees and above thought qualified to become division head within a 10-year period.
2. Lower middle management employees and higher thought qualified to attain at least a major department head (a top functional or product head position) within a 10-year period.
3. Lower middle management employees thought qualified to advance to a specified organization level within a 10-year period.
4. Young employees at lower organizational levels thought to possess the potential for very substantial managerial advancement.

A special report is prepared for each individual included in categories 1 and 2.

Provision is made for indicating for each individual the:

--Specific outstanding achievements and contributions particularly during the past year which are indicative of the forecast potential.

--Positions for which the individual is ready for promotion within one year.

--Positions for which the individual will be ready for promotion within one to three years.

--Whether the individual should be considered for transfer from a line to a staff position.

--Plans for the next three years for further development beyond the experience on his current position.

The term *promotability forecast* used by DuPont is a most descriptive one, it is more descriptive of the process we recommend than the more traditional term of *replacement planning*.

In the DuPont method an executive is being asked to think thoroughly and plan deliberately insofar as future high-level managers are concerned. Appendix E provides additional information on replacement planning.

We already have noted in chapter 2, having to do with top management, that there is a very beneficial process which we referred to as a manpower review. The manpower review presupposes that an executive has gone through a replacement planning process such as we have just described. The valuable part of the manpower review process then becomes the opportunity for interaction between top levels of executives about the future of the organization. Note again the inter-relationship between two segments of an overall system: the replacement planning process and top management action.

SUMMARY

Deciding what it is that should be accomplished is a sound step to take in initiating a systematic approach to executive continuity. This brought us to the third requirement to be stressed, namely, anticipating future needs.

Three studies which help us to grapple with the challenge of anticipating future needs were presented. One described the characteristics of current presidents of large enterprises. Another looked at motivational requirements of top level positions. Finally, an in-company study illustrated a process for establishing position specifications.

The impact of structure on definition of future needs was demonstrated by looking at the varied requirements for companies in the oil industry, in divisionalized manufacturing, in a large functional organization, and in banks.

The impact of the business cycle on future needs adds to the complexity by calling attention to the change in abilities required by a given business at different stages in its life cycle.

Four procedural suggestions were given for analyzing future executive needs. Age and mobility studies were illustrated. Finally, a criticism of traditional replacement planning provided a basis for a modification which can more appropriately be called promotability forecasting.

5

Objective data

The fourth major requirement for an effective overall systems approach to executive continuity is objective data.

The basic outcome of the entire approach is in terms of "units"—individuals who can achieve satisfactory results when appointed to key executive positions. The outcome is a steady flow of such competent executives. It is instructive to see how much time and effort is devoted to getting data by managers in professional sports so owners can get winning teams. Elaborate volumes of data are gathered prior to the annual drafting of college football and basketball players. Computers are utilized. A steady flow of weekly statistics on college players flows into the computer. Scouts add the perspective which comes from direct observation and interviews. Video tapes provide either complete coverage or a sample of actual performance of key candidates. Special budgets are set up for securing, processing, and presenting this vital data in a timely manner. Necessity can well be said to have become the mother of invention in professional sports. The costs of player personnel are extremely high. The box office receipts are directly affected by the drawing power of the sensational rookie, who eventually becomes an established star. So no expense is spared to get the data to permit making smart acquisitions annually.

The same basic position is implied for executive continuity by giving fourth priority to the requirement for objective data. Organizations that are really serious about executive continuity must invest in getting the data about personnel needed to make smart decisions.

Let us briefly review the relationship of objective data to points made in earlier chapters. The major components of an overall system approach was stressed in chapter one. The critical ingredient which directly impacts the effectiveness of every component is objective data. Few of the suggested actions to be taken by top management, as stressed in chapter 2 can be done effectively in the absence of objective data. It is impossible for top management to personally get the needed data. This is one of the primary contributions to be made by an effective staff group. Chapter 4 identified ways to determine the future talent needs of a business organization. As a result of action recommended in determining future needs, we will assume that the number of future executives, and certainly some assumptions about desirable characteristics, will have been made. Now is when objective data about available individuals is needed to build the ability to match executive position specifications and the qualifications of individual executives.

This chapter will grapple with the tough challenge of getting objective data. Once we have defined what is meant by "good" data, attention will be given to the reasons why most organizations currently have inadequate data. The major sources of objective data will be evaluated. Finally, a special process, tested over a period of years, for getting objective data at the executive level will be described. It is called the *Accomplishment Analysis Program.*

A DEFINITION OF "GOOD" DATA

We have frequently used the term objective data. Just what is meant by objective data? We could also say that in this chapter we will be searching for ways to get "good" data. There are several characteristics which go to make good data. For one thing, data needs to be reliable, that is the data holds up when the same information is secured the second or third time. There are no unexplained swings in the basic information about a given individual. Information which seems to be consistent is usually referred to as being reliable. Managers can depend on the information.

Another requirement for good data is that it be pertinent. It is possible to secure an enormous amount of data; but useful data is that type of information which is most pertinent to the decisions to be made. It also is necessary that the data be seen as relevant by everyone concerned. Two groups who are concerned about relevancy are the candidates themselves and the executives who are making decisions about these candidates.

Another characteristic of good data is that there is a minimum amount of bias. This, of course, is another way of saying that the information is accurate. It is unlikely that we are going to achieve data that is completely free of bias; however, to be useful the data should have a minimum of bias.

Data is also proved good to the extent that it permits the making of comparisons among quite diverse candidates. If individuals are being considered from different segments of the organization, if they have quite different functional backgrounds—such as finance and marketing—this makes for considerable difficulty in making choices. Therefore, top management is quite desirous of having information that permits the making of comparisons under such circumstances. It is this enthusiasm for comparability that leads many organizations to experiment with and make use of psychological tests. We will discuss tests later.

WHY IS OBJECTIVE DATA SO IMPORTANT?

Objective data about individual executives is of critical importance. Top management is "betting blue chips" when it selects an executive for a key position. If the executive fails it may cost thousands of dollars or even millions. It also costs in morale, disruption, and loss of confidence in top management both internally and externally.

The selection decision requires matching one or more candidates with the required specifications. Having a good fix on the current abilities, skills, interests, attitudes and values of an individual is essential to anticipating or predicting the individual's future behavior.

Two patterns are frequently found in large organizations in making promotional decisions. One pattern is for the top executive to promote his "buddies," the other is for the top executive to go outside the organization. In effect, he develops more confidence in strangers. If the systems approach is going to make these two patterns obsolete, and it must to fulfill its promise, then top executives will have to have good data available on all potential candidates.

MOST ORGANIZATIONS HAVE INADEQUATE DATA

It is a very rare company that has information available on candidates for executive positions that is accurate and useful. In fact, it is ironic that many top management people talk about their personnel as being valuable resources. One look at the data that executives in most large companies utilized in making critical executive continuity decisions reveals there is very little helpful information there. Unless the executive is personally acquainted with the individuals, he has little or no information upon which to make decisions.

Why is it that so few organizations have worthwhile information about candidates for top level positions? There are a variety of reasons.

In many instances top management of a company has not come to realize the need for such information. This is particularly true in moderately sized companies where the top executive is rarely called upon to appoint an executive. Another important reason is that many top executives do not realize that it is possible to get such information, hence they do not ask for it. In most companies the traditional pattern of personal knowledge is relied upon. This usually means that top management gets information on the basis of dramatic events, such as an important success or an important failure.

Some organizations rely on getting certain data such as a work history, and this is the extent of their demand for good information. In some cases such information has been put on to computers, and once this has been accomplished many top management groups feel that something has been accomplished. The fact that this computer information is rarely of value in making decisions about candidates for executive positions is not discovered. Another reason why such information is not readily available is that there is a traditional practice of collecting opinions from those who have known an individual. A random assortment of "halos" are collected. Usually this is done when a decision is iminent. The imminence of decisions quite often has an adverse impact upon getting accurate data. Some organizations require a written performance appraisal. Executives have quite often relied on this information. Most organizations eventually come to realize that the traditional performance appraisal process leaves a great deal to be desired. The basic difficulty is that it is difficult to determine when such information is accurate and when such information can be trusted. Managers, in general, are reluctant to put negative data into the record and let it become part of an individual's historical record.

For these reasons most organizations fail to have worthwhile information about candidates for top level positions. This constitutes a very serious handicap in making developmental plans and in making selection decisions. Let us now consider how to go about securing objective, descriptive information.

MAJOR SOURCES OF INFORMATION

There are six basic sources of such information. The first and simplest one is usually referred to as a personal history record. This consists of such basic data as age, education, salary progression, and title of positions held. Another source of information is that of self-description or self-analysis. A typical example here is one in which individuals are asked to prepare a statement of their accomplishments for the preceding year. A third source of information is performance appraisals prepared by superiors. In some organizations this information is collected by means of a group discussion. The written record is usually reflected as group consensus. Another source of information is the evaluation prepared by a trained psychologist. Some organizations have their own internal psychologists, others make use of outside professional organizations. This type of information is derived primarily from psychological tests and depth interviews. The information consists, primarily, of psychological observations and insights. Another source of information is that of a reference check with former bosses. A final source of information is the Accomplishment Analysis process. The Accomplishment Analysis process represents an attempt to get information about the managerial abilities of candidates by a thorough exploration of past accomplishments, or lack of accomplishments, and the practices of management that were used in achieving these accomplishments. Let us analyze each of these sources more closely.

ANALYSIS OF SOURCES

Personal history records are necessary. They do reveal certain past experiences of an individual. They give certain basic data about age and education which is necessary to consider. However, at their best, they are limited to providing data which is of minimum help in making decisions about a developmental plan, or about promotional moves. Personal history records are limited, particularly in providing data about how the manager actually manages and about his personal characteristics.

Self-descriptive information is a tricky type of data, both to collect and to use effectively. It is possible to get managers to prepare descriptive reports about their own annual accomplishments. Many managers provide a very accurate description of what they accomplished and what they did not accomplish. These descriptions often prove to be very helpful. However, there is a wide difference in both the ability and willingness to provide accurate data so that it is impossible to place great reliance upon self-descriptions. Another way of saying it is that it is difficult to determine when one can rely upon self-descriptive information.

The limitations of performance appraisals are quite apparent to executives who have endeavored to make use of such data. Some appraisals may be very accurate, very objective. Others may be very distorted, very inaccurate. In order to determine how much reliance can be placed upon a performance appraisal one needs to know both the subordinate and the superior. Consequently, the usual performance appraisals are of limited value in providing objective, worthwhile data, particularly in a large organization where data is sent from one of many components to a central headquarters group. In fact, the process of sending performance appraisals to headquarters in and of itself quite often leads to "contamination." Some efforts have been made to have group appraisals in which three individuals or more get together and discuss a given individual. This does offset the bias of the individual superior. Such group appraisals have proven to be of value in some organizations. However, the time required usually results in the death of group processes after several years. There are very few organizations that sustain this process for a period of five years or more.

While we have noted that performance appraisals have weaknesses, there may still be a need, particularly in large organizations, to ask for regular performance appraisals for the total managerial group. However, we will argue later that the critical decisions having to do with candidates for future executive positions are too important to rely upon written performance appraisals.

The general acceptance of the limitations of the previously mentioned sources of information have been recognized by many executives. This has led many of them to become enthusiastic about psychological appraisals. Executives tend to feel that this gives them objective data, that it gives them data that permits them to make comparisons. Our own position on psychological appraisals of experienced executives is definitely negative. Our reasons for this position are as follows. Tests have not yet been devised that help in determining managerial ability. A trained psychologist can describe personality characteristics with some accuracy. However, basing predictions of future managerial performance on these characteristics is an artistic feat without a demonstrable high record of accuracy. Further, we feel the actual record of performance is the best available indicator of past performance. We have found that an effort aimed at doing this is much more productive of "good" data. While we would perfer not to test experienced men, we do believe in the use of tests.

We would give a comprehensive test battery to all technical and professional personnel after about three or four years of service with an organization. Preferably this would be done when the employee is about 27 years of age. The individual employee would then receive a full explanation of the results to help him in his own career planning. The data would be retained by the personnel department. This department would be expected to interpret the data for managers upon request.

Use might be made of psychological appraisals when hiring experienced men from the outside as an additional precaution against making mistakes. It should not be necessary to ask experienced executives within a company to take psychological tests.

Use can also be made of psychological appraisals by a professional psychologist when very complex problem cases develop. This would be particularly true when an executive seems to have considerable potential but it is difficult to realize on this potential. In these cases such psychological appraisals would only be done with the full consent of the individual and with the definite intention of helping the individual.

Reference checks can be a useful source of information when they are secured in a thorough manner. Experience suggests that information of this type can best be secured by a personal interview or by telephone interview. Again all executives who have relied upon reference checks, particularly in a large organization, have found that there are occasions when the information they have been given proves to be accurate; on other occasions, for a variety of reasons, the information they have secured proves to be highly inaccurate.

The limitations of the previously mentioned sources led Mahler Associates to develop a process which we refer to as the Accomplishment Analysis Process. This process has been developed and tested in more than a dozen large organizations over the last decade. Admittedly, it is not the magic answer, it does not do everything; however, it is a process which top management has often found to be helpful. A description of this process follows.

THE ACCOMPLISHMENT ANALYSIS PROGRAM

Attention will be given to the following:
--The purpose of the Accomplishment Analysis Program.
--The historical development of the process.
--A description of the process.
--The requirements for optimum results.

Purpose

One purpose of the Accomplishment Analysis Program might well be stated as helping an organization avoid being victimized by the Peter Principle. Individuals are not promoted to a level of incompetence.

Making decisions on appointments to key positions is a challenge for every top executive. Such decisions can have a critical impact upon the future success of the enterprise. Most experienced top executives have long sought multiple sources of information when faced with a critical decision. Here is where the Accomplishment Analysis Program comes into play. The top executive has two sources of information. One from executives in the regular line-of-authority. The other source is the staff man or men doing accomplishment analyses.

As previously mentioned, in our experience in numerous large organizations, about half of the names on replacement charts do not belong on the chart. But which half? Here is a second purpose of the Accomplishment Analysis Program—to validate the replacement chart. The staff man who studies 30 executives by means of the accomplishment analysis has one distinct advantage. No one else in the company has as sound a base for judging the 30 men as the staff man. The staff man puts his reputation on the line regularly by indicating whether he feels a given nominee has potential to do the predicted job.

Since this process usually takes place before critical decisions are made, differences between executives' replacement planning thinking and accomplishment analysis thinking can be discussed thoroughly. Differences can lead to an alert being set up to permit closer observation before a critical decision is made.

There is a third purpose served by the Accomplishment Analysis Program, namely, that of stimulating growth and development. The analysis process puts the staff man in an excellent position to identify important developmental needs and then do something about them.

Studying scores of executives who are about the same age permits insightful analysis on developmental needs. The chance to first interview in depth and then talk frankly with both a nominee and his superior makes for real ease in establishing an effective counseling relationship.

In summary, the Accomplishment Analysis Program is designed to contribute to:

--increased accuracy in making critical executive appointments,

--achieving optimum growth and development of those executives deemed promotable.

Historical development

Some years ago the president of Uniroyal observed that both capital appropriation requests and executive appointments were critical decisions he was called upon to make or approve. In the former instance, he had more information than he needed prior to making the decision. In the latter case, he had little or no data he could really trust. He challenged the authors to remedy this. After several non-productive efforts, we settled on the Accomplishment Analysis Program. Among the methods which did not prove to be useful were psychological tests. It is generally accepted by behavioral scientists and by laymen that the best indicator of future performance is recent past performance. The interview process was built on this foundation. To keep the process from getting unwieldy, we limited the input to two sources—the nominee on a replacement chart and his immediate superior. Both were asked the same questions. The subordinate interview requires about three hours, the superior interview about two. About half of each interview is devoted to a review of accomplishments and lack of accomplishments. The remaining portion of the interview covers the processes of managing—planning, organizing, leading, controlling, and innovating.

It is important to note that the questions are, primarily, journalistic rather than editorial. Interviewees are asked to report, to describe, to give specific examples, to illustrate their comments. Rarely are they asked for an opinion. For example, a manager is not asked to report on his evaluation of how good a planner a subordinate is. However, the manager is asked to describe how a candidate actually does his planning. Admittedly, there is considerable variation in the ability of executives to describe such behavior. There is also considerable variation in the amount of knowledge that superiors have about how a subordinate actually does various elements of his management job. In this manner, the complex problem of endeavoring to equate opinions, to offset the halos of quite diverse supervisors of managers is avoided.

The type of data to be secured is influenced directly by the type of executive deemed desirable in the future as discussed in Chapter 4. The more thoroughly the requirements have been defined, the more helpful this is in designing the questions to be included in the interview process. It also aids in making the written report helpful to top managers in their decision making. Examples of the interview questions are provided in Appendix D. Not all of the questions are included. Space prevents including a complete copy of the interview questions used for both supervisors and subordinates.

The accomplishment analysis report is that of the staff man. He endeavors to report objectively on accomplishments or lack thereof. He restricts himself to those accomplishments on which both superior and subordinate are in agreement. In describing the management's practices he endeavors to concentrate on those characteristics which are revealed in the interviews with both the subordinate and the superior. In reporting on both accomplishments and on strengths and limitations, the interviewer endeavors to report as objectively as possible. However, there are two specific ways in which he sticks his neck out, in which he places his judgment on the line. In the placement section of his report he indicates whether or not, in his opinion, the candidate should be considered as having potential to become an executive at a given level. He also may suggest suitable placement alternatives. In addition, in the development section he suggests appropriate developmental actions and appropriate timing thereof.

In interviews with executives about subordinates it is not uncommon to find some individuals who do not have a precise idea of what a subordinate has accomplished. In addition, some executives do not have knowledge about how a subordinate actually manages. If a skilled interviewer is unable to obtain such information from a superior, how much dependence can be placed upon getting a written appraisal or getting a recommendation from such an executive as to whether or not his subordinate is qualified for promotion? One of the main reasons why many decisions turn out to be wrong goes back to the fact that the executive when asked for an opinion, of course, gives his opinion. When it is based upon a considerable lack of knowledge of accomplishments and actual management practices the likelihood of accurate prediction is not very great.

Process

The steps in the process are as follows:
1. A name is selected from the replacement chart to be interviewed. (We will call them nominees.)
2. The nominee is interviewed first.
3. The immediate superior of the nominee is then interviewed. Experience suggests the superior should have had one and preferably two or more years of direct supervision to make the interview most fruitful. In some instances, a prior superior will be interviewed.
4. The interviewer prepares an Accomplishment Analysis Report. Examples of such reports are given in Appendix D.
5. The report is discussed with the immediate superior. Any factual errors are corrected. Should a superior differ, this difference is noted on the report.
6. The report is discussed with the nominee. He is encouraged to see this as an opportunity to benefit from counseling with a presumably objective third party.
7. Periodically, a set of reports are discussed with top level executives.
8. Copies of the reports are retained in the staff man's possession. Those who are entitled to review the reports are encouraged to do so with the staff man who wrote the report.

As a general rule, the process requires about two man-days of time on the part of the staff man.

Experience demonstrates that an outside consultant should not do accomplishment analyses. The only exception might be in a relatively small organization.

Requirements

There are several requirements that are essential to a successful accomplishment analysis:
--Top management must have a strong desire to get and use a second source of data.

--A respected, astute staff man. The two man-days per accomplish-
ment analysis report must also be included in the staffing consider-
ations.
--Identification of the basic position specifications for key positions.
--A replacement planning process.
--A habit of company-wide promotions.

There is sometimes concern on the part of some organizations about
a staff man being asked to prepare accomplishment analysis reports. It
is feared he may become a kingmaker. Here again the entire system
must be kept in mind. We will discuss how the report fits into the overall
system shortly. This offsets the likelihood of kingmakers developing.

In actual practice, the greatest value of the Accomplishment Analysis
Program has proven to be in identifying executives who do have potential but for whom appropriate developmental experiences are not being
provided. We call these executives ones who are overdue to move. The
Accomplishment Analysis Program also helps to identify acute situations where there is no one below a given executive who is deemed to
be qualified to be his potential successor. The report also helps top
management to make sharp replacement decisions and to make them
earlier. They are in a better position to match a given individual with
a given superior or a given individual with a given situation. In organization after organization top management has come to have real confidence in and appreciation for the information provided by the accomplishment analysis.

With regard to data about executive candidates, an organization
should design a rather comprehensive approach, making use of as many
sources of information as possible. It is quite obvious that we would
place heavy reliance on the Accomplishment Analysis Program. The
time consuming aspects of this process requires that it be restricted to
those candidates who are deemed to have high potential for general-
manager-type positions.

It is not possible in a book such as this to define the process in
sufficient depth to enable an individual to go out and conduct such an
interview. The process is a skill process that requires thorough instruction, it requires practice, it requires skillful critique to develop the
necessary skill in getting the data, interpreting the data and preparing
an effective report. An analysis of the accuracy of accomplishment
analysis predictions in one company is given in Appendix D.

SUMMARY

Each requirement seems to be as important as the previous ones.
This is certainly true of the requirement for objective data. The inter-
relatedness of requirements is well demonstrated by the impact of data

on all other requirements. "Good" data is reliable, pertinent, contains a minimum of bias, and permits differentiation. Even though the need for good data is generally appreciated, most organizations have inadequate data on executive personnel. Often top management doesn't realize that it is possible to get good data.

There are six basic sources of information: personal history, self descriptions, performance appraisals, psychological evaluations, reference checks, and accomplishment analyses.

We see value in using each of these methods without relying on any one method entirely.

6

Accelerated development

Accelerated development is the fifth requirement of major importance in the design of an overall system. Accelerated development applies to the first 10 to 12 years of an individual's experience in an organization. Special efforts can be made to increase the amount of learning which takes place, or the natural course of events can be permitted to occur. Before considering how best to provide such learning experience, let us consider the prevailing practice.

For many years we have strongly advocated early identification of high-potential younger executives and their accelerated development. We observed that a few organizations really accepted the need for this type of action and, over a period of years, actually implemented such an effort. Most organizations did little or nothing about accelerated development. This led us to conduct a study, in cooperation with several large enterprises, of the current pattern of executive development. We decided to analyze the people flow within large, divisionalized companies. We found it helpful to do this by identifying four critical career crossroads. In this chapter we would like to report on the results of the career crossroad study and then consider how the accelerated development can be implemented.

FOUR CRITICAL CAREER CROSSROADS

A critical crossroad refers to a change in a position requiring a drastic change in behavior. A significant turn has to be made. Figure 6–1

FIGURE 6–1
Critical career crossroads in a large business organization

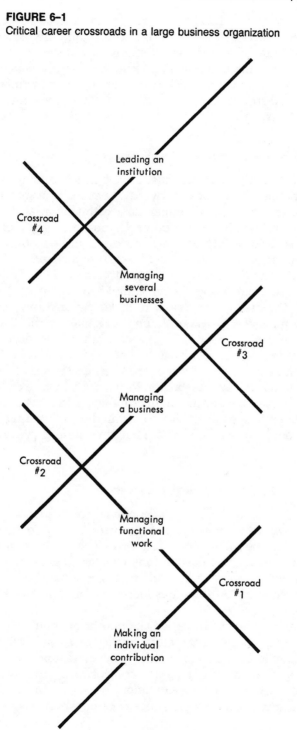

identifies four such critical crossroads found in all large, divisionalized business organizations. One could, of course, identify additional small or intermediate crossroads between any two of the crossroads identified. This additional detail will be avoided to permit concentration on the most critical crossroads. The implications for growth and development derived from these four will, in all likelihood, pertain to intermediate crossroads.

Crossroad #1—shift to a functional manager

The prevailing practice in most large business organizations is for a college graduate, who looks forward to becoming a manager, to first serve several years as an engineer, an accountant, a salesman, or some other type of individual contributor. In most companies crossroad #1 is the initial critical turn for the future executive to make. This turn is not quite the full left angle type. The first supervisory position usually involves direction of a small group, with considerable time still spent on doing one's old work. As the individual moves up the manager hierarchy, the pressure increases to make the turn toward more time spent as a manager. Consider an engineer making this transition. Initially, he sees himself as an engineer whose value derives from his engineering ability. Gradually, as his knowledge becomes obsolete with time and his management scope enlarges, his "value added" shifts to his managerial ability. He begins to have a concept of himself as a manager, but a manager of engineering work. In most companies, the engineering manager will move up within the engineering department until he comes to crossroad #2. The same pattern prevails for other functions.

Crossroad #2—shift to managing a business

The shift from a manager of functional work, such as engineering or marketing, to a manager of a business is a sharp turn. Trade-off decisions must be made across functions. The top man must now rely on the managers in each of the functional areas except, of course, the one from which the new business manager came. Strategic thinking becomes necessary. Ambiguities increase. Different pressures are encountered.

A few managers may have had an opportunity to manage more than one functional component before hitting crossroad #2. Some large organizations force the issue on this type of cross-functional experience. But managers in most companies are not likely to have had direct experience in more than one function.

The transition is often a challenge. The new business manager must learn a great deal about other functions so he can make wise trade-off decisions. He must find out what the unique work of a general manager is. He has to shift his concept of himself to being a manager of a business. He begins to work against a balance sheet rather than a cost statement or a sales forecast.

He slowly begins to realize that his thinking, his reacting, his decision-making processes have been conditioned or set by his prior functional experience and are no longer appropriate. So Crossroad #2 becomes a difficult and challenging turn to be made. Some fail to make the transition. Drucker makes this rather startling statement: "In my experience, two out of three men promoted to top management don't make it; they stay middle management. As a middle manager he controlled operations and fought fires. As a top manager, he hasn't the foggiest notion how one goes about making entrepreneurial or policy decisions".[1]

Crossroad #3—shift to managing several businesses

One would think that this turn might not be so sharp. After all, if one could run one business successfully, what could be so different about running two or more. Several complexities begin to occur. Supervising general managers is different from making trade-off decisions across functional managers. One has to begin to get satisfaction out of others being successful businessmen—a most challenging attitudinal change for many executives. Often the new businesses are unique, but the new manager relies on his past experience with one business for the strong convictions that influence his decision making. Adverse operating results quite often shatter the old convictions.

At this crossroad, the interaction with the central governing body becomes of prime importance. "Maze-brightness" must be added to other sterling characteristics required on this new road of multiple businesses. Other complexities are added having to do with community, industry, governmental, and ceremonial activities. The decisions are bigger, the risks greater, the time spans longer, the uncertainties increase, the anxiety and pressures are high. One's concept of one's self as a broad-gauged businessman evolves. Having gotten this far, some now begin to set their sights on the next crossroad.

Crossroad #4—shift to institutional leadership

This crossroad is not one that many individuals are asked to consider. It is one that is particularly challenging. Many a top executive does not make the turn at all because he does not even see it as a turn which is necessary. He keeps on doing the same thing he did when managing several businesses, except he now scales it up to cover the remaining businesses.

A change in self-concept is required here, as it has been for each previous crossroad. The executive who becomes a leader of an institution begins to see himself quite differently. He now begins to be more concerned about the corporate image than about his own self-centered image building. Decisions are made with an eye to long-term policy implications. The realization that his value is determined, in a large measure, by three or four strategic decisions in a given year begins to dawn, somewhat threateningly. Quick decisions and busyness begin to be seen as irrelevant on this road.

The larger an institution, the more important it becomes that the top executives make this #4 turn. Unfortunately, few executives have a prior model of institutional leadership to follow. The big challenge is not only one of ability, it is changing one's concept of one's self. One must change from an executive who runs several businesses to one who is leading the entire institution. Most critically, one has to begin to get a deep sense of satisfaction out of efforts aimed at creating an institution.

Let us consider actual crossroad data gathered from six large business organizations, reported in Table 6–1.

CROSSROAD DATA IN SELECTED COMPANIES

Six major manufacturing organizations supplied career crossroad data for all executives who held general manager positions. The positions ranged from general managers of an operating component to the chief executive officer.

Company A is a multibillion dollar manufacturing enterprise. They have a hierarchy of profit-center managers, group vice presidents, and president. The reported results are for 89 managers in these four levels.

Company B does over a billion dollars in sales. The hierarchy involves profit-center general managers, group vice presidents, and a president, The reported results are for the entire hierarchy, involving 22 executives.

Company C has over two billion dollars in sales. Their hierarchy also involves profit-center general managers, group vice presidents, and a president. The reported results are for a total of 15 executives.

Company D does nearly two billion dollars in sales. The hierarchy is similar to Companies B and C. The number of executives is 12.

Company E is a multibillion dollar organization doing business on a global basis. The hierarchy is similar to that of Company A. The reported results are for 20 executives.

TABLE 6–1
Critical career crossroad data

	Company						Average
	A	B	C	D	E	F	
Number of years as an individual contributor	8	6	6	9	7	5	7
Number of years as a functional manager	11	13	13	11	12	16	12
Number of years as a general manager (one business)	4	7	7	5	5	4	5
Number of years as a group executive (several businesses)	6	13	1	2	5	6	5
Age upon becoming a supervisor	31	30	30	34	29	30	31
Age upon becoming a general manager	42	43	43	45	41	46	43
Age upon becoming a group executive	46	48	50	50	46	50	48
Age upon becoming a chief executive (or office of chief executive)	52	53	51	52	50	51	52
Percent having experience in two or more major functions	59	90	47	58	70	90	69

Company F is a multibillion dollar organization also doing business on a global basis. The report covers the 20 top executive positions in the company. In effect, this includes all general manager positions at four levels.

IMPLICATIONS OF CROSSROADS DATA

It is interesting to note how similar the results reported in Table 6–1 are for each of the six large organizations. Let us consider the fact that in these organizations the pattern is for their current "general-type" executive to have spent seven years as an individual contributor, becoming a supervisor at the age of 31. Does this really make sense? We are dealing here with the early formative years. They are spent operating as an individual contributor, working under direct supervision, carrying out assigned tasks and projects. It would certainly be difficult to argue that seven years of such experience is necessary. We would argue just the opposite. Seven years at the formative stage of the young executive's career spent as an individual contributor is likely to be a serious handicap. It is likely to develop habits which are going to be inappropriate some 12 years later when the individual becomes a general manager.

Let us consider a second fact that these same executives spent 12 years as a manager of a function before becoming a general manager. Is this a desirable pattern? Here one has to differentiate between an executive who is going to become a generalist over several functions and one who is going to be in a top functional position. Again, it would appear to us that 12 years spent in one function does not really make sense for the development of future general managers. In Chapter 4 we talked about requirements of future general managers. Let us consider three requisites for success as a general manager from the discussion in chapter four. A general manager should:

--think like a generalist

--make decisions like an entrepreneur

--be able to lead quite diverse groups of people.

Certainly an individual who works in one function for 12 years gets little opportunity to develop any of these three characteristics. They are most likely developed, if at all, after appointment as a general manager. The "tuition" for learning after being appointed can be devastatingly high.

In two organizations there was a strong likelihood that the executives would have had experience in more than one function. In these cases the 12 years may make sense. In only one case was the time shortened for individual work and added to cross-functional opportunities.

We draw another inference from the data. The flow of personnel from initial recruiting to appointment to successive levels of general management positions has never been rationalized. Habits and traditions govern the process. We conclude that this traditional process is not likely to produce the desired number nor type of general manager needed in the future.

We think there are definite factors which influence the growth of general managers and managers of large functional groups. We would like to see these factors built-in to the first 20 years of development of future executives. Let us consider these factors.

FACTORS INFLUENCING GROWTH OF MANAGERS

We are concerned here with factors of importance in influencing growth of managers to fill the critical positions in the organization. More often than not these positions will be general-manager-type positions. In some instances they will be top level functional positions. The following factors, we feel, are of critical importance in influencing growth:

- --Early opportunity to supervise, to take significant risk, to take full responsibility.
- --A variety of models of competent executives to emulate.
- --Appropriate length of time in a given position.
- --An experience with adversity—learning by undoing.
- --Experience in more than one function.
- --Constructive coaching by a superior.
- --Periodic educational experiences of short duration when one is "learning prone."

Early opportunities

We would argue that it is of critical importance that an individual get an opportunity to become a supervisor quite early, preferably before 30. This will insure that an individual will begin to get a concept of himself or herself as one who gets results through others and not by dint of personal effort.

The young supervisor needs to have a position with full responsibility. Opportunities are needed to calculate and take risks. Experience suggests it is possible to find individuals who can readily take on the challenge to be a youthful supervisor. However, severe resistance is usually encountered in providing such opportunities.

Variety of models

Young managers learn much of their management style by watching their elders. It is a fortunate young man who has an opportunity to be exposed to a variety of superiors who are competent but use quite varied styles.

Timely assignments

It is difficult to learn if one is in a position a short time. The length of time depends on the particular rhythm of a business. A young supervisor needs to get feedback on the effectiveness of actions and decisions. He needs to see how some of his decisions turned out. It has traditionally been said that people learn by doing. They also learn by undoing.

It also is a waste of time to stay on a job too long. Again too long depends on the rhythm of the business. Usually, optimum learning occurs when an individual can get one and possibly two feedbacks on his decisions. Thereafter diminishing returns set in.

Experience with adversity

This is a somewhat novel suggestion but extremely important. Some executives climb a long way up the ladder, often to the very top, without ever experiencing a soul-searching period of business adversity. One would not deliberately program an individual for failure at an early stage in a career. However, assignments of extreme difficulty could well be arranged to provide this experience with adversity. This is particularly helpful to the cocky individual who may otherwise get impatient or stop learning.

Multifunction experience

We noted earlier that about half of the general managers in large companies providing data for the crossroads analysis had had experience in only one function. Certainly a manager who is considered to be a potential general manager could benefit much more by one five-year experience in one function and a second five-year experience in another function. Most critical here is that the function conditions the way a manager makes decisions and the way he manages. Experience in more than one function makes this apparent to the individual. He can then correct for this condition.

Coaching

Periodic coaching by a superior can contribute greatly to the ability of a manager to learn fully from his own experiences. Few individuals can be objective in their own introspections. Those individuals who are going to be accorded opportunities for accelerated development are likely to be quite self-confident. It is easy for this to shade over to conceit. When it does, learning ceases. Here is where coaching is critical.

Educational experiences

Education can contribute. It appears that bigger dividends occur if education is provided in short periods at regular intervals. In particular, managers seem to be learning prone at certain times. This is likely to be true as they take on new assignments, especially those involving a critical career crossroad. Educational experiences should be scheduled during these learning-prone periods.

We would argue that these factors influencing growth of managers need to be incorporated into the methods and policies of the overall system. Let us now give attention to personal factors pertaining to executive growth.

PERSONAL FACTORS PERTAINING TO GROWTH

The prior discussion of the challenge presented in making each cross-road turn permits several "driving suggestions" on what it takes for the individual executive to make smooth turns. In the final analysis, each executive must "make the turns" himself.

Anticipation is certainly appropriate. Ambitious individuals should begin to think through the transition which will be required by the next critical crossroad. It is necessary to be successful on the current stretch, but that is not sufficient. The individual executive may well press for lateral moves that will stand him in good stead when a crossroad turn is to be made. Few individuals volunteer for a lateral move. It involves risks. It also demonstrates that the executive is willing to sacrifice to learn. Such a demonstration certainly attracts the favorable attention of those making promotional decisions.

A change in self-concept is a basic requirement. The basic pattern of an executive's behavior is controlled by his self-concept. The challenge of competition is exciting. Winning leads to confidence. Often confidence changes to conceit. The conceited executive has great difficulty engaging in self-analysis.

He rejects inputs that suggest he may need to change his concept of himself. He looks back with satisfaction on his successes on the straightways. Little does he realize that he is likely to skid on the critical crossroad.

An ambitious executive needs to begin to map out a deliberate change in his concept of his self, complemented by changing habits of managing. It is safest to consider all past habits suspect at each crossroad transition.

Do not rely on current models. Many executives pattern themselves after a more experienced executive. This is dangerously misleading. The future is likely to be so different from the past that many new and different abilities, talents, and styles are likely to be required at each critical crossroad.

A change in work definition is also required. Making a smooth turn at critical crossroads requires a change in definition of work at each turn. Many executives are surprised after a crossroad promotion. "My job is quite different now," is a frequent verbalization. The executive now begins to spend time on different things, to work on different decisions, to work with different people, to have different concerns and different anxieties. It is necessary to search out the work which is pivotal and which can best be done by the executive in his new position.

The sooner one recognizes that a dramatic change in work definition is required, the more likely the crossroad turn will be made with a minimum of "burning rubber."

In chapter 1 we noted Drucker's early concern with the likelihood that organizations would stress technique and method and fail to get real development. The early experience of Uniroyal, as reported upon in chapter 1, revealed Drucker's concern to be a genuine one. Many companies are now busy with elaborate processes, yet plagued with a lack of real top management talent. We would argue that the career crossroads data from six large, progressive companies explains why results are not forthcoming. Careers are not being managed, directed, or programmed. They just happen. The failure to direct attention to the first ten years appears to be most critical. The continued analysis of career-crossroad-type data is beginning to dramatize the fact that in most cases no amount of developmental actions provided for men after they are 40 can really make much difference. Such developmental efforts are many years too late.

We suggested that an accelerated development program become a part of the overall executive continuity system.

We have used the term "people flow" or the pipeline analogy to stress the continuous nature of the process. These terms also dramatize the inevitability of the process. What a company eventually realizes in the way of executive competence is dependent upon the number and quality of the initial recruits, and their subsequent development and retention. In data processing one hears the phrase "garbage in, garbage out." The same phrase certainly applies to the people flow process.

The accelerated development requirement forces one to take a close look at the nature of experiences newcomers get in their first ten years with the organization. Organizations that have taken such a close look have done so in four major areas:
--College recruiting
--Career planning
--Early work experience
--Early identification of potential executives
Attention will be devoted to each of these four areas.

COLLEGE RECRUITING AND ACCELERATED DEVELOPMENT

There are several basic questions which each company must ask about the area of recruitment:

1. How is the company viewed by people it would like to hire? Do they see the company as socially concerned? Do they see the company as willing to give them genuine responsibility when they join?

2. Are you hiring new recruits with primary concern about their ability to do individual contribution work, or are you hiring new recruits with primary concern about their ability to be future middle level or higher level managers?

3. Is the selection process discriminating enough to bring in those best suited and reject the others? Are those who clearly will not prosper in the company separated early in their careers, both for their own good and the company's good?

4. Are the early formative years of promising young people being used effectively?

If a person is to develop in management, is he given an opportunity as quickly as possible to supervise people? Have assignments of new men gone to bosses who have demonstrated the ability to guide growth of young men and women? Has the first boss been trained to be effective in guiding the newcomer's development?

5. Are young newcomers assuming responsibility for their own growth?

Some young newcomers want passively to be developed. Does each boss seek to bring this responsibility home to the newcomers early in their careers? Are they helped to be experimental, to try new ways, to keep learning?

College recruiting is a habit for most business organizations. A few wily organizations, noting that most new recruits seem likely to quit within two or three years, only hire those who have worked in one or more companies. However, most organizations go through an annual process of setting quotas, mobilizing for campus visitations, and the final selection of college recruits. Few organizations have really thought through the relationship between college recruiting and the subsequent availability of executive candidates some 20 years later. Such a confrontation would lead to numerous changes in the traditional college recruiting process. You can test whether this statement applies to your own organization by the nature of your responses to the previous questions.

Let us now consider remedial actions. We will not concern ourselves with the regular recruiting processes. Rather we will consider several novel actions which are particularly pertinent to the executive continuity challenge.

A special recruit is needed

One large chemical company finally decided that they would at least use a parallel system. Some college recruits would be hired in hopes they would become future top managers of a given function, such as marketing or manufacturing, or possibly a general manager over functional managers. Other college recruits would be hired, somewhat traditionally, into individual contributor assignments without any prior assumptions about their eventual destination.

The specifications for the future manager-type college recruit were:

"Those recruits who are hopefully destined to be our middle level managers or higher will have to have a technical degree. In addition, we want a broad-gauged recruit who has graduated from a 5-year engineering program which stresses liberal arts as well as technical education. He may be a B.S. with an M.B.A."

While each organization will want to work out its own unique specifications, this chemical company example illustrates one change in the approach to college recruiting which is necessary for achieving the objectives of the executive continuity program. It requires deciding to look for a special kind of college recruit from the very beginning. We will discuss later the nature of the work experience to be accorded these special recruits.

Another alternative for getting a new type of recruit is the hiring of junior military officers. A trend has developed in recent years for companies to hire junior military officers whose governmental obligations have been completed. They are hired into managerial positions as well as professional and technical positions.

Such organizations are impressed with several characteristics frequently manifested by junior military officers: maturity, ability to lead, ability to work under pressure, and career motivated and realism about the way large bureaucracies work.

The recruiting spigot cannot be turned on and off

Many large organizations turn off the recruiting spigot at the first economic downturn. This is a sure sign that top management has not really thought about why they have college recruiting. It is also likely to occur with top managers who have not really got serious about an executive continuity program.

The smart company will have thought out several basic policy positions regarding college recruits. These policies will be designed to last through both fair weather and foul. At least the spigot will not be turned off entirely. Here are several such policies and programs:

1. Arbitrary recruiting ration. Usually the recruiting quota is negotiated each year. The quotas are heavily influenced by recent business conditions. The logic of a given quota is usually rather tenuous, whether it be high or low.

One company reasoned that they were hiring new management recruits to be sure they had managers some 10 to 20 years later. It was possible to make some minor money savings by not hiring any recruits in a given year. However, this was, in effect, deliberately handicapping a subsequent generation of top management. They finally concluded that it was uneconomic and foolhardy and could be avoided by a policy

that would endure during both economic peaks and valleys. The policy was to establish a quota as a percentage of the number of exempt personnel (exempt meaning essentially professional, technical, and managerial personnel). This percentage figure was determined with reference to such statistics as:
- --growth predictions
- --manager-sales ratios
- --age-level data
- --turnover data

Once established, this figure was not modified except for a periodic review of the initial actuarial assumptions.

Experience in this organization over a period of years demonstrated that the ratio of college recruits to exempt population will remain fairly constant unless there is an unusual effort to bring in college graduates. Even then the change in the ratio will be slight under normal circumstances because of the reluctance on the part of line management to add to the personnel count or to terminate doubtful performers to make room for the new recruits. Business cycles tend to level out the ratio over the years. When business is on the up side more recruits are hired, but more exempt non-graduates are also hired. Turnover tends to increase because jobs are easy to get. When the cycle turns down college recruiting is reduced, exempt ranks are reduced, and graduates on the payroll are generally reduced because cuts in personnel follow the rule of "last on, first off."

The main value of the arbitrary recruiting ratio was that it forced the people-flow to happen. It was apparent that the initial input had a most critical impact on the eventual depth of management. By establishing a firm but conservative figure this company was able to put recruiting on a stable, predictable basis. This made for much better relationship with educational institutions. It also provided a critical stability for the entire system at the very genesis of the whole process.

2. Central funding. Another basic policy which has rarely been adopted but has considerable merit in getting sound college recruiting is central funding. The chief financial officer is asked to set up a plan based on the monetary requirements of the estimated yearly recruiting plans and carry this as an investment in manpower for the future of the company. The recruiting and hiring is then done by the most capable men in the company and the recruits are assigned to company components for a period of time. At a predetermined time the location must decide if they want the man permanently. If so, they put the man on their payroll.

The above plan, like all others, has advantages and disadvantages. Here are some of the advantages:

a) All recruiting can be done on a year-round basis by specialists, rather than at one period of the year on a part-time basis by many individuals.
b) A few full-time recruiters can establish closer relationships with colleges and thereby strengthen their ability to obtain top recruits.
c) The ability to make hiring offers on the spot, rather than the prevalent referral to locations, sharpens the recruiters' decisions and reduces one of the greatest areas of expense and slippage in the traditional recruiting practices. The go–no go decision makes the recruiter and recruit enter into the whole process on an action basis rather than an exploratory basis.
d) Locations have an opportunity to see a man in action and can place him as a need may occur during the trial period instead of hiring a number of men at a given time regardless of current need.
e) A decision to move a recruit to a new location or different function can be made on the basis of observable performance. Many recruits find after a period of time that they might make a better contribution in a different kind of work.
f) A distinct advantage can be gained in selection of outstanding graduates when a stable approach to recruiting is maintained while other companies are initiating recruiting moratoriums.

The disadvantages are:

a) Locations may resent having recruits hired for them.
b) Peers and superiors may consider them as outsiders.
c) When jobs are open the locations may fill from outside because they do not consider the recruit as their man.

A change in orientation is needed

Most companies, as revealed by annual studies conducted by Northwestern University, lose about half of the graduates they have hired by the end of the third year of employment. The Uniroyal people conducted an extensive study to determine why this occurred in their organization. Heading the list of reasons were such things as lack of challenge, poor supervision, lack of opportunity. We will consider the implication of these results shortly. It also was quite apparent that the transition from campus to corporation life was difficult. Some companies are beginning to recognize that the new recruit can be helped with this transition. Uniroyal is one such organization. They initiated a special program to facilitate this transition. A seminar for college graduates was established. The format was simple. Sometime within 6 to 18 months of employment all graduates were invited to a seminar.

A group of 25 men and women from different locations, with different jobs and educational backgrounds were brought together. The participants worked on their own under expert guidance. They addressed themselves to such subjects as:

What were my expectations on joining the company?

Discussion of the breadth and depth of company, products they make, and so on. (Each person told about his own location and products.)

Discussion of the company's annual report.

Discussion of company training, benefits, policies, and procedures. (This subject is never covered completely at the time of hire.)

Discussion of case studies of men who have left the company and why—their fault or company's?

What does the company expect of individuals like me?

These discussions, plus bull sessions with peers from all over the company and the chance to get a view of the overall company picture and meet the men who hold important positions (at least six top officers

College recruits	Number	Percent who quit
Seminar attendees	469	21.5
Non-seminar attendees	540	39.6

attend parts of the sessions), reinforced the graduate's critical decision to make a career at Uniroyal. It was not possible to get all graduates to the seminars; this resulted in a control group against which to compare turnover. Studies over a five-year period have shown a much lower turnover for those attending the seminars. This example is not intended as a recommendation. It demonstrates the fact that the transition from campus to corporate life is a difficult one. Companies need to provide for a "decompression effect." To do so enables many new recruits to make the adjustment in the first organization they join rather than in a series of organizations.

CAREER PLANNING AND ACCELERATED DEVELOPMENT

Several large organizations have undertaken a career planning process for their college recruits. They have found that most young employees are acutely concerned about themselves and their careers. The first purpose of the career planning program is to provide such employees with basic data about themselves and to provide them with the benefit of an effective career discussion with an experienced personnel specialist. As we noted in chapter 5, most large organizations have difficulty getting useful information about their professional, technical, and managerial talent. This is particularly true of the younger employee. Therefore, a second purpose of the career planning program is to insure that an organization has certain basic, uniform data on all recent college recruits. This basic data assists in more skillfully planning career moves, making placements, and planning developmental actions.

The career planning program in these organizations is designed to be administered by regular personnel specialists. All college recruits who have been with the organization three years (approximately) are invited to participate. Participation is voluntary. The three-year period is arbitrary. Its main virtue is that the individual in whom one invests for this program will likely remain with the organization.

All instruments are written, and selected for ease in interpretation. The measurement instruments contain some tests which must be administered under strict standards on procedure and time. These instruments are administered by an experienced personnel specialist in a group setting. Group time requires about 4-½ hours. The remaining instruments are completed on an individual basis at work or after office hours, requiring another four to five hours.

The interpretation and career discussion with participants are conducted by an experienced personnel specialist. The participant gets a "profile" report. The basic data remains in a confidential individual personnel file. Access to the data is only provided to a manager in the presence of a personnel representative.

An explanation of the instruments and the profile report is to be found in Appendix F.

INITIAL WORK EXPERIENCE AND ACCELERATED DEVELOPMENT

Over a period of years companies have found initial jobs for the college recruit which meet two basic critieria. They are easy to move new men into and then out of, and they are safe. The crossroad study of general managers in several companies reported upon in this chapter showed that the new recruit spends about seven years as an individual contributor before becoming a supervisor. This data supports the conclusion that much of this time is certainly non-productive from a developmental view point. The experience may well handicap the development of future executives.

Regarding the initial work assignments for the first five years for the special recruit they have selected for future management positions, companies need to ask themselves the following questions:

—Is the first job a challenging one? How about the second and third jobs? Are they demanding? Does the new employee get a real chance to test himself?

--Is the new employee's first manager a good model of a capable manager? Is he an effective coach? Does he understand the new recruit? Can he motivate the new recruit? Does the new recruit get regular, helpful performance appraisals?

Sterling Livingston, professor of business administration at the Harvard Business School, suggests that a young man's first manager is likely to be the most influential person in his career.[2] If this manager is unable or unwilling to help develop the skills the young man needs to perform effectively, the latter will set lower standards for himself than he is capable of achieving, his self-image will be impaired, and he will develop negative attitudes toward his job, his employer, and—in all probability—his career in business. Since his chances of building a successful career with his employer will decline rapidly, he will leave, if he has high aspirations, in hope of finding a better opportunity. If, on the other hand, his manager helps him achieve his maximum potential, he will build the foundation for a successful career.

The early years in a business organization, when a young man can be strongly influenced by managerial expectations, are critical in determining his future performance and career progress. This is shown by a study at American Telephone & Telegraph Company. David Berlew and Douglas Hall found that what the company initially expected of college graduates who were management level employees was the most critical factor in their subsequent performance and success.[3] The researchers concluded: "The high correlation between how much a company expects of a man in his first year and how much he contributes during the next five years is too compelling to be ignored."

Berlew and Hall summarized their research by stating:

> Something important is happening in the first year . . . Meeting high company expectations in the critical first year leads to the internalization of positive job attitudes and high standards; these attitudes and standards, in turn, would first lead to and be reinforced by strong performance and success in later years. It should also follow that a new manager who meets the challenge of one highly demanding job will be given subsequently a more demanding job, and his level of contribution will rise as he responds to the company's growing expectations of him. The key . . . is the concept of the first year as a *critical period for learning,* a time when the trainee is uniquely ready to develop.

Roy W. Walters, Jr., former director of college employment at the American Telephone & Telegraph Company, contends that: "Initial bosses of new college hires must be the best in the organization. Unfortunately, however, most companies practice exactly the opposite." Walters observes that rarely do new graduates work closely with experienced middle managers or upper-level executives. Normally, they are bossed by first-line managers who tend to be the least experienced and least effective in the organization. While there are exceptions, first-line managers generally are either "old pros" who have been judged as lacking competence for higher levels of responsibility, or they are younger men who are making the transition from "doing" to "managing." Often, these managers lack the knowledge and skill required to develop the productive capabilities of their subordinates. As a consequence, many college graduates begin their careers in business under the worst possible circumstances. Since they know their abilities are not being developed or used, they quite naturally become negative toward their jobs, employers, and business careers.

Failure to have positive answers to the questions raised earlier about initial work experiences means that a company is guilty of under-development, under-utilization, and ineffective management and use of a valuable resource—its young managerial and professional talent.

Tradition says a new college recruit is assigned to an individual contributor type position for five to ten years before giving him a supervisory position. The tenor of the previous chapters and this one leads to the conclusion that this pattern is undesirable for recruits into management. The recruit we are concerned about is hired to be a manager. We would argue that the sooner he becomes a supervisor the better. One extremely large business organization has done just this. After a brief orientation of about a month, the recruit is assigned to a supervisory position. It is, in effect, a second level position. He is given an initial year. If he makes good, he continues. If he does not, he is asked to leave the company.

This organization has found that properly selected recruits have no trouble making this transition. However, they also found that the biggest roadblock was the unwillingness of older managers to really entrust responsibility to the young recruits. This organization also discovered that quite dramatic savings could be achieved. Fewer recruits needed to be hired. Turnover was substantially reduced.

EARLY IDENTIFICATION IS A NECESSITY

As the overall system begins to come into focus, it becomes apparent that many developmental actions cannot be accomplished unless plans are undertaken early in the career of a manager. This leads to a requirement of an "early identification program." The establishment of an early identification program does not necessarily guarantee results; however, the absence of such a program seriously threatens successful results.

Let us consider three rather critical specifications which previously have been discussed as being important for a future executive.

One is that the executive thinks like a generalist, that he, in effect, be a generalist before he is appointed to a general manager position. The second one is that he make decisions like an entrepreneur. This means that the individual calculates risks and then takes these calculated risks. And, finally, the individual must be able to lead quite diverse groups of people.

If an executive is going to meet these three characteristics before appointment as a general manager, then it becomes necessary to give him certain experiences early in his career. For example, the ability to think like a generalist is certainly enhanced by having actual experience in directing two or more functions. If an individual is going to decide like an entrepreneur, then all the evidence suggests that he must have an opportunity to make important decisions at an early stage in his career. If he has not had this opportunity early, in effect the organization has conditioned him for 15 years or more to accept decisions made by others. Subsequently, when he is placed in a position where entrepreneur-type thinking is required, the typical executive is handicapped seriously by the lack of any entrepreneur-type experience at an early age.

The ability to lead quite diverse groups, as well as large groups, is not something that can be learned from a book. It requires the actual experience of managing quite diverse groups, hopefully under the skillful coaching of an experienced superior.

The DuPont organization has thought through the timing on the appointment to the position of vice presidential general manager in their divisionalized organization. Their analysis, going back over a period of years, showed that men were about 50 years of age when appointed to a general manager position. This led them to conclude that they had to identify young men with high potential and give them opportunities to move across functions and operating components. This same conclusion may not necessarily be appropriate for another organization. However, it is an interesting exercise for each organization to endeavor to arrive at an age figure as to when a general manager is likely to be appointed. Then those experiences that are deemed to be highly desirable for a general manager need to be identified. Once this type of analysis is engaged in, the almost inevitable conclusion is that it will be absolutely necessary to identify candidates quite early in their career so that it is possible to give them a variety of desirable experiences. Analyses in a variety of companies suggest that individuals need to be identified at about age 26 and then given an accelerated opportunity to develop.

There is an underlying assumption that needs to be made explicit with regard to this type of analysis. It is assumed that those experiences that develop an effective functional manager, such as a manager of manufacturing, are not likely to be sufficient for the development of general managers. We have previously identified three rather critical requirements for a general manager position. If an organization is serious about having these requirements met by candidates for general manager positions, they can best be fulfilled by providing early opportunities for risk-taking experiences. Some type of early identification program becomes a necessity. If meaningful experiences are to be provided it will be necessary to identify individuals quite early in their careers and to give them an accelerated opportunity to have such experiences.

It is predictable that organizations will meet resistance in launching an accelerated development program. Few organizations actually endeavor to do this in a deliberate manner. The DuPont organization encourages this to happen by keeping a box score by divisions on the extent to which managers deemed to have potential are receiving cross-functional experience. It is necessary that top management decide whether or not this requirement is going to be a matter of policy. If it is, then the policy must be encouraged. In some instances considerable persuasion is necessary. There is a basic reluctance on the part of functional managers to permit cross-functional moves. Marketing managers are aghast when a manufacturing individual is brought into their midst and vice versa. Admittedly, there are risks involved in such moves. This is one reason why it has to be done at an early age and at a lower level in the organization.

DuPont has had a policy encouraging cross-fertilization in effect for several decades. Managers are moved between locations and functions, such as sales and manufacturing. They are also moved from one operating component to another and from line to staff positions and vice versa. An indication of their dedication to cross-fertilization is reflected in the following figures for their middle and upper level managers:

--Over 60 percent have worked in more than one functional field.

--Over 40 percent have worked in more than one operating department.

A special group are younger, lower organizational level employees considered to have very substantial managerial advancement capabilities. In a recent analysis this group of several hundred averaged 32 years of age and have been with DuPont about eight years. Already, about one-third have worked in more than one major function.

There is also advantage, particularly in multi-divisional kind of companies, in encouraging managers to have experience in more than one division. This is particularly true for a relatively small number of individuals who might eventually be given consideration as future top managers; such as a president or a group vice president. Here again a considerable amount of pressure on the organization is required to insure that the cross-divisional transfers are made. Among the types of pressure which can be exerted are the requirements that five candidates be considered in making appointments to executive positions, three of which must be from outside a given organization.

There is valuable experience to be gained from having managers work not only in line positions where they are exerting line authority, but also to have experience in working in a staff position where they must use the authority of staff groups. If this experience is with a central group in the headquarters, they get an opportunity not only to learn about the complexities of staff work, but also the complexities of the headquarters operation. Experience in staff positions is valuable in enabling managers to understand and exercise power in a skillful manner. It also enables one to better understand how to get the optimum contribution of staff groups.

Year by year involvement by line management, from bottom to top, is essential to the success of an accelerated development program. The payoff from such a program begins to bear fruit after about five years of consistent effort. This is not an activity that can be delegated to the personnel staff. It must be handled by each level of management. At Uniroyal, for example, the selection reviews are made by the plant manager level, then reviewed and further refined to meet program goals by the general manager and his staff. The final review is held with top corporate officers and all general managers for the corporation. An explanation of the Uniroyal program is provided in Appendix G.

At the annual corporate review in Uniroyal a limited number of candidates are selected for "cross-pollination" between divisions. A rule of thumb is that each division gives up two and takes two. The Uniroyal policy statement on "cross-pollination" is also included in the Appendix G.

The philosophy behind the Uniroyal "cross-pollination" program can be summed up as follows:
1. Involvement of line management.
2. Selection based on performance.
3. Everyone has opportunity (college, non-college, men, women, any race or creed).
4. Importance of entire process is enhanced by having final selections reviewed by top management.
5. Annual selections—wipe slate clean—avoid select group of "fair-haired" individuals.
6. Compels management to do rotation. (Training by challenge of new experience.)
7. Forces interdivisional transfers.
8. Makes visible a large number of young (under 35-years-old) candidates to all officers of the company.

SUMMARY

Four critical career crossroads were identified. They constituted the shift from
  --Individual contributor to functional manager,
  --Functional manager to general manager,
  --Managing one business to managing several businesses,
  --Managing several businesses to being an institutional leader
Data from six large companies showed quite comparable results. The main implications of the results seriously questions the pattern of future general managers spending 7 years as an individual contributor and 12 more years as a functional manager.

Factors influencing the growth of managers and personal factors pertaining to growth were discussed.

Planning for accelerated development called for serious attention being given to college recruiting, career planning, early work experience, and early identification.

7

Effective coaching

The sixth requirement for a comprehensive approach to executive continuity is that of effective coaching. Effective coaching refers to the discussions between a superior and a subordinate which help the latter to develop and grow. It is likely that effective coaching is the requirement that has been stressed the longest. Professor Myles Mace first stressed the importance of coaching in 1949 in his book entitled *The Growth and Development of Executives*. The book was based upon his survey of numerous company activities. He concluded "that the most effective way of providing for the growth and development of people in manufacturing organizations is through the conscious coaching of subordinates by their immediate superiors." He went on to say, "The objective of the executive's job, in other words the coach's job, is to utilize the abilities and capacities of others. Effective utilization means developing the latent potential of subordinates. Coaching subordinates is, therefore, not some technique to be adopted and used by administrators as a tool, a method or a device. It is a way of administration: it is administration." [1]

His studies lead him to stress that managers should:

--Give their subordinates an opportunity to perform.
--Provide an atmosphere of confidence.
--Establish standards of performance.
--Create an effective team.
--Counsel subordinates on their work performance.

Mace then went on to devote an entire chapter to "Getting the

87

Coaches to Coach." One might assume that effective coaching would now be commonplace after having been stressed more than two decades ago. Surveys we have conducted at the president level and at the middle level of many organizations reveal that just the opposite is true. We will review these surveys of coaching and then consider how coaching practices of executives can be improved.

COACHING PRACTICES OF COMPANY PRESIDENTS

Over a number of years several thousand executives have participated in a Coaching Practices Survey conducted by Mahler Associates. Twenty-one of these executives were presidents of their companies. The subordinates, numbering 137, completed a survey questionnaire on their superiors' coaching practices. The survey covered nine types of coaching which had to do with:
--Responsibilities and goals
--Delegation
--Knowledge of performance
--Assistance as needed
--Motivation
--Working relationships
--Benefiting from experience
--Group activities
--Future responsibilities
Five questions were asked pertaining to each type of coaching. Each question asked for an indication of the frequency of a given superior's coaching practice as seen by his subordinate. For example:

> "To what extent has your supervisor explained to you the basis upon which your salary increases will be granted?"
> _____1. He has not explained this at all.
> _____2. He has explained this in general terms.
> _____3. He has explained this in some detail.
> _____4. He has explained this quite thoroughly.

A tenth factor covered attitude toward the coaching practices. In addition, subordinates were given an opportunity to select up to seven specific coaching practices that they would like to see increased. In total, 45 coaching practices were studied. It will be of interest to look at the coaching practices carried out most frequently and those carried out least frequently. In the latter case we will also look at the frequency with which subordinates said they would like to see an increase.

Table 7-1 suggests that certain types of coaching are done with a high frequency by the presidents participating in this survey. The pattern of the ten practices done most frequently points to a high level of activities leading to a good working relationship. Information, back-

TABLE 7-1
Coaching practices done frequently

Coaching practices	Percent saying it was done quite frequently
Superior discusses such things as the needs of the business, changes in direction of the business, long-term results needed.	91
Superior provides support and backing when it would be helpful.	89
Superior evidences interest in my opinions and suggestions on important subjects.	89
Superior provides opportunities to communicate with him on matters of importance.	88
Superior permits me to establish most of the things to be done.	88
Superior places stress on achieving both current results and longer-range results.	87
Superior follows up more on significant aspects than on details of subordinate's work.	87
When discussing problems and undertakings, the superior endeavors to understand the subordinate's viewpoint.	86
Superior uses group meetings with his subordinates to get across his philosophy of doing business, his standards, and so on.	85
Superior insists on commitments (goals) being specific in nature.	82

ground briefing, support, and interest are provided. Attention is given to defining what is expected. Note that few, if any, of the most frequent coaching activities would really help an individual to grow and develop. Let us look at the other side of the coin: the coaching practices done infrequently. In this instance we will also look at the percent requesting an increase in a given activity.

How well do the 21 presidents coach subordinates? The data in Table 7-2 suggests that three-fourths of the subordinates have not had a discussion on ways they might improve their managerial skills. One-fourth considered it important enough to ask for an increase. Five practices having to do with career questions were conducted infrequently. We often say that no one talks to anyone about his future unless he is being invited to a farewell party.

The results for several thousand middle level managers are quite similar to the results reported for presidents. Based upon these results, we would conclude that few executives can be credited with contributing to the growth and development of their subordinates. If coaching by superiors is really important, if it really is necessary, if it really does make a difference, then most organizations are short-changing them-

TABLE 7-2
Coaching practices done infrequently

Coaching practices	Percent saying it was done infrequently	Percent saying they would like to see it increased
Telling a subordinate the requirements expected of one to qualify for larger responsibilities in the future.	83	22
Discussion with a subordinate about ways in which he might improve his leadership or management skills.	78	23
Giving a subordinate suggestions for improvements he needs to make.	63	20
Discussing specific things a subordinate might do to better qualify for taking on greater responsibility in the future.	62	27
Encouraging a subordinate to do specific things to better prepare for advancement.	60	12
Explaining the "ground rules" concerning compensation decisions.	59	17
Talking with a subordinate about his future opportunities.	55	15
Discussing a subordinate's ambitions and aspirations.	55	19
Talking with a subordinate about your evaluation of his performance.	54	21
Discussing authority of a subordinate.	53	4

selves. We believe that effective coaching can contribute greatly to the growth and development of executives. However, getting executives to provide effective coaching constitutes a real challenge. Before considering how this challenge might be met, let us review the results of a study aimed at determining whether formal coaching really makes a difference.

DOES FORMAL COACHING MAKE A DIFFERENCE?

In the course of giving coaching practices surveys to many different organizations, we had occasion to study three organizations to determine just what differences seem to exist in the coaching practices of those managers who conduct "regular coaching interviews" and those managers who do not conduct such interviews.

Managers were asked to report on the nature of the coaching practices of their superiors. By checking responses to multiple-choice type questions, these coaching practices referred to either practices or results which might be obtained by either formal, systematic coaching interviews or by informal, unsystematic coaching efforts, or by a combination of both.

Those who reported they had never had a coaching interview were assigned to a "not coached" group, and those who reported having had a coaching interview sometime in the past were assigned to a "coached" group. Before looking at the results for these groups on nine different aspects of coaching, let us first briefly describe the groups.

Group A consists of the 100 top management people in an organization of about 15,000. This is a single plant in a large manufacturing organization having to do with national defense type products. Thirty-five of the 100 individuals answering the survey reported that they had never received a formal interview.

Group B consists of 79 middle and lower-level managers in several supermarket organizations. Twenty-one (27 percent) of the 79 reported they had never had a formal interview.

Group C consists of 31 middle-level managers in a large electrical organization. Of this number, 11 (35 percent) indicated they had never had a formal interview.

The results represent the percent responding to the question as indicated:

TABLE 7–3
Coaching practices survey

Coaching question	Coached group			Not-coached group		
	A	B	C	A	B	C
I have a very good idea or know exactly what is expected of me	85%	88%	64%	59%	62%	35%
My manager supervises me about right (he delegates).	78	88	82	46	57	60
My manager supervises me too loosely.	16	7	9	44	38	35
I have a very good idea of what my manager thinks of my work	60	56	64	26	38	10
My manager is frank in telling me what he thinks of my performance	59	55	64	34	38	10
Within the last six months my manager has made suggestions on responsibilities on which I need to improve.	66	77	64	34	34	20
My manager gives me considerable assistance in improving my performance	47	64	54	18	38	39
My manager motivates me in appropriate ways to do my best.	76	84	82	32	43	17
I like the idea of an annual coaching interview.	82	91	100	86	81	94

Conclusion

The differences between the coached group and the non-coached group are of great magnitude in all cases, except one.

The manager who sees value in providing regular coaching interviews is seen by his subordinates as an individual who is likely to:

1. Let them know what is expected of them.
2. Let them know how they stand.
3. Supervise them about right.
4. Provide frank statements about their performance.
5. Provide suggestions and assistance when needed.
6. Utilize appropriate motivational methods.

It is impossible to establish a cause-and-effect relationship between the conduct of regular coaching interviews and a positive report by subordinates on other coaching practices. However, the results do suggest that those managers who are willing to provide formal coaching interviews differ considerably in their coaching practices from those who do not provide such interviews. The results also suggest that implementing the requirement of effective coaching will indeed be a significant challenge. The importance of facing up to this challenge is well documented by the "Pygmalion Effect." Let's now consider this interesting concept.

THE PYGMALION EFFECT IN EXECUTIVE COACHING

Sterling Livingston, Professor of Management at Harvard, has contributed valuable insight into the dynamics of the coaching relationship between an executive and a subordinate. He calls it the "Pygmalion Effect."[2]

In George Bernard Shaw's *Pygmalion,* Eliza Doolittle explains:

"You see, really and truly, apart from the things anyone can pick up (the dressing and the proper way of speaking and so on), the difference between a lady and a flower girl is not how she behaves, but how she's treated. I shall always be a flower girl to Professor Higgins, because he always treats me as a flower girl, and always will; but I know I can be a lady to you, because you always treat me as a lady, and always will."

Some managers always treat their subordinates in a way that leads to superior performance. But most managers, says Livingston, like Professor Higgins, unintentionally treat their subordinates in a way that leads to lower performance than they are capable of achieving. The way managers treat their subordinates is subtly influenced by what they expect of them. If a manager's expectations are high, productivity is likely to be excellent. If his expectations are low, productivity is likely to be poor. It is as though there were a law that caused a subordinate's performance to rise or fall to meet his manager's expectations.

The powerful influence of one person's expectations on another's behavior has long been recognized by physicians and behavioral scientists and, more recently, by teachers. But heretofore the importance of managerial expectations for individual and group performances has not been widely understood. Livingston documented this phenomenon in a number of case studies prepared during the past decade for major industrial concerns. These cases and other evidence available from behavioral research now reveal:

   --What a manager expects of his subordinates and the way he treats them largely determine their performance and career progress.
   --A unique characteristic of superior managers is their ability to create high performance expectations that subordinates fulfill.
   --Less effective managers fail to develop similar expectations and, as a consequence, the productivity of their subordinates suffers.
   --Subordinates, more often than not, appear to do what they believe they are expected to do.

Livingston argues that managers cannot avoid the depressing cycle of events that flow from low expectations merely by hiding their feelings from subordinates. If a manager believes a subordinate will perform poorly, it is virtually impossible for him to mask his expectations, because the message usually is communicated unintentionally without conscious action on his part.

Indeed, a manager often communicates most when he believes he is communicating least. For instance, when he says nothing, when he becomes cold and uncommunicative, it usually is a sign that he is displeased by a subordinate or believes he is hopeless. The silent treatment communicates negative feelings even more effectively, at times, than a tongue-lashing does. What seems to be critical in the communication of expectations is not what the boss says, so much as the *way he behaves.* Indifferent and noncommittal treatment, more often than not, is the kind of treatment that communicates low expectations and leads to poor performance.

Livingston suggests that managers are more effective in communicating low expectations to their subordinates than in communicating high expectations to them, even though most managers believe exactly the opposite. It usually is astonishingly difficult for them to recognize the clarity with which they transmit negative feelings to subordinates.

Livingston suggests that something takes place in the minds of superior managers that does not occur in the minds of those who are less effective. While superior managers are consistently able to create high performance expectations that their subordinates fulfill, weaker managers are not successful in obtaining a similar response. What accounts for the difference?

The answer, says Livingston, seems to be that superior managers have greater confidence than other managers in their own ability to develop the talents of their subordinates. Contrary to what might be assumed, the high expectations of superior managers are based primarily on what they think about themselves—about their own ability to select, train, and motivate their subordinates. What the manager believes about himself subtly influences what he believes about his subordinates, what he expects of them, and how he treats them. If he has confidence in his ability to develop and stimulate them to high levels of performance, he will expect much of them and will treat them with confidence that his expectations will be met. But if he has doubts about his ability to stimulate them, he will expect less of them and will treat them with less confidence.

Stated in another way, the superior manager's record of success and his confidence in his ability give his high expectations credibility. As a consequence, his subordinates accept his expectations as realistic and try hard to achieve them.

Let us review several main points which have been developed:

--Effective coaching has long been recommended.

--Effective coaching which leads to development is still rare at ex-ecutive levels.

--Effective coaching does make a significant difference.

This means we must grapple more effectively with means of achieving effective coaching at the executive level.

SUGGESTIONS FOR IMPROVING THE COACHING PRACTICES OF EXECUTIVES

The above studies of coaching practices confirm the fact that it is difficult to improve the coaching practices of managers. But it can be done, provided a sound series of actions is carried out. Let us consider six possible actions and then discuss each briefly. We would suggest that it is necessary to:

1. Plan a series of efforts to be undertaken over a period of years.
2. Give attention to improving both day-to-day coaching as well as formal coaching, such as annual performance interviews.
3. Provide individual managers with a bench mark of their current coaching practices and repeat this measurement periodically.
4. Provide periodic instruction on coaching techniques and do so in such a way that actual improvement in coaching skills results from the instruction.

5. Identify "good" and "poor" coaches and plan appropriate action for managers in each group.
6. Get a coaching benefit from an objectives program.

1. Plan a series of efforts to be undertaken over a period of years. Coaching practices of executives can be changed. But to change the practices of an appreciable number of executives must be looked upon as a long-term undertaking. In truth, the job is never done. But some observable progress might be seen by planning and carrying out a sound effort over several years. In the past some organizations have expected a short course to be sufficient stimulus to get and sustain a change in habit. Mace's suggestion that coaching is administration reveals the underlying nature of our problem. We are actually trying to get managers to change their way of managing. This complex challenge requires a sustained effort.

2. Concentrate attention upon improving the informal, day-to-day coaching as well as formal coaching practices. This suggestion is particularly important. Traditionally, considerable effort has been concentrated on formal, annual appraisal programs. It was the thing to do. The reaction of many executives, as the above studies show, has been to avoid doing the formal interviews. Many argued, with considerable merit, that the important coaching was the day-to-day coaching. It is, therefore, suggested that the challenge be defined as aiding executives to improve on both their day-to-day coaching and their more formal coaching efforts.

In this connection we have identified 12 ways by which an executive can improve his day-to-day coaching. The twelve suggestions are to be found in Appendix I where they have been included in a check list by which executives can check their day-to-day coaching practices.

3. Provide bench-mark measures for individual executives. It is interesting that companies so often overlook one of the better known and well accepted principles of learning; that an individual must have a measure of his progress in order to learn and be stimulated to learn. Certainly getting some improvement in day-to-day coaching necessitates getting such information. One way to do this is to provide coaching practices survey results to an executive.

In our experience, we have found it desirable to report the data in such a way that each manager gets his own results and no one else gets to see them. This process is much more likely to get the manager to accept the data. It avoids the stimulation of resistances which may arise if a manager feels he may be subjected to superior criticism if his results are poor. Helpful suggestions will be found in Appendix J.

4. Provide periodic instruction. Having an effective two-way discussion with a subordinate, aimed at getting an improvement in his performance, is a skill. Some executives do this naturally. But most executives do not. For example, previous study results show that about every second executive has difficulty being frank in discussing a subordinate's performance. Most efforts at providing instruction have been short in length and long on theory. We would urge that a series of instruction sessions be planned. In our experience, the initial instruction sessions should be devoted to the presentation and discussion of coaching survey results. This proves to be a way of getting started which is seen as helpful and practical by executives.

It is helpful for executives to have some sound principles upon which to guide their coaching efforts. In addition, executives must actually practice to develop skill. Role playing is the most effective process to date for developing skills in inter-personal techniques.

5. *Identify "good" and "poor" coaches.* Our extensive surveys of coaching practices have demonstrated that there is great variability in coaching practices of executives. It is quite apparent that a general course, no matter how well designed, cannot be equally effective when such heterogeneity is present. We have come to consider the "poor" coach as a special problem. Preliminary research results tend to show that poor coaches are also considered by their superiors to be poor managers. Usually some basic underlying difficulties exist. It may be a lack of confidence, a lack of willingness to exercise power, a lack of knowledge of the work itself. In any case, we have found that the poor coaches need special sessions of their own and they need frequent help to improve on both their ability and willingness to coach.

6. *Get a coaching benefit from an objectives program.* Many organizations have developed a management-by-objectives program. Such a program can serve several purposes. One purpose is coaching for development. A well designed objectives document involves setting objectives for self-improvement for current responsibilities and to prepare for future responsibilities. Quarterly reviews between superior and subordinate give the superior an opportunity to act as a coach rather than a critic. Here is another example of interdependence between two management activities: coaching and managing-by-objectives. Getting the benefits of such interaction is an example of the benefits to be secured from a systems approach.

SUMMARY

Coaching has been generally recognized as a most important factor in the development of executives. To date, the evidence reveals that getting executives to improve their coaching practices is extremely difficult. However, improvement can be secured if a comprehensive series of efforts is programmed and then implemented.

8

Educational programs

We see an educational program as a seventh requirement for an overall executive continuity system. We hasten to add that the educational program will, in the future, have to be quite different from current educational programs if it is to make the expected contribution to the overall system.

Educational programs for the experienced executives have been with us now for a quarter of a century. Harvard held its first Advanced Management Program in 1945. General Electric can be credited with initiating the first long-term internal educational program for executives in 1955 with its own nine-week Advanced Management Course.

A diligent search of the literature and discussions with many large organizations suggests that we do not have sound data upon which to base an answer to the question of the value of formal classroom education for the executive. One astute observer has stated with regard to educational programs for executives, that never has so much money been invested with so little evidence of an adequate return. Another observer with a good vantage point for generalization is Prof. J. Sterling Livingston of the Harvard Graduate School of Business Administration. He contends that a well-educated manager is a myth.[1] He argues that the successful manager must:

    ––Be skilled at problem-finding.

    ––Be skilled at opportunity-finding.

    ––Be effective in implementing action.

    ––Have the capacity for empathy, or the ability to cope with the emotional reactions that are inevitable.

Livingston states: "Many highly intelligent and ambitious men are not learning from either their formal education or their own experience what they most need to know to build successful careers in management." He and others have questioned the heavy reliance upon formal university education in developing managers. They argue that formal education, in and of itself, is not really capable of developing managers. We would state our position a bit differently. A company should not expect a formal education program to produce future executives. Achieving this result requires a comprehensive systems approach. However, we see needed contributions which can best be provided by an effective educational program.

In this chapter we will review briefly the prevailing pattern of advanced educational programs. We will identify certain pitfalls or limitations resulting from the prevailing pattern. Attention will then be given to the needs which might well be met by a well designed program. We will then consider some trends and some developments which give promise of producing educational programs that do make a significant contribution.

PREVAILING PATTERNS OF ADVANCED MANAGEMENT PROGRAMS

Both business and non-business organizations have made extensive use of formal educational programs. Practically every major university has an advanced management program. The American Management Association has conducted a four-week management course for more than a decade. A few large companies have their own advanced management programs. Many other organizations rely on short courses. These may be conducted as an internal program or part of an external program. Let us give attention to each of these basic alternatives.

University-sponsored programs

George Bricker has been a concerned observer of university-sponsored executive development programs for more than 20 years. His annual *Bricker's Directory* provides an up-to-date picture of such programs.[2]

Bricker identifies ten university-sponsored executive programs that are designed for top management in medium and large size companies. The universities are: Harvard, Carnegie-Mellon, M.I.T., Stanford, Columbia, Hawaii, California (at Berkeley), Columbia, Northwestern, Southern California. An analysis of these ten programs will reflect the prevailing pattern for top level executive programs.

The program length averages just about 7 weeks, with a range from 4 to 13 weeks. The average cost for tuition and board and room is about

$500 per week. The average number of participants is 66, and their average age is 43. With rare exceptions, the instruction is provided by regular university faculty members.

The subject matter covered by a majority of the programs includes the following, in order of frequency:

Financial management (financial controls, accounting)
Business and society (government, business ethics)
Marketing
Economics
Management science (decision making, quantitative data, computer systems)
Planning
Organizing
Human Behavior
Control

Other subjects, represented in less than half of the programs, include business policy, business simulation, labor relations, international business, production, research and development, and urbanization.

The most frequent instructional methods are the case methods and lecture with discussion and, in some instances, a combination of both.

The definition of purpose shows a great similarity for all programs. They aim to "broaden," to expose participants to new horizons and to enlarge their outlook toward the events taking place around them. In addition, many programs do stress the development of managerial abilities. The abilities most often stressed have to do with new methods of analysis, decision making, and strategic planning.

Andrews study

Professor Kenneth R. Andrews of the Harvard Graduate School of Business Administration undertook to measure the effectiveness of university management development programs.[3]

The complexities of measurement led to the use of a questionnaire. Andrews' conclusions are based upon responses from more than 6,000 businessmen who had attended courses in 39 universities. Even though his study was conducted in the mid-1960s, it is likely that the same results would be obtained if a repeat study were conducted today.

Andrews reports that the purpose of practically all programs was stated in very general terms. The programs were designed to help executives function more effectively in their present positions and to help prepare them for promotion to greater responsibility. The programs were intended to make generalists out of specialists. An increased tolerance and understanding of other departmental functions, recognition of the importance of human relationships, and expanded awareness and understanding of the economic, political, and social environment of business are commonly stated purposes of the major programs.

All the programs aimed to broaden, to expose men to new horizons, and to enlarge their outlook. The laudable purpose carried with it, as Andrews notes, the virtual impossibility of quantifying results.

Participants were asked, "What do you think happened to you (as a result of attending the program)?" The predominant response was, "the program broadened me." Mention was made of learning about other businesses, other functions; about the importance of human relations; about the desirability of being more flexible in searching for solutions to problems.

The great majority of participants reported a favorable attitude toward their educational program. It was seen as being worth the time, effort, and separation from family and job. The most frequent report of impact of the management education experience upon the participant's managerial skill and knowledge is that of "broadening." Those who conduct studies based upon reactions to educational programs come to expect a euphoric reaction. They are rarely disappointed. So this initial conclusion of Andrews does not add up to very strong evidence of effectiveness.

Andrews drew numerous implications for university action:
--Faculty effectiveness is very critical and difficult to achieve.
--There is a need to be much more specific about purpose and outcomes to be expected.
--There is a need to decide more specifically what level of participant universities aim to enroll.
--There is a need for development of truly advanced programs.
--There is a need for closer working relationships between universities and the sponsoring companies.
--There is a need to question whether shorter programs are really the appropriate answer.
--Universities need to work out the unique educational contribution which they can best make.

He also drew numerous implications for company action:
--Using companies should expect no dramatic change in the subsequent behaviors in the men they send.
--A single experience will not provide as much as can be achieved from a succession of formal programs.
--Companies need to select men who are promotable and have a positive attitude toward learning, and are at the level appropriate for the program.
--Companies need to program to achieve continuous individual development.

The 1960s saw an increased use by business and non-business organizations of company-sponsored educational programs. The economic down-turn of the early 1970s caused reassessments to occur on both sides. This is fortunate, for the potential benefits of educational programs certainly have yet to be achieved by the prevailing practices. Let us consider in-company programs before addressing ourselves to the challenge of getting improved results from educational programs.

In-company

Several organizations have established their own management institutes. One of the most venerable is GE's Management Development Center at Crotonville, New York. It started in 1955 with a nine-week advanced management program. Over a period of five years approximately 1,500 managers took the Advanced Management Course. In recent years the course has been shortened to four weeks. About 200 top managers attend each year.

International Business Machines has had an advanced management school at Sands Point for more than a decade. A combination of outside resources and in-company executives are used as faculty. The four-week program provides insight into company background and developments and a broad view of management's role in society.

Motorola set up their own Management Institute, complete with campus, near Tuscon. With the help of professors from leading business schools, they devised curricula for executives with a unique blend of the latest in graduate-level education and specific knowledge about their own industry.

CPC International, with its far flung overseas operations, sees the problem as both education and communications. At its Management Development Center in Brussels, the company regularly conducts business-school like courses to introduce executives to the latest techniques in information systems, planning and control, discounted cash flow, and risk analyses. One goal is to give all executives a common set of working tools.

Very few business organizations have gone as far as GE, IBM, Motorola, and CPC. However, many organizations have sponsored courses of one- to four-weeks duration without establishing their own physical facilities. The pattern seems to be for such programs to flourish for several years, then be dropped, only to be revived again some years later.

A most interesting management education experiment is being conducted in Belgium. It might well be called an "executive-swapping" program. It is sponsored jointly by Belgium industry and the country's largest universities as a way of advancing management education. The program is ten months in duration. The "fellows" start out by taking a university management course of several months duration. They then move on to two months of problem analysis with the host company. To make the swap, each participating company chooses an executive to go to one of the other companies. Then each host company spells out what it considers to be a main strategic problem and the executive, or "fellow," attempts to solve it. The fellow is sent to a company whose business is as different as possible from that of his own.

One day a week is spent back at the university with a group of other fellows for a discussion of their various projects. The final months of the program are devoted to the crucial effort of putting their recommendations into effect.

One might well call this the laboratory portion of a theory course. To date, there is little evidence of such exciting experiments going on in the United States. However, there is likely to be much more experimentation by both companies and universities as they attempt to reach a higher level of effectiveness.

POTENTIAL PITFALLS

The prevailing practice of educational programs, whether done externally or internally, have failed to produce the needed results because of recurring pitfalls.

A basic pitfall occurred with the advent of advanced management education. Harvard assumed there was a market. They designed a program tailored after their undergraduate program. The initial purpose was stated broadly. Trial and error led to some adjustments to accommodate experienced executives' reaction to a formal educational experience. Most other universities followed in the steps of Harvard. However, some had no tradition of case studies so they relied on their undergraduate style of lecture and discussion.

This initial basic pitfall is the absence of a thorough need-determination process which governs the choice of subject matter, size of group, educational method, and type of instructor.

A second pitfall has to do with the heterogenous nature of participants. The instructor in the average university program is faced with 66 quite diverse students. They come from organizations differing greatly in size, from quite different types of business, with quite different backgrounds and quite unique personal needs. The instructor must strike a general pattern which appeals to most of the students, most of the time.

A general course is designed for the entire student population. Such a general course seldom meets specific needs. For example, the newly appointed general manager has some rather specific educational needs that are quite different from the established general manager. These different needs are seldom met with an appropriately designed educational effort. Consider another example. The technical or engineering-oriented manager who aspires to become a general manager usually has quite a different set of needs than does the manager who has a marketing orientation or a finance orientation. In each case these managers would benefit from having specialized instruction that would assist them in offsetting some of the characteristics that tend to persist due to the nature of the educational background and the nature of the functional work which has characterized their career.

The third potential pitfall to be found in educational programs, whether done externally or internally, is that top management will assume that the educational activities will do the job of developing their future managers and so they neglect many of the other requirements identified as being necessary for the overall system. In effect, they are placing too great a reliance on the educational process for developing managers.

A fourth pitfall has to do with the participant. In many organizations the executive who can be made available for six weeks is sent. This means that the real comers often miss out on an educational experience. It also confuses the organization as to the interpretation to be placed upon being selected to attend a program. In some instances, the entire process is done in such a way that the participant arrives at the course with a distinctly negative attitude.

A fifth pitfall is that the educational process is not programmed as a continuous effort over the entire career of a manager. Very few organizations have thought through the appropriate educational experience for a manager when he is 25, when he is 30, when he is 35, when his is 40, and so forth. Once in a manager's career, usually at some random interval, he is given an opportunity to take a six-weeks educational program. Often this constitutes the first and last formal educational experience he is to receive. Such a one-time-only experience is unlikely to assist a manager in keeping up to date with knowledge explosions of both a managerial and technological nature.

A sixth pitfall has to do with the need to improve managerial ability. Educational programs have as their avowed purpose that of broadening an executive's knowledge and awareness. Application of this knowledge calls for skills. These skills are almost never included in an advanced management program. We are not necessarily implying that current programs should be replaced with ones stressing managerial skills. We are stressing that managerial skills can and should be developed by appropriately designed educational programs.

Let us next consider some of the requirements for growth and development of executives in continuity programs that might be met by an educational program.

REQUIREMENTS THAT MIGHT BE MET BY AN
EDUCATIONAL PROGRAM

In chapter 6 four critical career crossroads were identified. They had to do with the transitions from:
1. Individual contribution to functional manager.
2. Functional manager to general manager.
3. Managing one business to managing several businesses.
4. Managing several businesses to being an institutional leader.

In making the initial transition, the individual has to change his concept of himself. He has to rely on others to do work he used to do. He has to become comfortable in doing managerial tasks. He has to get satisfaction out of others doing well. He has to master supervisory skills and methods. This transition requires changes in attitude, acquisition of new knowledge, and development of new skills.

This transition requires a well-designed educational program for the new supervisor. It is amazing how few, even large companies, have regular programs which insure that new supervisors do receive training. In most organizations the logistics require that supervisory education be done internally. As we suggested in chapter 6, we see a need for an increasing number of young high-potential personnel to become supervisors before the age of 30. This group, as well as others, should have the benefit of education in supervision.

Once in supervision an individual usually stays in one function for some time. He is expected to master this function. Here again is a need for the acquisition of specialized functional knowledge and skills. This type of instruction is best accomplished with some homogeneity of participants. Large organizations can support their own internal effort. An increasing number of smaller organizations are using a trade association as a cooperative alternative. Some organizations in a given city are also considering cooperative arrangements. Collaboration with universities is particularly fruitful in this functional area. Joint need-determination can be done, leading to design of programs which meet specific needs. This suggestion leads to the design of a functional course, such as marketing, tailored to a special type of business, such as industrial selling.

Let us consider the transition from managing functional work to general-manager work. The individual has to be able to understand each major function so he can both direct the functional manager and integrate across functions, making appropriate and timely trade-offs. Often the individual has to recognize that his way of thinking, deciding, and managing has been strongly conditioned by his experience in one function. This usually proves a handicap in managing several functions so unlearning as well as learning has to take place.

During this transition the individual has to shift from a supportive role to the dominant role in direction of the business. Business judgment is required. Ability to understand and lead quite diverse groups becomes critical. Here again we see a real value in an educational program. Becoming a general manager requires becoming quite knowledgeable about other major functions. The processes of planning, organizing, and controlling become more critical. Leadership and application of behavorial knowledge become a necessity. We see many of the present university programs meeting the need for gaining broader knowledge about functions and business in general. The original GE program was designed to do just this.

However, as we noted in talking about pitfalls, few advanced management programs really aim at skill development. We see a big need for skill training of general managers in management processes. Such an educational program has to be well designed. The designers have to be ahead of practical, experienced managers in their recommendations. An example of such a program is given in Appendix H.

The transition to managing several businesses is a challenge to most executives. A shift has to be made from directing a business to leading, inspiring, and controlling general managers. The general managers are often more experienced in a given line than their supervisor.

Here again there is so much to be learned that a class or group effort becomes a necessity. We see an opportunity here for a specially designed program which relies heavily upon higher-level managers. Their prior experience in managing several businesses can be shared with the newly-appointed group executives. It is also possible to use outside resources. One innovative design for a group of such executives involved the choice of five resource experts in the fields of economics, business planning, human behavior, environmental issues, and management sciences. The resource personnel were not permitted to make a speech or give a lecture. Subgroups of executives were required to plan how best to use each resource person for a two-day period.

Finally, a few individuals are asked to make the transition to being an institutional leader. They must now set the direction, secure and allocate resources. They have to establish policies and values for the enterprise and protect the integrity of the institution. New learning, new attitudes, new skills are required. Rarely are there models available to be emulated. Again, the amount of learning required of the institutional leader suggests a group effort can make a real contribution.

Imagine working with a select group of chief executives, each one new in his position. Here is a group which could benefit from such subjects as business policy, business ethics, business in society. Such a group process could make a great contribution to the tough challenge of making the change in concept required in moving from an operational leader to an institutional leader.

Let us next consider some trends which offer some optimism in securing the contribution from education programs which we should be getting.

TRENDS IN EXECUTIVE EDUCATION

There are several trends, some well established, some just beginning, which argue well for achieving the potential inherent in an effective educational program. Among the trends are the following:

1.   Cooperative action on existing program improvement. The previous pitfalls can be attributed to educators in some instances, in other instances the "customers" of education are at fault. Actually, both educators and customers are coming to realize that criticizing each other is of little consequence. Achieving improved executive education results requires joint exploration and planning. An increasing number of educators and business executives are beginning to invest time in interacting on educational issues. Some large associations, such as the American Banking Association, have had a history of collaborating with educators in the design and conduct of managerial courses.

A recent phenomena is the establishment of a non-profit corporation, by a score of companies in a given city. The corporation is set up to design and conduct an advanced management course tailored to the local companies' needs. This cooperative approach should provide a critical requirement—namely the discipline of specific objectives. Specific objectives need to be established jointly by both customers and the educators. The specific objectives will then permit making optimizing decisions about homogeneity, about course size, about educational methods, about course schedules and course leaders.

2.   Both general and specific programs. At the present almost all university-sponsored educational programs can be called general programs. They provide a certain type of educational program. We see these programs continuing. The current skepticism about such programs will hopefully lead to their improvement. However, executive education in the future will see the development of well-designed specialized programs. The specialization will have to do with subject matter, with participants, and with purpose.

The trends to date suggest that universities will continue to offer generalized educational programs. It is somewhat ironic that educational organizations manifest a rigidity that prevents consideration of any substantial changes.

However, the "customer" organizations are beginning to understand that educational outcomes can be defined and secured by an appropriate investment. More and more customer organizations are beginning to see educational outcomes as a necessity and not a nice thing to do. In effect, the customer is becoming more sophisticated. This is leading individual companies and collaborative groupings of companies to invest in the design of specialized educational programs. We see a very desirable mixture of generalized and specialized educational programs evolving in the future.

3. Periodic, career-long education. A few companies are considering establishing a policy that every manager will have an educational experience every two years. Others have added follow-on course after follow-on course to an initial internal program. This has now settled into a pattern of providing certain programs for each major level of management.

While not a dominant trend, it can be predicted that as the importance of manager continuity becomes more and more obvious, the standards, the expectations, of education will rise substantially. One consequence will be periodic education for executives over their entire career.

Certainly the definition of requirements in terms of the crossroads suggests the need for specialized educational programs at different stages in careers. A number of large organizations now have a pattern of programs which begin with the first level of supervision and extend to upper middle managers. Formal programs for top level executives are still rare. Most are episodic.

Venezuela has an interesting regulation. If a business organization does not spend a certain percent of its sales for employee training, it is taxed. The provides a strong incentive for regular employee and managerial education. It is possible other countries will begin to use the same regulation.

4. Developmental costs dealt with cooperatively. The current situation finds each university designing its own management educational programs. Some of the programs just barely justify the word design. A considerable amount of follow-the-leader takes place. Each business organization concentrates, individually, on doing its own thing as far as educational courses for managers are concerned. There are several results from the current pattern. It is extremely rare that enough money is spent on the development of a soundly conceived and well-tested educational course. This is true both of universities and companies. It is also true that the innovations in management education over the last ten years have been extremely meager.

A trend is beginning to appear for a cooperative approach to management education. It is quite likely that both costs and higher standards will force more cooperative development of management education. This will permit more money to be spent both on development and testing of innovations and on incorporating innovations into program designs.

5.   Education and experimentation combined. Organizations want to see executives improve their managerial abilities, which in turn leads to getting improved organizational results. At their best, educational activities can only be preparation for improving one's managerial ability. The improvement comes from "experimentation" on the job. Stress has long been placed on the importance of learning by doing. One sharp observer of managerial ability has also stressed that learning also comes from undoing. Doing and undoing implies actual trying of new alternatives on the job. The adult educator becomes a catalyst in helping the adult to develop confidence and skills needed to experiment. The development of managerial ability is being seen as a progressive, continuous process requiring both education and experimentation.

Note that a rather close working relationship has to be established between superiors in an organization and educators to combine education and experimentation. The superior is in a unique position both before and after a learning experience to encourage application. There is a trend, just beginning, for more planning to achieve a combination of education and experimentation.

6.   Managers taught by managers. As soon as an organization decides to provide an educational experience for managers every two years (or some other frequency), it is faced with the logistics of available instructors or leaders. Professors, consultants, and internal staff individuals turn out to be in short supply. The expense also becomes critical. Therefore, organizations are turning to their own managers to be the instructors for other managers. Railroads, insurance companies, banks, chemical companies are among the quite diverse types of organizations to do this quite successfully.

7.   Managers will have more of a say in designing their own educational experience. This cannot be called a trend yet. The examples of this happening are quite rare. However, adult learning theory certainly supports the trend. Necessity also will be on the side of this trend. As it becomes absolutely necessary that people grow and develop, experiments, using long known adult learning theory, will increase. Both developing a skill and using it is highly conditioned by the adult's attitude. Hence, involvement and participation will be needed to get a positive attitude and an eventual behavioral change.

SUMMARY

In spite of the frequent criticism of executive educational programs we see an educational program as a seventh requirement for an overall executive continuity system. The prevailing pattern of educational programs in universities and in-company efforts are generalized programs aimed at broad functional knowledge and knowledge of management processes, such as planning and controlling. The prevailing programs do not produce the needed results because of recurring pitfalls. Six such pitfalls were examined. Consideration was given to requirements in executive development which might be met by an educational program. The stages in careers, revealed by our critical career crossroad analysis, provided a basis for highlighting requirements. Finally, seven trends in executive education were described. These trends hold promise that the contribution needed from educational programs can be achieved.

9

Organization-wide selection and placement

We now come to the eighth requirement in the overall executive continuity system. We started out saying the first requirement was most important. Each subsequent requirement was also considered to be extremely critical. To use a baseball analogy, the sum total of the previous requirements should begin to produce a farm system with some depth. However, the eighth requirement, namely, an organization-wide approach to selection and placement is a necessity to realize the ultimate result—namely, key positions being filled by well qualified personnel.

Deciding what needs to be done is relatively straightforward. However, implementing this requirement is a long, arduous task.

An M.I.T. research study by Theodore Alfred has analyzed how the typical internal promotion process works in business organizations.[1] He reports that:

1. Most corporate practices make it possible for managers to hoard good people to the detriment of the total organization.
2. Most corporate practices make it possible for a manager to promote from within his own department or from among his acquaintances without considering others in the organization.
3. An individual's opportunity to be considered for other jobs in the organization depends to a large extent upon his present supervisor's opinion and knowledge.
4. When a promotion is announced, those who did not get the job do not learn whether they were considered at all and, if they were, why they did not get the job.

5. The present system causes individuals to have doubts about their future in the organization, increasing their susceptibility to quitting.

Alfred suggests there are two basic causes for these five conditions. One is the lack of adequate information. The second is lack of overall company policies that do not leave unnecessary authority with individual managers. Alfred argues for better manpower information and for a change in the power structure. We find ourselves in complete agreement with Alfred's analysis of typical practices and basic causes.

The traditional practice in most organizations is for the executive making a selection decision to be permitted to select from those he knows well. As often as not, he picks men with whom he feels comfortable, men who will be loyal, men who are "buddies." There may be numerous candidates who have equal or even superior qualifications. But in large company after large company, such candidates are not considered because corporate-wide selection has not been recognized as a necessity by top management. Each division of a large enterprise is permitted to approach the problem of selection as though it were a completely independent organization. Parochialism takes over. The corporation fails to capitalize upon one of its advantages as a large enterprise, namely, the ability to pick from a large pool of talent and to move people across the entire organization. There are a very few organizations that have a well thought out corporate-wide approach to the selection of general managers.

The five major factors required to achieve a sound corporate-wide selection process will be considered. This will be followed by a look at the major steps to be taken in the selection process.

MAJOR FACTORS

There are five major factors involved in getting an effective organization-wide selection and placement effort. They are:
- --Depth of management
- --Sound knowledge of candidates
- --Basic policies and procedures
- --Direct involvement by top management
- --A skillful staff contribution

Depth of management

Let us return for a moment to our baseball analogy. Baseball has been known for years for its farm system. At one time, the dynasty of the Yankees was perpetuated by the productivity of their farm system. A new star appeared to replace the fading star. In recent years the farm system appears to have failed the Yankees organization. In business and industry such a situation is called "lack of management depth."

In chapter 1 ten basic requirements were stressed to provide the needed people flow, the needed depth of management. In a subsequent chapter stress will be placed on the importance of tying the numerous requirements into an overall system.

Let us assume that the system is working. There is a people flow of talent coming along to fill future executive spots. If this is the case, executives will not be tempted to hoard talent. They may still be reluctant to release a good man, but they won't block it altogether. The system also requires that each major component must keep its high-potential young men moving along. Promotions to another component provide the needed mobility to keep this unique talent moving along.

It is obvious that the value to be gained from a corporate-wide selection program is dependent upon the existence of an adequate depth of management.

Sound knowledge of candidates

A factor critical to the effective working of a corporate-wide selection process is sound knowledge of candidates. It is interesting to contrast the amount of data professional football teams have on their potential and current players with the data on key talent within business and industrial organizations. One is tempted to do it by quantity. Measured in either pounds or inches, the football organization has about ten times as much data. When measured in terms of quality, that is soundness or usefulness of data, the professional football team does not have to take a back seat. Much of the data is factual. Football organizations know that their success depends on the abilities of the talent they field. They invest in getting voluminous data to better protect their overall franchise investments.

Chapter 5 was devoted to the challenge of getting "good" data about personnel. The relevance of such knowledge to corporate-wide selection is revealed by considering the three users of the data. Top management has to have a final approval on appointments to all key positions. A staff group will have to make recommendations of those to be considered. Finally, the decision-making executive has to go through a process of choosing from the recommended candidates. The more confidence these three parties have in the basic data about candidates, the more easily the entire corporate-wide selection process operates.

Basic policies and procedures

Once qualified individuals are available for consideration, then the interesting challenge is that of getting corporate-wide attention given to such talent. Here it becomes necessary for top management to be both persuasive and persistent. It is inappropriate for top management to force a given candidate for a promotion on a reluctant executive. This tends to decrease the likelihood that the candidate will succeed. The process must be a more subtle one. Some organizations have a policy that requires that five candidates be considered for appointment to a key executive position and three be from outside the immediate component. This forces the appointing executive to make use of the staff contribution as a means of giving company-wide consideration to talent. An example of such a policy of the Uniroyal organization on corporate-wide selection is found in Appendix K. Other organizations have begun to insist on cross-functional and cross-divisional experience. Hence it becomes necessary for divisions to begin to cooperate in order to meet these requirements.

A procedure requiring cooperation of operating divisions in implementing a "cross-pollination" program as conducted in the Uniroyal organization was referred to in chapter 6.

Some organizations have established a policy to avoid getting trapped by putting the best available man into a position when the best available man is not qualified. The policy states that a position must be filled by a qualified man and if no one is available within the immediate organization, then they will go outside to fill such a position.

Another means of stimulating a corporate-wide approach is to require that all key executive selection decisions use a candidate analysis process. This process requires that the manager who is making the selection answer three basic questions:

What is the nature of the job to be done?

What are the important requirements?

How well do the candidates meet these requirements?

Forms provided for this purpose facilitate the decision-making process.

Standard Oil of Ohio has a policy, applied to their entire exempt group, which states that all employees will be made available, without exception or delay, for a promotional opportunity anywhere in the company. The central staff does not need to "negotiate" prior to placing an individual on a slate.

Multi-national companies quite often have a policy that in each country their companies will be staffed and run entirely by nationals. Johnson & Johnson and IBM are two such organizations. The multi-national company can benefit by having a well formulated policy on the assignment of individuals off-shore. It takes a sound policy and consistent adherence to the policy to get well qualified individuals to accept assignments and to get the potential developmental benefits of foreign assignments. An example of an international policy of the Uniroyal organization is found in Appendix L.

Direct involvement of top management

Considerable stress was placed upon the importance of top management action and involvement in chapter 2. Let us be quite specific. A corporate-wide selection program does not have a chance unless top management really understands its importance and is directly involved in the program. Left to their own devices, lower level executives will almost always select someone they know. If an executive has grown up in one component, he moves his "buddies" up behind him. It takes strong top executive action to overcome this "incestuous tendency."

We noted in chapter six that the final crossroad was the shift from managing several businesses to that of becoming a leader of an institution. Direct involvement by top management in implementing a corporate-wide approach to executive placement is a good example of the institutional role.

A skillful staff contribution

Experience in many large institutions demonstrates again and again that an effective corporate-wide selection effort requires a skillful staff contribution. The main challenge to a staff is to act as a catalyst in getting the conditions required to generate people flow. In addition, it takes a really competent staff contribution to get sound data on candidates and encourage consideration of individuals on a corporate-wide basis. The staff will also find that they will be expected to devote considerable time to counseling executives with career concerns. Action to assist in placement of executives who are removed also constitutes another contribution expected of a staff.

The stress on the five major factors mentioned in this chapter, serves to reinforce again the need to take a systems approach. However, an effective company-wide selection process requires a variety of specific procedures. Let us now consider specific procedures that are needed.

SELECTION PROCEDURES*

There are two major variables in the selection situation: the candidates and the open position.

Selection, then, involves using relevant information on these two variables to make predictions about the future. It involves extrapolating from what we think we know about each candidate's past behavior and accomplishments to his likely future performance in a given position.

---

* The content of this chapter is dependent upon a reference guide prepared by Theodore LeVino.

That in turn requires making assumptions about the position and its environment. Questions such as the following need to be considered. What will be the crucial things that need to be accomplished? How will various influences affect each candidate's likely performance?

Let us look at the enemies of effective selection. They include nepotism in all forms, prejudice, halos, selecting exclusively in one's own image or for how "comfortable" the hiring manager or his boss would be with a given candidate, and all the more common forms of subjectivity error. Warding off such enemies requires objectivity, selecting for strength as opposed to avoidance of weakness, making the best assumptions about the future job imperatives, and striving for an excellent match of men and position.

Let us be clear. While the selection process is still more art than science, we advocate logic versus emotion, evidence versus ignorance, order versus randomness, system versus sloppiness, method versus luck, and discipline versus inconsistency. We advocate the selector having and using as much valid data about the candidates and the opening as possible, and *then* making the visceral decision.

Let us now consider the basic procedures of the selection process.

Position specifications

Deciding on position specifications is the beginning of the selection process. Position specifications are the four or five personal characteristics which will make the difference between success and failure in the next two to three years on the job. These have been aptly called "the critical makes or breaks." They differ from the previously discussed general specifications in their specificity, timeliness, and immediate orientation.

Position specifications will vary widely between businesses and even for the same business at different points in time, as we noted with regard to the life cycle of a business in chapter 4. Specifications are not helpful if they are general or reflect universal expectations. They need to be specifically related to the business situation at hand.

Some managers may be very systematic about writing position specifications; others may resist doing it. It is not easy work! It requires thinking hard about the realities of the near-term future. It means understanding or learning enough about the status of the job situation now to know what it is that needs to be changed. It means, in some cases, exposing past mistakes and failures.

We suggest that position specifications be prepared as a two-step process.

The first step is to identify 5 to 7 of the important results which must be accomplished by the newly appointed executive. These should be specific, they should include the more critical results. They should stress the changes which might be required in the future.

Examples of such statements are:

--Take the business from a loss to a profit in short order.

--Meet the technological challenges of major competitors.

--Clean house. Strengthen management.

--Reduce excess employees.

--Rebuild morale and achieve teamwork.

Frequently, where only man specifications exist, they are drawn from an image or background of the successful former incumbent, or are the characteristics thought to be missing in an unsuccessful one. This may be a useful line of thought. But sometimes even with success in the past, we deliberately want to change a number of things. There is no substitute for making sure of what we want done before jumping to the conclusion that someone just like or the opposite of the former incumbent is what is needed. An example of a form which facilitates the above action is found in Appendix M.

A final point on job requirements and man specifications. Our observation is that many selections that do not turn out well are the result of inadequate visualization of job requirements, rather than inadequate data on people. Many cases of later "failure" result from changes in job requirements rather than selecting the wrong individual. That is, the selection initially may have been reasonable, but the job changed during the incumbent's tenure such that it no longer played to the incumbent's long suits, and may even have played to weakness. Jobs change much more rapidly and dramatically than is realized.

For these reasons, a real effort is needed to understand and describe the position to prevent poor selections.

Candidate sources

The selection procedure described so far has dealt with getting agreement and understanding of the opening to be filled. The next step is to share that understanding with appropriate candidate sources. It is important to have some discipline at this point to make sure that all reasonable sources are tapped. Our bias is that the manpower staff man is a natural control point for the selection procedure. If he is responsible from the start for getting the opening described, the next logical step is to have him coordinate the candidate search.

"Appropriate" sources obviously vary with the level and nature of the opening. That is, the sources tapped for candidates for a lower level manager in a highly specialized engineering discipline will most certainly be different than those used in a higher level manager of a business.

Occasionally it may seem necessary to seek candidates before there is common knowledge that a search is underway. These covert searches have obvious disadvantages, not the least of which is that they rarely stay secret very long. If the idea is to get something accomplished before the incumbent or some others hear about the search, the advantage of telling them before the search is started had better be reexamined. A second disadvantage is that some of the natural sources are closed, with the attendant unavailability of certain channels of names and evaluative or corroborative data. Third, and perhaps the most severe and subtle shortcoming, is the resentment caused among those who felt they should have been considered for the job or called upon to contribute candidates.

Candidate screening

The process of screening candidates involves an initial screening of potential candidates' names. In actual practice, "first-pass" screening usually involves separating candidates into three categories:
1. Those about whom enough is known to have confidence they *should* be considered.
2. Those about whom enough is known to have confidence they *lack* the key ingredients being sought.
3. Those about whom *not enough* is known to put in (1) or (2).

Screening obviously means studying available data and looking for individuals whose strengths match the requirements of the opening. All available data should be considered. Where there is a substantial amount, corroborative insights or cross-checks are usually received from more than one source. Sometimes there are contradictions. This review and analysis should provide leads for follow-up inquiry after screening. In the case of individuals in category (1) above, there may be an interview, or reference checks. In the event the data are skimpy or too thin to come to any conclusions, as in category (3), the analysis should produce leads on where to go for more data. In any event, the screener should note why a candidate was put in (1) or (2). Writing this down is good self-discipline. If the reason cited is fuzzy, obscure, or indefensible, further examination or data are required.

Slate preparation and approval

Once all potential candidates are screened, a final candidate slate has to be decided on. The staff man who did the initial screening must decide which names and what data to present to the hiring manager for consideration, and in what form.

Our preference is to submit the names of all worthy nominees to the hiring manager. We feel that he should know who was suggested by whom, and for what reason the screening put each individual into contention. By this approach, the hiring manager has the option of accepting the manpower staff man's judgments or applying his own. Without the full list, he does not have such a choice. Those screened out can simply be listed by name, level, title, source and reason for exclusion.

Those screened "in" for further consideration should number approximately ten. There is nothing hard and fast about this number. Individual managerial preferences, amount and quality of data reviewed, number known personally, known availability, and similar data, may cause substantial variances. Assuming average attrition for reasons of availability, interest, and the hiring manager's screening, ten candidates will shrink to five—a reasonable number to interview and seriously consider. A much smaller number than ten after initial screening may result in too few final candidates. A larger number may be too cumbersome and raise questions of whether the specifications are "tight" enough.

The manpower staff man will have to determine what constitutes a satisfactory candidate slate for the organization. This involves individual managerial preferences and approaches, the amount of data available, the experience, skill and credibility of the manpower staff man, and the nature of the opening.

The best single guideline is to do what is necessary to assure honest consideration of the best potential candidates. The practices which accomplish that, constitute the "right" candidate slate approach.

Finally, there is the need to secure approval of the slate. Approval may be sought before final screening, or afterward but before interviews. Obviously the purpose of any approval step is to leave open the possibility of change as a result of the approval manager's inputs. To this end, the approval manager should want to know who was screened in, and why others were screened out. He may want to add inputs on existing candidates, probe the tentative ranking, or add names for consideration. If the hiring manager gets so far along in the candidate selection process that he is already pretty well committed to a given decision, the approving manager is put in either the "rubber stamp" or "autocrat" position. Both are ineffective, and damaging to process credibility.

Here is where the systems approach comes into play. If a thorough discussion took place during the annual manpower review, as recommended in chapter 2, then widely divergent views will have been resolved prior to a critical decision.

In some cases, the approving manager is the normal one-over-one. In most instances, this provides sufficient balance, experience and perspective. Some special cases—like general manager appointments—may warrant an additional layer of concern. Here, a higher level executive may want to be influential in freeing a candidate who was—by all normal ground rules and considerations—not considered available. Or the higher level executive may feel that an individual can't be made available.

Candidate availability

We commented earlier on the tendency to hoard good men. One dimension of executive mobility deserves further exploration—the matter of when an individual should or should not have the opportunity to be considered for another position. Making this determination is a logical consideration at this point in the selection process. That is, it is premature to check all potential candidates' availability and interest before screening, but the final screening should include candidates who are genuinely available.

Some companies have a basic policy that two years is a reasonable minimum period for individuals to stay in one position before being considered ready for another position. Except for very special situations such as the individual not working out or being very unhappy with his situation, or where the job did not materialize as contemplated, an individual should expect to "amortize" the expense of his transfer and training and to contribute positively to the business over a period of at least two years. The policy often indicates that special situations may temper this guideline—in effect to make it reasonable to lengthen or shorten the period.

When at all possible, the individual should be given the opportunity to make the decision himself. Most managers strive to see that this happens. Their experience indicates there are far fewer moves than feared as a result. Not only are people less mobile than we have come to believe, but if they know they will be considered for future opportunities—they are far less likely to jump at the first one that comes along.

On some occasions it is necessary to declare an individual unavailable for a given opportunity. To prepare for such an eventuality or to minimize any problems resulting from having to do so, the following managerial practices are recommended.

1. Executives should have an understanding with each subordinate about the probable timing, terms, and conditions of his availability. This can be done at appraisal or career discussion time or whenever it is appropriate. However, it should be done *before* there is an immediate issue. Subordinates will then have been conditioned to negative decisions on quick moves.

2. An executive will usually find it wise to tell a subordinate promptly of any negative decision on availability. Chances are good that he has heard or will hear of his potential candidacy. One is not likely to win when betting against the efficiency of the "grapevine." It is much better, in the long run, for the manager to have mentioned it—whether or not he is first.

3. The executive should tell or remind the individual what is planned to be done about his availability in the future. If it is only a matter of timing, set a date when he will be available. If it is a matter of performance, make sure the standards are known.

Finally, although touched on before, this is a good place to add an additional comment on parochialism. Taking the narrow, selfish, own-best-interest point of view in business situations may be natural, understandable, and sometimes logical and necessary. But the overly parochial decision, whether it is by an isolated executive, by a major function, or by a subdivision, can have some very negative consequences on people flow. We are talking about the kind of provincialism characterized by walls being built such that no one gets into the component except at the bottom, and no one gets out unless he removes himself.

If executives always select from within their own function or component, they may be deceiving themselves about the quality of person who is available. At least they are denying themselves the opportunity to get calibrated on the kind of job someone from outside might do and the ideas he might bring.

They may also be growing their own people too narrowly and thereby seriously limiting their future opportunities. They are not allowing their men to be tested in different environments, against others' opinions, judgments, and screens. Over a long period of time with no movement in and out, the three or four levels of management comprising a component can get very complacent. They go to seed. Their people-judgments are not only self-reinforcing but become self-fulfilling. Provincialism often ends up in a disaster with an entire management being swept out at once.

Selection interviews and decision

The interviews of final candidates should serve the dual purpose of developing additional information on which to base the final selection decision, and of further expanding the candidates' knowledge of the opening. This quid pro quo nature of these interviews is overlooked by some managers. If an executive spends all the interview explaining and selling the job, he does not find out anything more about the candidate. Furthermore, the candidate may react negatively to not being asked or allowed to talk about himself, and to the executive's apparent lack of interviewing sophistication.

On the other hand, one should not spend the entire available time probing for candidate information. The executive may feel that he knows the candidates, but they may not be satisfied they know what they might be getting into. Similarly, if candidates spend all or too much of their time responding to questions about themselves, they may not feel adequately "wooed." They may infer that *their* questions and concerns never would get adequate time with that executive.

So a balance is definitely desirable. The executive and the candidate should have about equal "air time" for selling and asking questions. This may vary some depending on prior knowledge of the job, its environment, and of each other. Most situations, though, call for give and take. This is true no matter how much time is allotted or available. There is always a practical limit to the time which can be used for interviewing, and by the time that is reached, both parties should feel they have had equal chances to explore their questions.

This interview time should be spent following up leads and questions developed during the screening phase. In looking over the data on final candidates and perhaps even after doing some reference checking on them, some specific areas for probing will have been noted. These may involve finding out why certain job moves occurred, what was accomplished on a given job and how significant it was, whom the candidate worked for, and so on. Similarly, the job specifications suggest areas to be covered. The hiring executive will want to be able to evaluate each candidate's ability to meet each specification. If the screening data did not provide all that is required to make these assessments, the interviews can fill in the gap. So in addition to getting a feel for the candidate, the hiring executive should be taking the time necessary to plug data gaps. He may ask the manpower staff man to assist in this task, or the manpower staff man may be the one to suggest what these areas are and how they might be probed.

Still another way to accomplish the total inquiry task, and at least to get additional impressions, is to have the other managers with whom the new man would work interview the candidate. Most candidates welcome the opportunity to meet and interview their prospective peers. This gives the candidate the chance to get several different points of view about the opening and the environment. The candidate may well ask the hiring executive about his philosophy of management and then check his subordinates to see if he comes across this way. These subordinates can be asked to help inform or "sell" candidates, but they can also be assigned a specific line of inquiry to pursue with a given candidate.

Several times we have mentioned "selling the opening" to the candidates. In so doing we are not advocating a snow job. Quite the contrary. For everyone's benefit, describing the opening completely and honestly is a must. This means revealing the routine aspects along with the creative opportunities, the dull along with the exciting, the potential conflicts and risks along with the rewards and challenges. To deliberately mislead a candidate is obviously unethical and self-defeating.

However, some "selling" is necessary. Many good candidates come away from an interview visit with the feeling of having been taken for granted. No attempts were made to interest them in the position. Their interest in the job was assumed and never explored, cultivated, or aroused. Too much of the visit time had been spent in trying to determine how they fit the opening, and not enough in expressing interest in them. Put another way, it is quite proper to find out what they can do for you; but you must also show what the new position can do for them.

Some executives arrange to have the best one or two candidates back for a second visit. This gives both the hiring executive and the candidates a chance to reflect on the first visit and to bring up questions arising from or not fully answered in that initial session. It also may be used to provide a tour for the candidate and his wife in the community, to give them an impression of housing, schools, and the mortgage situation. Other managers like to combine these two trips into one two-day visit to avoid the additional travel expense.

In a previous section we covered the one-over-one executive role in approval of slates. In addition some executives want to interview candidates for positions two organizational levels down. This may be occasioned by the approving executive not knowing some candidates, or because of the extreme importance of the open position. Some executives may do interviews in all situations. Doing so provides an additional perspective and impression evaluatively, and gives the candidates a chance to size up the one-over-one part of the environment.

We think it is important that the one-over-one executive play a role in selection, but we do not feel this necessarily has to involve interviews. If the hiring executive is new or inexperienced, or has not demonstrated outstanding selection ability in the past, the one-over-one executive and the manpower staff man may want to do some coaching or possibly interviews. Conversely, a one-over-one executive who does a perfunctory interview may be mislead by this, and may actually get in the way of those with more and better information.

In most situations, the one-over-one executive can exhibit his concern for the outcome of the selection decision by reviewing the hiring executive's rationale for the selection decision, by requiring formal evaluation of each candidate against the job specifications, and by probing the soundness of the evaluative decisions. To go much beyond this raises the question of who is actually making the selection decision.

Finally, there is the need to make a selection decision. The interviewing is over, the results and impressions synthesized, and all the data analyzed against the requirements. The objective and intellectual process is complete. Assuming that no one candidate stands a foot taller than the others, now is the time for the "gut" feel to take over. Almost all selection decisions at this point involve compromise. Rarely does any one candidate possess all the strengths being sought. There rarely is a case where following the strategy of trying to choose the "best man" results in an easy answer. It is more often a case of "dead heats" between individuals bringing different combinations of strength and limitations, which taken totally are about equally desirable.

Some executives are frustrated by going through a thorough, analytical and objective selection process only to wind up at an impasse which must be resolved subjectively. But far better to wind up there with the intellectual homework done, than to make the essential "gut" decision without it.

Selection follow-up

Once the hiring executive has made a decision, it needs to be communicated to a number of persons. First of all, the candidate selected needs to be informed. The individual does not always say yes, or at least right away. He may be competing for other jobs at the same time; he may impose some conditions which take time to investigate; he may want his wife to visit the community if this has not been done. In short, it is never wise to inform unsuccessful candidates until the person selected has accepted the offered position.

These comments may seem overly obvious, but we still hear and see cases involving imperfect communication, premature disclosure, and unwarranted assumptions that result in embarrassing situations. The manpower staff man can help by making certain the hiring executive and successful candidate have resolved all the loose ends. It may involve something as simple as agreeing to delay moving the family until after the school year ends. It may be something more complex in the negotiating that follows an agreement in principle. Housing today, for instance, represents a significantly complicated enough problem to warrant early and detailed attention.

In advising the other candidates that they were not selected, a telephone call from the hiring executive is in order. This is warmer than a letter and gives the manager a chance to adequately phrase and explain his reasons for the selection he made. It is not necessary to counsel the individual on his strengths and weaknesses. However, at times the hiring executive can provide data which help the individual gain insight which will stand him in good stead on future interviews.

THE SELECTION PROCESS AT THE TOP

An interesting study of top management succession in 13 large corporations was conducted for the Committee for Economic Development.[2] Based upon interviews with top executives, the study concluded that the development and succession of the few top managers is not simply an extension of the same process that governs the selection and progress of the intermediate ranks of management. In a sense, the process is seen as reverting to a small business context. The interplay between parties is more intimate. The top men rely upon personal contact or direct observation. The process of arriving at an announced decision was seen as taking place over a couple of years. The evolutionary decision process brings to the fore one or two contenders for a top-level position. In some instances, the organization was structured around the people. Congruent with the small company atmosphere is the element of luck associated with being promoted to top management. Decision makers experienced difficulty in finding objective differences in highly selected individuals. As a consequence, trivial differences among candidates often determined the choice.

The authors find themselves agreeing with the CED study. It does describe the current state of affairs.

The "small company" syndrome does seem to apply at the top of large companies. However, we do not consider this to be a state which is desirable. Why should the small company syndrome be accepted as inevitable?

As we observe the situation, a chief executive, soon after being appointed, makes a decision to run a one-man show, set up a partnership, or possibly establish a troica or office-of-the chief executive "consortium."

This decision then results in organizational changes at the next two levels. Appointments to new positions are made. This pattern does seem to be inevitable. However, the executive continuity system should do two things. It should produce qualified candidates in sufficient numbers to provide a choice. The decision-making process should be a thorough, systematic one. In effect, the most critical stage in the entire continuity pipeline should be dealt with in an objective manner. "Big piles of blue chips" are being wagered on critical top-level decisions. We see real merit in a systematic process involving the chief executive and the board of directors.

REMOVALS

Occasionally it is necessary for an executive to remove a subordinate from his position. The appropriate technique will vary with the reason for removal and attendant circumstances. That is, what might be appropriate in the case of gross misconduct would not be applicable in the case of the individual who is reorganized out of a job. Similarly, treatment may vary depending on the individual's past contributions, level, and length of service.

Because of this variation and our basic desire to treat people as individuals, it is difficult to suggest specific rules or guidelines. Fairness and reasonable consistency are two criteria for an executive to keep in mind. This requires large amounts of understanding, good judgment, honesty, objectivity, and, in some instances, being generous under conditions which may be highly charged with emotion. These situations should involve the combined perspectives of several levels of management, plus the manpower staff man, and other appropriate individuals.

Many of these situations defy preconceived solutions. The *best* advice to those involved is to *seek* advice when the case comes up. But let us briefly examine the subject of removal because of failure to perform, as an example, and at least cover some of the pertinent considerations.

Before an executive is removed from a position because he is not delivering the expected results, several conditions should have been met. He should have had:

--adequate warning, orally and in writing;

--a clear understanding of results expected and the critical variances;

--a reasonable time to make the needed improvement;

--help in trying to get the desired results.

If after these conditions have been met there still has not been sufficient improvement, removal is justified. The questions now are what kind of position and where the individual can perform well, and what does he want to do? Do the reasons for his lack of performance in this position preclude consideration for all other positions in the company? Was this position just a poor match? Some executives are inclined to look at "failure" as absolute and final. Too often, they are so concerned over the limitations that caused the removal that they overlook the strengths still there that caused the appointment. This one-failure-and-out syndrome is wasteful. This is particularly so if we consider the possibility that an individual may have learned from the mistakes.

To be sure, the individual removed from a position may not want to return to positions he could do well. He may have status problems in "going back a notch." Even if we recognize his ability to perform well on a given type of position and are willing to try to find one for him, he may not be interested. In any case, an exploration of worthy alternatives, both inside and outside, needs to be made jointly.

INTERNATIONAL PLACEMENT

Multinational companies have both interesting difficulties and exciting opportunities. A definition of the opportunity of crossbreeding of key men is provided by Sir David Barran, chairman of Royal/Dutch Shell. He is quoted by *Forbes Magazine* as saying: "If individual companies within our group are always going to breed their own top staff, the purpose of belonging to a multi-national organization is lost." For decades the Royal/Dutch Shell group have moved men regularly from one national affiliate to another.

An interesting advantage of a U.S. company's international operations as a training ground for future executive officers is found in the nature of foreign subsidiaries. Normally, the operations are smaller, and that makes it easier for a man to obtain experience in all phases of the business. The executive gets more opportunities for decision-making on his own than he would in a larger U.S. operation. At the same time, the foreign operation usually introduces more complexities having to do with competitive conditions, governmental relations, and local values and traditions.

There is a small trend for American companies to appoint nationals to key positions in the U.S. IBM has appointed Jacques G. Maisonrouge, a Frenchman, as head of their World Trade Corporation. Dow has named an Italian, a Canadian, and a Hungarian-born naturalized Canadian to its board. H. J. Heinz has moved a young Irishman from its British operations to head up the biggest operating division in Pittsburgh. Carborundum appointed an Englishman as its number two man in the United States. GE appointed a Belgian to head up its medical electronic division. Merck appointed its Dutch-born former chief of foreign operations to the position of president.

SUMMARY

The eighth requirement in the overall executive continuity system has to do with organization-wide selection and placement. Lack of policies and a strong centralized approach are quite usual phenomena. Five major factors are required in getting an effective organization-wide selection and placement effort. They are a depth of management, a sound knowledge of candidates, basic policies and procedures, direct involvement of top management, and a skillful staff contribution. Specific suggestions were given for procedures having to do with position specifications, candidate sources, candidate screening, slate preparation and approval, candidate availability, selection interviews and decision, selection follow-up, and removals.

10

Interaction of an executive
continuity system with other
management processes and
personnel programs

The ninth requirement is not actually a component of the executive continuity system which has been described in the previous eight chapters. Rather, this requirement calls for the executive continuity system to be synchronized with other management processes and personnel programs. Strenuous efforts to develop executive talent are quite often handicapped by an inconsistency in a management policy or a personnel program. For example, one company in a large, volatile industry kept losing its talent. They were leaving to become presidents of other smaller companies. For several years this organization refused to accept a frequently used device, namely, that of giving their major operating heads the title of president of their respective divisions and naming them corporate vice presidents. The device did not cost a cent. It did require changing an established pattern. This change, plus a few others were made and the loss of talent was reduced considerably.

In this chapter attention will be given to interrelationship of the executive continuity effort with five management processes:
--Business planning
--Management by objectives
--Organization planning
--Managerial controls
--Top management leadership style
In addition, the interrelationship with four personnel programs will be considered. They are:
--Compensation

--Retirement policies
--Executive communication practices
--The displaced executive

BUSINESS PLANNING

Large enterprises have developed a variety of business planning processes. There is usually a process for such functional areas as market planning, for product planning, for financial planning, and for research planning. George Steiner, cited in Chapter 2, suggests that comprehensive planning is composed of three types of plans: strategic, medium range program plans, and short-range, detailed plans and budgets. As organizations get more systematic about planning, the necessity of relating manpower planning to the more established planning processes is recognized. We have noted innumerable opportunities for this relationship in earlier chapters.

For example, once long-term business planning pertaining to the growth and nature of the business has been accomplished, it is possible to raise questions about such concerns as the following:

--The number of general managers needed in the future.
--The changes required in qualifications of future general managers.
--Potential personnel obsolescence problems.
--Potential personnel oversupply problems.

One large organization has shifted its approach to long-range planning in an interesting manner. They followed the traditional approach to projecting sales and profits each year for five years. They discovered that their stable businesses could do the projections with considerable accuracy. Of course, the value was not great. Their unstable businesses could not forecast with accuracy. The value would have been great if this organization could have made accurate forecasts, for many of their businesses were unstable. But years of effort failed to really produce a longer term projection which could be accepted with confidence.

This particular company decided to engage in a thorough process of "long-range thinking." The top 30 men in the company were asked to do two types of homework over a period of several months. First, they read books such as Herman Kahn's and Anthony Wilner's *The Year 2000.*[1] Then they concentrated on reading additional futuristic references on selected areas such as technology and human resources. Each individual prepared a set of assumptions about conditions ten years hence in five areas:

--Socio-economic conditions
--The industries in which they were engaged
--Their own organization

--Competitive conditions
--Executive continuity implications
The individual reports were compiled into an overall report. A three-day conference was devoted to talking out, arguing, and arriving at consensus on assumptions about the future. This process, in their opinion, did encourage long-range thinking. A reference report was prepared. It has been used in two ways. All profit-center managers are asked to prepare business plans for each of the next two years. They must also identify those specific things they are going to do or stop doing in the next two years because of their assumptions about the future. It became quite apparent as to those who are really acting on long-term assumptions and those who were playing games. The entire process contributed greatly to anticipating major changes required of the enterprise. The importance of an effective executive continuity effort was certainly reenforced.

The second use was to devote a special session once every two years to reviewing and revising the long-term assumptions.

Many of the suggestions provided in chapter 4 on Anticipation of Future Needs are pertinent to the integration of business planning and executive continuity planning.

Business planning is in a state of ferment with a great deal of trial and error experimentation. The predictable outcome is for organizations to be more systematic and more effective in preparing and using plans. We see an opportunity for the staff group associated with the executive continuity effort to act as a catalyst in ferreting out the implications for executive continuity action of major business plans. The state of the art is still in an elementary stage. However, the frequency with which executive talent has become a critical limiting factor is occurring sufficiently often that top managers are according priority to integration of business plans and executive continuity plans.

MANAGEMENT BY OBJECTIVES

Many organizations are experimenting with different approaches to setting objectives. There are numerous approaches. One basic approach utilized by several of the largest enterprises is referred to as the Responsibility-Indicator-Objective approach. The major characteristics of this method are:
--Objectives are "anchored" to responsibilities.
--A device, termed "indicators," is used to bridge from responsibilities to objectives.
--Objectives are usually short term. However, both short-term and long-term objectives are set on occasion.

--The responsibilities usually number about ten. Most have to do with operating results. Several have to do with personnel.

--Subordinates are expected to set their own objectives, subject to higher review and approval.

--Subordinates are expected to "manage" themselves against their objectives document.

--The objectives document is also used as a communications device with superiors and subordinates. Usually there is a regular quarterly review.

A review of an objectives document for a president of a large organization provides an illustration of the important relationship between an objectives program and an executive continuity effort. One section of the document is presented below.

Responsibility: Selection, development, and motivation of key executives*

	Indicator	Objective	Goal
a.	Number of executives who quit	None	None
b.	Number of key positions filled with competent performers	All	Identify exceptions and program action.
c.	Number of choices of qualified performers we have when making appointments to key positions	Eventually, two as a minimum	Replacement plans prepared
d.	Compensation competitive on appropriate comparisons (internal and external)	No major changes needed	Analyses made, any needed corrections made
e.	Development action for each key executive implemented per schedule	No exception	No exception
f.	Number of key executives implementing a goals program	All	All
g.	Up-to-date basic data on all key personnel	No exception	No exception, age analysis completed by July 1
h.	Number of appointments made from outside the company	Positive trend each year to where no more than one in ten are from outside	Secure data and set realistic goal for this year.

* Key executives are those one and two levels removed.

It is apparent that an effective objectives program certainly concerns itself with items directly related to the executive continuity system.

A comment needs to be made on the process as well as the content. Subordinates are expected to set their own objectives. They will likely have a knowledge of their superior's objectives. They are expected to manage themselves against the objectives document. On a regular quarterly basis the subordinate reviews his progress with his superior. Important variances are dealt with on a problem-solving basis. In effect, the superior is put in the role of a coach. At the end of the year the subordinate prepares an accomplishment report. Such report becomes a part of the cumulative record of the individual.

The above process contributes greatly to individual development. The subordinate gets both greater freedom and timely advice and counsel. Attention is given to doing the total job. Attention is also given to self-improvement pertaining to both the present and the future.

The impact of an objectives effort on self-improvement was dramatically revealed in a large manufacturing plant. An objectives program was installed in this plant for 500 supervisory, professional, and technical personnel. At the end of the second year the amount of money spent on tuition refund had doubled. No drive had been conducted. The necessity to establish an objective for self-improvement led many individuals to get off "dead center" and take a course.

Those organizations with a formal objectives program can evaluate the extent to which objectives pertaining to executive continuity are to being set and followed up. Those organizations without an objectives program may well want to consider initiating such a program.

ORGANIZATION PLANNING

The organizational structure has important impact on the executive continuity system. For example, it is possible to set up special developmental positions to help in achieving the overall objectives of the continuity effort. Some organizations, such as DuPont and American Cyanamid, have set up assistant general manager positions with a very deliberate policy to assist the enterprise in the development of future managers. Other organizations have made effective use of the project, or program, or product-manager type positions as a part of the overall matrix organization to give young managers experience in making tradeoff decisions across functions.

Another interesting organization planning problem has to do with companies making the transition from a domestic to a global operation. The historical evolution of companies in the United States from a domestic to a global basis seems to be characterized by certain rather predictable phenomenon. As a given company moves from an export to a manufacturing and marketing organization doing business on a global basis, a phenomenon which can best be described as "coagulation of crude" occurs. Seemingly, all of the unsuccessful individuals in the enterprise gravitate to the international division over a period of years. In subsequent years when the company decides to get serious about going global, it becomes apparent that one of their most critical problems is the lack of proper talent. At this point it becomes necessary to take a serious look at both the organizational structure and the competence of personnel for doing business on a global basis. One large consumer-product organization dealt forthrightly with this phenomenon. The new president abruptly shifted all domestic executives to international positions and vice versa.

Another interesting organization planning problem occurs when a large divisionalized company decides to consolidate. Some large enterprises find that they have divisionalized too far. They then reduce the number of major profit centers substantially. The move is usually well justified in terms of the operating results. However, such a move has a drastic impact upon ambitious executives. First, some managers who have had the excitement of being a general manager are asked to return to being a functional manager. Many of these managers perfer to quit at this point. Second, the number of general managers needed in the future is reduced drastically. At each level of management ambitious individuals have to wait. They find themselves staying in the same position twice as long as they had expected. While the new general manager positions are obviously bigger, the competition is obviously also going to be tougher.

Thus it is that major changes of an organization planning nature directly affects the executive continuity effort. In addition, the structure itself can be planned to facilitate attracting, developing, and testing of general manager talent.

MANAGERIAL CONTROLS

Over a period of years companies build up a reporting and control system. The ITT organization is renowned for its tight control system. One sage observer of the management scene has stated: "Executives do what their superiors inspect." Some control systems contribute to executive continuity efforts. Most do not, and some inhibit continuity efforts. The traditional control system concentrates on short term financial results. The message which comes through to executives is that top management is only concerned about immediate financial results. Companies that have been operating on this basis for years will have established a significant obstacle to any executive continuity effort. In some companies it has become an insurmountable barrier!

As mentioned earlier, the DuPont organization developed several criteria indicative of each division's effectiveness in management development. Annually a report is prepared comparing each division against each criteria; i.e., the percentage of managers with multifunctional and multidivisional experience, and so on. Those divisions which show up poorly on such comparisons are motivated to do something about it because they do not like to be "low on the totem pole."

Another large organization has designed an Executive Manpower Status Report. The report is designed to give a "numerical" picture of the status of the executive manpower effort. An example of such a report is provided in Appendix O.

Forbes Magazine reports on the impact of compensation policies of Johnson & Johnson as follows: "One of the reasons Johnson & Johnson works so well is that it's managers, unlike those of most big companies, have an enormous stake in making it work."[2]

Forbes goes on to comment on the use of high salaries, deferred compensation, stock options, and stock grants. *Forbes* also attributes Johnson & Johnson's success to their organization structure. There are 88 autonomous companies, each with its own president and board. Some are hundreds of millions of dollars in size, some are less than a million in size.

This hierarchy of different sizes of autonomous companies permits progressive testing of general managers.

Several organizations have made use of a control process designed for the people area. It is called a "ten-ten" program. The program identifies the top and bottom ten percent of a given employee population. Appropriate action plans are called for and follow-up takes place to insure action is taken. This highly visible approach does stimulate action. The action does contribute to keeping the pipeline open for people flow, thus enhancing chances for executive continuity. A description of such a program is found in Appendix N.

TOP MANAGEMENT LEADERSHIP STYLE

Some chief executives attract talent and some repel talent because of their personal leadership style. The latter tendency is seen quite frequently in the financially oriented leaders of conglomerates. Some of these organizations have a 30 percent to 40 percent turnover in executive ranks annually. Top management of acquired companies have rather brief tenure. These same organizations have great difficulty in developing their own future key executives. Therefore, they pay a premium price for their executive talent by acquiring them on the open market. Conglomerates, under such leadership, are missing one of the potential competitive advantages they have. They are large enough to have a sound executive continuity program. The full cost of such short-sightedness will be paid by the unfortunate successors of such leaders. A few conglomerates might be referred to as financial-managerial enterprises. The top leader, priding himself on both leadership ability and financial acumen, stresses programs for achieving the vitally needed executive continuity.

The ability to attract or to repel is also seen in well established enterprises. A chief executive who repels is soon known to executive recruiters. He makes them rich. With little effort they can place the repelled talent, often with competition. It is a rare executive who does not take one or two capable men with him. Some take an entire regiment.

The underlying secret of the ability to attract executives can be derived from statements made by subordinates of such men:

--He's a statesman.

--He can be trusted.

--He's got character.

--He respects the dignity of an individual.

--He challenges in such a way as to get the best from everyone.

--No one ever wants to let him down.

--He's concerned about people as well as operating results.

--He's mature, he's stable.

It adds up to the assumption that an individual executive has a good opportunity to achieve his own career objectives under this kind of a leader.

Interestingly, the pattern of leadership which generates this kind of reaction is likely to be perpetuated for two reasons. The selection criteria often include a requirement for such leadership. In addition, the chief executive has set a model which is likely to be emulated by his successors.

The chief executive who repels has already rationalized this sad condition. He is not likely to change. It becomes a fiduciary responsibility of his board of directors to look at the real economics of such situations.

COMPENSATION

The compensation policies have a very important bearing on the attraction of high-potential talent. They also have an important bearing on the retention of high-potential personnel.

It is interesting to note that in Alfred P. Sloan's book on his career with General Motors, little credit is given to the compensation policies as one of the more important devices in the success with which General Motors has developed and retained executive talent. Some observers credit this one policy as being the most important contributor to the success of the overall enterprise. For example, when it is possible to secure double one's annual salary in a bonus, this does motivate a considerable amount of performance.

The previously mentioned recommendations for cross-functional and cross-divisional moves makes it quite important that the salary is administered in a consistent manner across the entire organization. Failure to do this adds an additional handicap that is extremely difficult to overcome. Another interesting example of a compensation-created difficulty occurs in foreign assignments. If it is necessary to sweeten an individual's salary by giving him a two or three level jump when he takes a foreign assignment, then the interesting problem comes about when an individual is to return to the domestic organization. For his experience and age he usually finds himself out of the running or out of the market in his own organization. This leads some organizations to leave the base salary progressing along on a normal rate and add a special provisional payment for duty while on foreign assignments.

One entrepreneurial leader has a generous bonus program. His profit-center executives get half of the available bonus for achieving established profit goals. The second half is attained by achieving established growth goals. The stress on growth forces attention to such factors as critical executive manpower needs for achieving growth goals.

RETIREMENT POLICIES

It is necessary to consider the entire pipeline when planning for executive continuity. In an early chapter we called attention to the need to rethink the entire entry process by which future managerial talent joins an enterprise. It is also necessary to think through the entire exit process.

Retirement policies have been concerned with the value of an arbitrary retirement age in eliminating those who are becoming nonproductive. The value is the objectivity of the arbitrary age. Executive continuity aims at a flow to the top of the organizational pyramid. The peak of the pyramid allows for little mobility. It therefore is necessary to think through appropriate retirement policies with special concern for their impact on executive continuity.

All the evidence suggests the need for an arbitrary retirement date. This is particularly so at the very top level. There seems to be an occupational syndrome which operates at the top. Many a chief executive convinces himself he is indispensable. A given chief executive does not have to have this attitude long for it to be a true one. As likely as not, there is no genuine development effort to build depth. The thin reserves are thinned even more by the good young men who are too impatient to wait for years. Some who might have made it become too old in the process of waiting.

Some observers would add to the fixed retirement date by a tenure limitation. Mortimer Feinberg, professor of industrial psychology at Baruch College of the City University of New York and head of a New York firm that offers psychological consulting services to industry, says: "No man should be an incumbent (in one position) for more than eight years. Some men can make a contribution and renew themselves, but most can't. After awhile, the man runs out of ideas and options and becomes the captain of his own capture, the captive of his own previous idea."[3]

Feinburg suggests that after serving awhile at the top, an executive might consider stepping down to a lower position in his own company. "Why can't a general become a captain?", he asks. "If a man wants more challenge, why can't he just step down and start again?"

Retirement policies have seldom been established with the needs represented by the pipeline concept of executive continuity. A large electronics company, for example, provided a bonus of one year's pay for any executive who chose to voluntarily retire early. This was a one-time only decision to take care of an immediate acute need.

A large electrical company has reported on a novel, semi-retirement plan. The top executives in the future will "taper-off" at the age of 60. They will free themselves from the day-to-day decision making. Presumably, if this plan works out as planned top management positions will open up five years earlier than normal. The top executives are to be retained but assigned on a variety of significant long-range problems. It will be interesting to see if this novel concept is emulated widely.

A survey of some 1,900 corporate vice presidents and presidents made between 1965 and 1970 indicates that about 20 percent of them left their offices before mandatory retirement age. That compares with "no more than" 8 percent who left before mandatory retirement between 1948 and 1953. These figures do not include executives who left to take higher posts with another company.

Of the common management maladies that infect the U.S. corporation, one of the most irritating and potentially crippling to the company is the "hanging-on" syndrome. It shows up when a chief executive retires, prepares for retirement, or steps into a committee spot on his company's board of directors—but still calls the important policy and operating shots.

A variation of the ailment may be observed in older executives—frequently company founders or members of founding families—who remain in top management posts long past a normally accepted retirement time in their own organizations. And even when they announce that they are finally stepping aside, they keep on making the decisions and undercutting their alleged successor. Whatever form it takes, the syndrome brings on confusion over "who's in charge here" and serious conflicts in company goals. What is even more crucial, the malady stands in the way of developing and keeping efficient, professional managers.

Certain organizational situations seems to be fertile breeding grounds for the complaint. Family- or founder-dominated companies are particularly suspect, but the malaise also tends to creep into corporations where there is little corporate planning, a fuzzy organizational structure, poor executive promotion decisions, blocked communications, no firm retirement policies, and archaic management compensation practices.

POLICY ON TERMINATING EXECUTIVES

From the corporate standpoint, an executive termination represents lost time and money, and, perhaps, a reflection of management's ability to attract, develop, and hold competent managerial personnel. When the situation does arise, how should the company best proceed to terminate an executive?

Make certain there is no alternative. Basic and most important is an intelligent and clear cut determination that the executive cannot be effectively utilized in any other capacity. Under no circumstances, however, should the executive be retained simply to keep him on the payroll as a reward for seniority, loyalty, or as a balm to the company conscience. The problem certainly will not be remedied by transferring the man to a responsibility beneath his actual or imaged capabilities as this will simply aggravate the situation. The basic considerations must be for the dignity of the executive and the best interests of the company.

Face the situation squarely. The executive should be informed directly, candidly, and factually that he is being terminated and the reasons why. Tactics designed to freeze out an executive or to encourage him to resign only extend the unpleasantness of the situation and damage corporate efficiency and morale.

Do not prolong termination. In most cases it is wiser for the company to determine a fair severance arrangement and terminate the executive immediately. It is rarely advisable to maintain the executive on the payroll until he relocates, as his interest and energies obviously will be directed to his job hunt rather than to his corporate duties.

Provide help. There are many ways in which the corporation can be of assistance to the displaced executive. Letters from the executive's superior recommending consideration of his employment may be directed to a number of companies. Office and telephone facilities may be placed at his disposal for a predetermined length of time. The services of a psychologist may be offered to the executive for counseling and directive purposes. The circumstances of the termination should be factually discussed and understood so that the executive's version of his termination to future prospective employers will tally with the company's report in reference checks.

Maintain friendship. It is to the advantage of the company to maintain the displaced executive's good will, if at all possible. Poor handling of executive terminations can well tarnish a company's reputation.

SUMMARY

In effect the ninth requirement suggests that the executive community program works best when there is harmony with prevailing management processes and personnel programs for executive personnel. A close linkage needs to exist between business planning and executive manpower planning. An objectives program can contribute directly to continuity results, as can the control system. Organization planning becomes critical because any significant change has direct impact on executives and on future needs. Probably the single most critical interrelationship is between top management leadership style and executive continuity. Certain leadership styles preclude the achievement of any executive continuity on an internal basis.

In the executive personnel policy area compensation has an import impact on executive continuity efforts. Retirement policies have to be designed with care to facilitate people flow objectives as well as more traditional ones. Finally, the art of both retiring executives in a timely manner and of terminating them must be mastered.

11

Application of the systems approach

The tenth and final requirement—which was mentioned in chapter 1—is the need to design a systems approach to meet the unique requirements of a given organization. A reader will not likely reach this point unless he has a strong concern about executive continuity and has also begun to see a justification for the systems approach. We shall not, therefore, repeat the arguments which justify the increased complexity represented by a systems approach. Rather, in this chapter we will discuss the design of a system which will meet the unique needs of a given organization.

In the previous chapters both the theory and the methodology of nine critical requirements were covered.

In this chapter attention will be given to a process whereby an organization can design a new executive continuity approach. Many organizations have had some variation of a continuity program in operation. For such organizations, suggestions on assessing one's current program will be provided.

Let us first consider an example of a systems approach to executive continuity in a large business enterprise. Such an example will clarify what we mean by a comprehensive, integrated systems approach to executive continuity.

EXAMPLE OF A SYSTEMS APPROACH

The business enterprise is multibillion-dollar in size. It has a business group and product division type structure. There are over 100 general-manager- or profit-center-type positions. Considerable attention had been given in the past to managing professionally. However, little real attention had been given to the identification, development, and selection of general managers.

1. Central objective or mission

The central objective as stated by the chief executive was to have a continuity of competent general managers. Two secondary objectives provide a measure of the extent to which the central objective was accomplished. One secondary objective was that top management would have a tough choice to make from three well qualified candidates when filling general manager positions. The other secondary objective was that each general manager position would be filled by a competent manager.

2. Design process

The complexities of the situation, in terms of past practices, prevailing attitudes, and conflicting opinions about the desirability of more formal approaches led to the conduct of an initial diagnostic study. Among the more important findings of the study were the following:
--Few of the current general mangers had cross-functional experiences.
--Dialogues between a supervisor and subordinate about the latter's ability as a manager were quite rare.
--Data about the ability of executives was fragmentary.
--Considerable anxiety existed concerning potential crown princes and kingmakers problems.
This study led to the design of a comprehensive approach utilizing some well-known processes and several new ones. The design of the program took place over a period of a year. It was completed by a task force, with some consultant assistance.

3. The overall system design

The major components of the system were:
--Establishment of a supporting staff group
--An early identification program, supported by an assessment center process
--A major modification in college recruitment and new employee utilization
--An improved promotability forecast
--An annual manpower review process

--A company-wide selection and placement process
--An accomplishment analysis process
--A manager dialogue effort
--A revised company-wide educational effort
--An analysis or audit process

It was not expected that the entire design would be put into effect at once. It was programmed to introduce three or four components each year until the entire system was put into effect. In figure 11-1, a diagram of these components of the system shows the major relationships.

4. Description of components

A brief description of each component will provide a feel for the systems approach.

a. *College recruiting.* A special college recruiting program was designed. It was aimed at initial selection of individuals who might go up four levels or more in management. Briefly, the new college recruit, after brief indoctrination, was placed in a supervisory position. He has a year to prove he can make it or he is removed. The second lieutenant would be an appropriate analogy. This program is designed to assist in developing future upper level managers. The program has proved difficult to launch and sustain. This is not due to the recruits, it is due to the reluctance of managers in the organization to take risks.

b. *Early identification and accelerated development.* This program is aimed at developing future general managers. Men around the age of 30 are given an opportunity to get cross-functional experience, to get staff and line experience, to get domestic and offshore experience. The number identified is small, the program is not formally announced. Men in the program get one or two accelerated opportunities early in their career.

c. *Assessment center.* Since men selected in the early identification program have rarely had much supervisory experience, the assessment center endeavors to increase the likelihood that the men with real managerial potential are selected.

d. *Promotability forecasts.* At each level of general management, managers are asked to identify individuals they feel have potential to perform as general managers. They are not asked to nominate their own replacement.

e. *Annual manpower review.* Once a year general managers at each level have a review with their superior and a staff man. The review encourages thinking and discussion of: future organization structure, current managerial performance of key managers, promotability forecasts, the early identification program results, the college

FIGURE 11–1
Diagram of system

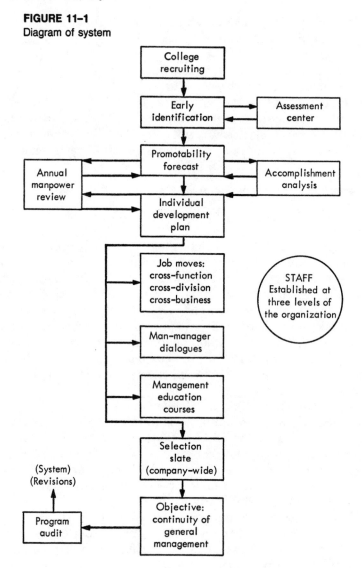

recruiting program results, and other aspects of the overall system. The feedback provided by a review may lead to revisions of plans for individuals.

Individual development plans. Stress is placed on specific plans for all men on the promotability forecasts. Most critical are plans for job moves of a cross-functional, cross-divisional, and cross-business nature. In addition, items for specific attention in management dialogues are identified.

Finally, scheduled attendance at specially designed management courses is included in the plans. The plans anticipate the actions to be take over a period of several years.

g. *Accomplishment analysis.* The traditional inventory type data was secured and converted to the computer data bank. Potential general manager candidates were also given an accomplishment analysis. A skilled interviewer interviewed each candidate and his immediate superior. Emphasis was given to getting descriptive reports on accomplishments and on managerial abilities. The accomplishment analysis process provides top management with a second source of data. The interaction between the interviewer and managers is designed to increase the accuracy of line management assessments and the specificity of their plans.

h. *Job moves.* The chief executive let it be known that he expected cross-functional, cross-divisional, and cross-business moves to be made. This was encouraged by the early identification program.

i. *The manager dialogue program.* The initial diagnostic study revealed an absence of dialogues between managers and subordinates, in spite of long stress on traditional performance appraisal processes. Skill training was provided to assist managers in having effective dialogues with subordinates concerning their managerial abilities.

j. *Company-wide educational effort.* Specially tailored courses were designed to help managers moving into new and bigger positions. Other special courses were designed to meet needs revealed in numerous accomplishment analysis studies of candidates. In addition, a few advanced management courses conducted by universities were made available for selected individuals deemed to have a special need.

k. *Company-wide selection process.* Managers are required to consider a minimum of five worthy candidates for general manager openings. Three of the candidates have to be "foreigners" from other components. This requirement encourages managers to use the central staff group.

l. *Program audit.* A specific measurement program was designed to assist in analyzing the established processes and the outcomes of the systems approach. The comparative results are discussed in the annual manpower review.

This approach comes pretty close to meeting all of the criteria of a genuine system mentioned in chapter 1. A central objective or mission was established. It was of real concern to top management. A variety of components were established. Provision was made for interaction among the components. Several feedback techniques were utilized. A staff was established to design, maintain and improve the system. Finally, a measurement program was provided to add an additional feedback mechanism.

DESIGNING A NEW APPROACH

The importance of a comprehensive systems approach has been a dominant theme throughout the entire book. It is now worth considering just how to go about designing and implementing such an overall approach. The major steps would include:

--Setting objectives for the executive continuity program.
--Establishing a staff function.
--Completing an analysis of the needs and the factors affecting achievement of the objectives of the executive continuity effort.
--Designing a comprehensive approach.
--Implementing it by phases.
--Institutionalizing the continuity approach.
--Periodic evaluation and modification.

Setting objectives

Setting objectives for an executive continuity program cannot be delegated by the chief executive officer. The objectives must reflect his real concerns, his real convictions.

Objectives are often set to reflect the need for executive continuity. We have just noted an interesting objective set by a chief executive of a multibillion dollar corporation. The executive continuity program would be considered successful if they had a tough choice to make from three qualified candidates in making appointments to key executive positions. Attention may need to be given to other objectives such as improving the competence of present incumbents, the extent of internal versus external selections, and the avoidance of loss of capable talent. The examples taken from objectives documents of a chief executive as shown in chapter nine is illustrative of executive continuity objectives.

The objectives may well reflect an immediate, short-range need brought on by imminent retirement. However, the objectives should reflect the executive continuity needs which will occur regularly for the entire future existence of the organization. The objectives should reflect the pipeline nature of executive continuity.

Establishing a staff function

Once objectives have been set, a decision will be needed on the nature of the staff function which will be required. Considerable attention was given to the importance of a staff function in chapter 3.

The critical question is whether or not to designate an individual who will devote full time to executive continuity. Some remarkably large organizations have a small number of key executive positions that would not justify such a position. Other diversified organizations, with a decentralized philosophy, might well justify a full-time position.

Several conditions argue for the setting up of a separate position or possibly a group:

--An acute need for results.

--An absence of currently qualified staff contributions.

--The need for setting up many fundamental programs (such as recruiting, executive compensation).

--A rapid growth in size and complexity.

--A global operation.

--A tradition of top management inattention to the executive continuity problem.

--A sizable annual loss of executive talent.

We have discussed the reporting alternatives and basic responsibilities of staff in chapter 3, so they will not be repeated here. Suffice it to say that the quality of the initial appointment has a vital impact upon the achievement of the continuity objectives.

Analysis of needs and conditions

This is a critical step. Many organizations omit this step. They rush out to find out what other companies are doing. They borrow a program here and a program there. It may or may not be relevant. The analysis of needs can be completed by the staff function. A task force, involving key executives, can undertake the analysis. An outside resource, such as a consultant, sometimes contributes objectively to a task force or a staff function.

Examples of two quite different ways of doing an initial analysis are provided in the Appendix. An "armchair" approach is described in Appendix P. This analysis process makes use of five questions for each of the ten requirements we have stressed as a part of the overall systems approach. The questionnaire can be completed by a task force made up of knowledgeable executives. Independent answers to each question can be prepared and then discussed to arrive at a consensus.

Obviously the analysis is no better than the objectivity of the task force members. There is an advantage in having each task force member read this particular book before answering the questions. This helps to provide a more uniform set of standards which the executives use in answering the questions.

A more comprehensive approach to need analysis is illustrated by an actual case in Appendix R. A diagnostic study was conducted by a consultant and an executive task force. The study both identified the needs and provided a design for an initial overall systems approach.

Design and implementation of a systems approach

If one follows the admonitions for designing a systems approach stressed in the previous chapters, numerous programs would have to be initiated in each of nine basic requirements. A systems approach is complex, it is comprehensive. The secret is to prepare a comprehensive design and then implement it in stages over a period of several years. The artistic nature of designing to meet unique organizational needs involves deciding on the priorities to be accorded the various programs. There is an advantage to undertaking three or four programs and getting them well established over a period of several years. Then another set of three or four programs can be undertaken. An interesting document has been prepared by Exxon as a guide for a new company or division undertaking management development. (See Appendix Q.)

Institutionalizing the continuity approach

The executive continuity approach can't result in the desired people flow unless it is an effort which is sustained decade after decade. In all likelihood the first chief executive who starts such an approach really will not get the benefit of it. His successors will. One organization started such an approach 18 years ago. One program was an early identification and accelerated development effort. Several candidates for chief operating office are currently under consideration. Both were in the first group to get an accelerated opportunity 18 years earlier. The successor of the president who initiated the program has benefited from the program as will his successors. That is, the successors will benefit if the continuity approach is institutionalized. Programs need to be maintained, improved, and upgraded. In addition, institutionalizing requires basic policies, it requires that successive chief executives understand and fulfill their role in the continuity system, it requires getting a succession of competent staff personnel. Above all, it requires the discipline to operate each program consistently and effectively year after year.

Periodic evaluation and modification

Needs change, conditions change, new methodologies occur. No matter how well designed and implemented a complex approach, like the executive continuity approach, it must be evaluated periodically and modifications made. Suggestions for accomplishing this follow.

ASSESSING AN ESTABLISHED PROGRAM

Several large enterprises established executive continuity programs 10 and, in some cases, 20 years ago. It is rare that these organizations make any significant changes in the program after the first five years. Executive officers change, staff personnel change, but the newcomers retain the established patterns. This complacency must be shaken if an established program is going to be assessed against the systems approach developed in this book.

Are objectives being achieved?

This is the basic question to be answered. In many instances an up-to-date statement of objectives is needed before undertaking to answer the question. Objective data can be secured to answer such basic questions. Subjective opinions of key executives are also relevant.

How about efficiency?

Programs get established and become a habit. Stepping back to look at ways for getting improved efficiency can be rewarding.

Are there opportunities for greater effectiveness?

The evidence suggests that few established executive continuity programs can be described as comprehensive. An Achilles' heel for many programs is the available evaluative data. Few organizations demand the quality of information that can be secured by the suggestions given in chapter 5. Few organizations have really thought through their educational philosophy. For example, few programs are timed with a concern for critical learning periods in an executive's career.

FUTURE ISSUES

Drucker was certainly prescient in 1953 when he warned that business and industry must achieve executive continuity or face governmental regulation. A recent Senate report blames lack of competent management for much of the tragic Penn-Central debacle. Studies of acquisitions and mergers reveal that a basic reason for the desire to sell is the absence of competent successors.

When we talk about the importance of executive continuity, we are certainly dealing with an issue of great consequence to individual organizations and to society as a whole. Fortunately, an increasing number of top managers are deeply concerned that they have an executive continuity effort and that it be effective. However, the evidence suggests that it is indeed a rare company that can be justifiably satisfied with results.

The current state of the art certainly is a distinct cut above prevailing practice of 15 years ago. However, significant advances are needed with regard to each of the ten basic requirements of the systems approach. We see a need for much more collaboration among all parties concerned with advancing the state of the art. Educators, businessmen, consultants, governmental officers all need to undertake cooperative efforts. Such efforts can justify substantial support over a period of years. This permits dealing with issues of consequence.

appendixes

There is a value in knowing about the philosophy, the policies, the methods and procedures of organizations that have been working at the challenge of executive continuity for some years. We have not endeavored to provide a large number of examples and illustrations. Rather we have selected examples which we believe merit serious consideration.

appendix A

Annual manpower reviews

Introduction

Many business organizations have an annual business review in which top management reviews the business results achieved by an operating manager. There is no doubt that top management is interested in business results.

The annual manpower review is analogous to the annual business review. Top management reviews the results achieved by an operating manager in securing, developing, and utilizing his manpower talent.

Objectives of the manpower review

1. To demonstrate top management interest in development and utilization of people.
2. To stimulate operating managers to give timely attention to their manpower problems.
3. To better inform top management of the depth of their management talent.
4. To secure better decisions on promotions, and more realistic manpower planning.

Procedure

1. The appropriate top manager (president, executive vice president, or general manager) advises each individual he supervises that a

151

manpower review will be held. Usually May or June is a good time to hold such a review, for fall months are often given over to budget reviews and business reviews. Initially a period of two to three hours is required.

2. An outline of the questions to be covered in the manpower review is given to each executive to aid him in his preparation.

    The operating executive cannot bring anyone along with him. It is a solo appearance. Fancy charts or presentations are taboo. The manager is expected to demonstrate a good, firsthand knowledge of all the topics mentioned in the outline.

3. Usually the review group consists of the president and the vice president of personnel or the director of management development. (If this is done at lower levels of the organization, the appropriate group would obviously have different titles.)

4. The review proceeds with the president posing the questions in about the order they are presented in the outline of questions to be covered in the manpower review. Notes need to be taken of major points that are covered.

    Usually, the need for action of various types is apparent during the review. The operating manager should be encouraged to be specific about *what* action will be taken and when.

ILLUSTRATIONS

Examples of two documents are included to illustrate the mechanics and the philosophy of the review process. An outline of the questions to be covered in an annual manpower review in General Electric follows. It is entitled "Manager Manpower Review Agenda."

An explanatory memorandum prepared by the Exxon organization for internal distribution is also included in this Appendix. The rationale for the review process is well stated in this document. The document is entitled "Development of Executives in Exxon."

GENERAL ELECTRIC MANAGER MANPOWER REVIEW AGENDA

I. Organization
    A. What organizational problems are you encountering?
    B. What organizational changes are you contemplating in the next 12–18 months?
II. Manpower needs
    A. Has the business situation changed or do you foresee changes which will have major effects on manager manpower needs? (Consider changes in technology, market place, competition, etc.)

B. What actions do you plan to meet these changes?

III. Individuals supervised directly

    A. Considering those who report to you, how well satisfied are you with each individual's performance?

    B. What are your plans to get improved performance or replace any less than satisfactory performers?

    C. For candidates for positions at your reporting level, you should be prepared to review each individual thoroughly with particular attention to development plans for each.

IV. Individuals two levels down

    A. Were there any significant differences between you and your managers regarding the promotability of individuals? What plans do you and these managers have to resolve these differences?

    B. How satisfied are you with the realism, specificity (action and timing) and probable value of the development plans prepared by your subordinates for their direct reports? How do you plan to improve on the process?

    C. How adequate is the depth and quality of candidates for in-line positions? If replacement strength is questionable, what are your plans to improve it?

    D. Do you foresee any replacement problems because of:

        --Organizational changes

        --Changing business situations

        --Age distribution of incumbent managers

        --Departures because of health or other personal reasons

        --Other causes

V. Follow up from last year's review

    A. Resolution of organization commitments

    B. Resolution of manpower commitments:

        --promotions

        --development plans

        --problems

VI. Other possible items for discussion are:

    --Losses of any high potential candidates

    --Early identification efforts

    --Implementation of a coaching program

    --Adequacy of performance appraisal procedures

    --Use of Crotonville and other educational programs

    --Age-level distribution among managers

    --Need for inter-component movement of managers

    --Recruiting efforts and results

    --Exempt manpower turnover and trends

    --Compensation trends or problems

    --Unique management development ideas to be shared

DEVELOPMENT OF EXECUTIVES IN EXXON

As business becomes more complex, the demand for well-qualified corporate executives is becoming increasingly difficult to satisfy. Exxon as a multinational corporation needs to give considerable attention to the development of management both in the United States and abroad. Exxon management accepts as a basic responsibility the need to provide well-qualified successors. Accordingly, today's management devotes a considerable amount of time and thought to the selection and development of their successors.

To resolve the problem on selecting and developing tomorrow's managers, certain minimum information is required, namely:
1. A means for identifying those individuals capable of progressing to senior management positions;
2. A means for determining how well potential managers are performing in their current assignments;
3. Assurance that individuals who are considered to have high potential obtain the experience needed for their development.

Recognizing the complexity of Exxon's business, it is imperative that a future manager be identified early in his career to permit the variety of assignments required for his development. In Exxon, the success of identifying managerial potential early in an executive's career results mainly from a corporate determination, fueled by the chief executive, to identify and develop managers. Exxon has no miraculous methodology for simply and accurately identifying and developing future managers.

Each Exxon manager has two primary annual review occasions for discussing his segment of the business. One of these reviews deals with stewardship for operations and the other for stewardship for personnel. These reviews start at the lowest operating level, cycling up to the top. Fundamental to the Exxon methodology on developing needed managerial talent is the concept of holding a manager accountable for the development of his executive resources as well as holding him accountable for operating effectiveness.

The stewardship review of personnel centers on three basic questions, namely:
1. What is the quality of performance of incumbents of senior-level positions in the reporting organization and what movement is planned in these positions?
2. What is the caliber and depth of the executive resources of the reporting organization and how will these resources be used?
3. Which individuals appear to have the potential to progress to the top of each organizational unit or to similar or higher level positions elsewhere in the organization? What is the highest level position each individual has potential for?

The annual review process with its appraisals of performance and estimate of potential for future assignments is both time-consuming and imprecise. Some of the reasons for this paradox are:

1. Exxon management does not expect that the potential estimates and rankings will have a high degree of accuracy. Most managers are uncomfortable with making long-range predictions of potential. The discomfort would be intolerable if they were expected to be accurate. The point is to establish a hypothesis as a basis for drawing a plan to test the hypothesis. Intelligent planning starts with the establishment of a target.

2. Why not let potential become manifest? Because there just isn't enough time. Exxon needs will not be met simply as a natural result of components meeting their own needs. The system must be stimulated if there is to be a choice among candidates for regional President and Director openings—a choice which includes candidates in their early-middle 40s.

3. If there were no other reason for undertaking this labor, it is enough that superior people will expect a system which looks for them and opens up channels for advancement.

4. It is necessary to use the development capability and apparatus of the total corporation in developing the highest potential resources. No single operating company offers the various work experiences that would be desirable.

5. Exxon experience suggests that if management is seriously over-optimistic in estimating potential of a 34 year old man an adjustment can be made without much harm on either side. If the same need for an adjustment becomes manifest at age 45, the bail-out can be a real problem. This is one of the arguments for forcing the organization to crystal-ball younger people in terms of potential.

How does Exxon get this done? As is often true in these matters, it is done despite its discomfort because the chief executive insists that it be done and sets the example by conducting a parallel exercise at the top. A plausible rationale helps also. Make a judgment and then test it. Do not be concerned if experience frequently proves a prior judgment was wrong. Predicting and testing the potential of individuals has to provide useful information which would not otherwise have been available. The result is an improved planning process.

A basic strength in the Exxon procedure for developing executives results from a review system which has someone looking over the shoulder of every manager regardless of his management level. This is significant merely because, understandably, each manager regardless of the size of the unit he is managing has a desire to obtain the greatest efficiency possible with the staff at his disposal. Occasionally, the effective development of future managers may require that a young executive be moved to another organizational unit under conditions where his replacement performs less effectively. The concept of the Exxon system is that a good manager not only will not resist such a move but, if the possibility comes to his attention, will suggest the move. In other words, the good manager looks at the organization's general interest as well as his immediate operating responsibility. One feature of the Exxon system designed to assure this type of planning is the requirement that the management echelon above each manager is responsible for development planning of the manager and of his replacement.

Emphasis is given to the movement of young executives even at the risk of impairing the operating effectiveness of a particular organizational unit because of the over-all importance of estimating or "guesstimating" which young executives appear to have the potential to reach senior management positions. As soon as possible after this type of estimate is made, it is important to test the judgment. Unless this part of the development process is carried out effectively, the rest of the total process for developing managers is placed in jeopardy. Major development moves designed to prepare executives to become senior managers are restricted in terms of the available talent. Talent that has not been identified at an early age and tested will probably be lost or unrecognized.

Exxon management believes the important thing is to specify what results are expected from each manager in spotting talent early and doing something about it. Relatively less emphasis is given to trying to control how he goes about it. Exxon does have a recommended set of tools but gives the operating companies a lot of leeway in deciding what they want to use. This reflects a number of things:
1. Some doubts about whether a clearly preferred method has yet emerged;
2. A desire to encourage a certain amount of experiment;
3. A desire to avoid an attitude that this is an exercise in completing forms and procedures;
4. A feeling that really capable managers respond best when told what results are wanted rather than how to get them.

Regardless of the methodology used, each regional and operating organization annually prepares lists of individuals with high potential. As young individuals are identified as potential corporate executives, the development and testing of their potential becomes a special concern of Exxon's top management.

appendix B

The manpower planner function in the General Electric Company

The General Electric Company is a large, divisionalized organization. The organizational hierarchy can be described, briefly, as follows:

Level 1. Chief executive office (chairman and vice chairman)
Level 2. Group executives
Level 3. Division general managers
Level 4. Department general managers (A department may be businesses or functional, such as a large sales component.)

There are manpower planners, usually called management manpower managers or consultants. They may be called managers, organization and manpower planning or managers, professional relations.

One manpower planning component serves Level 1. It is primarily concerned with overall systems design and with executive continuity issues at division general manager level and above.

The number of group executives varies from time to time. Generally, there are 10 or 12. Some group executives share a manpower planner consultant, some have their own. A few have set up a professional relations function with responsibility for executive continuity efforts and the traditional relations work for managerial and professional personnel. In any case, the manpower planners take on executive continuity responsibility for department level positions and above in their respective group.

The arrangement at the division level varies greatly. Some divisions may not have any staff assigned. Others may have a consultant only. Some may have a full-fledged relations function. Similar observations could be made of the department level situation.

The following information is provided:
1. Typical responsibilities of a manpower planner.
2. Generic specifications.
3. Manpower planner knowledge and skill needs.
4. An example of a position guide for a management manpower consultant.

Typical responsibilities of a manpower planner

A common way of examining roles is through specific position responsibilities. The role(s) can be inferred. The list of responsibilities below is typical in the sense that certain combinations of those listed typically appear in manpower planner position guides in General Electric. The term component refers to an organization such as a group, division, or department.
1. Design and modify as required the component's managerial manpower system to keep it tuned to the business needs, priorities, and opportunities.
2. Help component managers gain the information and skills necessary to make the managerial manpower system operate successfully.
3. Collect, analyze, and interpret data to aid the component's management in anticipating manpower needs and problems.
4. Help the component management identify managerial talent.
5. Collect and generate sound evaluative data on high-potential managerial talent, maintaining an inventory of the component's key promotable personnel.
6. Counsel component managers on their own or subordinates' development and career plans, following up to assure implementation.
7. Understand key managerial job openings and assure that job requirements are adequately described and agreed upon.
8. Perform candidate searches and assemble slates and evaluative data for key managerial openings.
9. Help component management prepare for and conduct the annual manpower reviews.
10. Review and make recommendations on key management compensation (including incentive compensation).
11. Be an internal consultant on management processes and on organization structure and development.
12. Develop own skills, abilities and knowledge base on a continuous basis, to be abreast of emerging concepts and able to apply them as needed.

13. Eventually, become the confidant of and broad-gauged consultant to key management, including business recommendations outside the manpower area.

Generic specifications

On several occasions groups of experienced and knowledgeable G.E. manpower planners have been asked to list the personnel characteristics they feel are desirable in one who would be effective in their work. As you might expect, the resultant lists were lengthy and diverse; but there was also a core of similarity. The core list is as follows:

Desirable Personal Characteristics of a Manpower Planner
1. Bright enough to compete intellectually in his environment. Capacity to think conceptually; to generalize effectively from bits and pieces.
2. Insightful and perceptive about and sensitive to others. Empathetic but objective. Emotions do not preclude the detached view.
3. Courageous. Willing to express his convictions even though they may be unpopular and may occasionally put him in jeopardy.
4. Persuasive and persistent. A realist about what can be accomplished but one who pushes hard for achievement. Well motivated with a high energy level.
5. Inquisitive, acquisitive, and good learner. Willing to consider new ideas. Knowledgeable and resourceful in his field.
6. Has poise, presence, and self-confidence; not in awe of rank.
7. Is "himself." Not a chameleon. Is consistent and predictable. Personally "calibratable."
8. Well organized; makes good use of time. Capable of shifting gears rapidly and dealing with unstructured and ambiguous situations.
9. High integrity. Trustworthy. Able to keep confidences and act with discretion.

These then are the most frequently mentioned characteristics of a manpower planner. It is also possible to identify knowledge and skills needed by a starting planner, an intermediate planner, and an advanced planner. A list of those might include:

Manpower Planner Knowledge and Skills Needed

A. Basic knowledge and information

   Starter
   1. His business: product, markets, competition,
   2. Management philosophy and processes

    3. Manpower system objectives
    4. Manpower system elements of work
    5. Professional and managerial relations concepts, principles, issues
    6. Field vis-a-vis corporate staff work

Intermediate
    1. Role alternatives
    2. Resources available
    3. Behavioral science theory (at least in survey)

Advanced
    1. Adult learning theory
    2. Personnel testing
    3. Diagnostic, audit, and measurement tools and techniques

B. Functional Knowledge and Skills

Starter
    1. Position design and evaluation
    2. Salary planning
    3. Work planning and review
    4. Performance appraisal
    5. Employee benefits

Intermediate
    1. Needs analysis (forecasting)
    2. Talent identification
    3. Personnel assessment
    4. Recruiting, placement, and selection
    5. Candidate slate preparation
    6. Equal opportunity/minority relations

Advanced
    1. Organization planning
    2. Organization development
    3. Succession modeling
    4. Development planning
    5. Career counseling

C. Personal Skills

Starter
    1. Speaking
    2. Writing
    3. Listening
    4. Reading

Intermediate
1. Interviewing
2. Consulting
3. Computer usage
4. Data synthesis/analysis/interpretation
5. Conference/course leadership and administration

Advanced
1. Counseling: directive/non-directive
2. Study design
3. Problem solving/decision making
4. Conflict resolution

These lists represent a consensus opinion of the characteristics, knowledge and skills an effective manpower planner should possess. Depending on assigned responsibilities and role, the importance and acquisition sequence and timing will vary from one manpower planning position to another. These lists represent a reasonably good model for the manpower planner's self-evaluation and development planning, and his setting management's expectations.

POSITION GUIDE
Management Manpower Consultant

General function: The management manpower consultant is expected to advise and assist the group executive and division general manager in planning for and taking the actions necessary to insure qualified candidates are available for appointment to general manager positions.

Responsibility	*Indicator of performance*
1. Candidate information: (Secure sound, comprehensive data on candidates; insure data is effectively used.) -- Complete accomplishment analysis. -- Design, prepare and maintain personal history record. -- Prepare analyses of data. -- Discuss data with general managers.	1. Number of accomplishment analyses completed. 2. Number of instances in which predicted performance has occurred. 3. Reaction of general managers to quality of data. 4. Completeness of personal history data. 5. Instances in which managers have acted upon implications of data.

2. Replacement planning: (Increase in the soundness with which general managers anticipate and meet their replacement needs for general managers.)
   -- Conduct "organization and re-placement planning" process with general managers.
   -- Stimulate managers to take actions to broaden and develop general managers.
   -- Encourage general managers to consider candidates from entire group.

   1. Number of planning processes completed.
   2. Extent to which replacement plans hold up.
   3. Number of placements made with developmental purpose.

3. Developmental actions by managers: (Increase in the frequency and skill with which general managers provide effective day-to-day coaching and annual performance reviews and other developmental actions.)
   -- Conduct coaching practices surveys.
   -- Develop new methods and techniques.
   -- Keep up-to-date on external educational opportunities.
   -- Advise managers on appropriate educational opportunities.

   1. Number of managers who have committed themselves to improve day-to-day coaching.
   2. Number of new methods and techniques introduced.
   3. Number of managers receiving instruction.
   4. Percent of annual performance reviews completed.
   5. Number of managers participating in external programs.
   6. Managers' opinion on results of managers' attendance at educational opportunities.

4. Selection of general managers: (Increase in the timeliness and soundness of selection decisions made for general manager open-ings.)
   -- Develop selection techniques and processes.
   -- Stimulate managers to use new techniques and methods.
   -- Provide suggestions of qualified candidates to general managers.
   -- Assist in outside recruiting efforts for general manager candidates.

   1. Average time required to fill open positions.
   2. New techniques and processes developed and used.
   3. Reaction of managers to candidates suggested.
   4. Success of outside recruiting efforts.

5. Department programs: (Stimulate departments to implement programs for personnel within departments vital to development of future general managers.)
   -- Prepare program instructions and guides, policies.
   -- Conduct informative and in-structional sessions.
   -- Stimulate departments to imple-ment selection and development programs.

   1. Number of department programs initiated.
   2. Number of informative and instruc-tional sessions.
   3. Number of requests for assistance.

6. Relationships: (Maintain effective working relationship with managers at all levels.)
   -- Provide timely assistance and advice to managers.
   -- Develop confidence of managers in your advice and assistance.
   -- Cooperate with other staff personnel.

   1. Frequency with which managers act upon your recommendations.
   2. Requests for assistance by managers.

7. Self-Development: (Plan and carry out a specific self-development program.)
   -- Plan and carry out appropriate reading program.
   -- Participate in internal and external instructional sessions.

   1. Nature of plans
   2. Actions taken.

appendix C

Position specifications

Executive position specifications come in a variety of shapes and sizes. The three examples included in this appendix are illustrative of different styles. We would encourage each organization to work out their own specifications. Specifications should represent strongly held convictions by top management of characteristics deemed essential for success in a given executive position.

Qualifications of a general manager

1. Past performance and personal history indicate that he has the skills, talents, and ability to get results—proven administrative experience. Experience preferably in running a line organization, such as a sales manager or factory manager.
2. Does he have a following?
    a. Has he won the respect of people?
    b. Do people seek him out?
    c. Do people have confidence in his thinking?
3. Is he basically broad-gauged and fair-minded?
    a. Can he see the overall interest in the enterprise as a whole?
    b. Can he fit the parts into the whole?
    c. Ability to see the concept as a whole.
4. Ability to take a group and build it into a team.
    a. Create high morale with a minimum of conflicts.
5. Ability to get the most out of individuals.
    a. Can motivate a man to give his best.

6. Ability to make decisions.
   a. Willing to make them.
   b. A high batting average on soundness.
7. Basically should have a high degree of force and persuasiveness.
8. Should have good common horse sense.
   a. Should be able to distinguish good from bad advice.
9. Should have a highly effective built-in radar.
   a. Ability to keep in tune.
   b. Able to take pulse of organization.
   c. Know what superiors, associates, and subordinates are thinking.
   d. Ability to shape policy and decisions within that framework.
   e. Effective grasp of politics—the art of the possible.
10. Ability to come up, regardless of circumstances, with an effective answer.

Characteristics of a high level executive

The following ten points are suggested as basic characteristics of an individual who is considered to be an excellent candidate for a high executive level in the company. No one person may be outstanding in all characteristics. He should not be lacking in any and he should be average in only a few. Proficiency and knowledge of jobs held is assumed; hence, training and experience is not specifically included. Also, consideration of age is not included.

1. A high level of intelligence as indicated by his performance in his field of activity, his ability to understand new problems or situations, and evidences of continuing growth of knowledge. A good memory is a strong attribute.

2. Should be able to communicate effectively both orally and in writing.

3. Health must be good and ability to carry on through strenuous periods is essential. Health and vigor should be stimulating to others.

4. Outstanding ability to work with people and to bring out effective performance by his subordinates in an atmosphere conducive to friendly associations.

5. Highly developed analytical ability to permit effective investigations and critical analyses.

6. Objectivity in handling problems, particularly with regard to people. Must be able to cope with emotional situations without becoming emotionally involved himself.

7. Outstanding ability to be creative as evidenced by suggestions indicating independent thought and the creation of basic broad plans.

8. Should be strong in courage of convictions and decisive, and yet be considerate of recommendations by other people.

9. An insatiable drive for accomplishment—the need to get things done—but, once the job is finished, to look eagerly ahead for the next challenge.

10. Should have a strong desire to succeed and to be a leader without sacrificing performance.

Specifications for general managers

A. Personal characteristics

1. Ability to relate effectively with others. Insight into human behavior—his own and others. Ability to live with and resolve conflict constructively.

2. Ability to sell self and his organization to his superiors—to develop their confidence in him.

3. Administrative strength. Delegates judiciously. Recognizes priorities. Efficient use of personal time.

4. Courage. Self-confidence. Willingness to take risks and unpopular stands. Deliberately decisive. Sets own course.

5. Flexibility. Open minded. Ability and desire to continue to learn. Can adapt to and manage change. Can handle many problems at one time.

6. High energy level. Can sustain long work hours. Well motivated. Takes the initiative. Willing to make personal sacrifices to get job done. Resolute and tenacious.

7. Integrity. No short cuts on ethics. Honest and objective with himself and others. Levels with people.

8. Leadership qualities. The capacity to get an organization moving.

9. Mental alertness. Above average intellectual powers and analytical abilities.

10. Stability. Capacity to produce results under pressure. Emotionally mature. Resourceful and calm in emergencies. Resilient and realistically optimistic. Not easily frustrated.

11. Toughness. High standards and results orientation. Measures self and associates against these. Willingness to reassign or replace incompetents.

B. Knowledge and skills

1. Behavioral concepts. Follows emerging concepts and remains healthily skeptical. Encourages experimentation without becoming a faddist. Understands human motivations and their organizational implications.

2. Business economics and finance. Knows what the signals are and how to read them. Can see the business implications in a

variety of financial statements and reports. Well developed instincts and judgments.

3. Communication. Speaks and writes well. Listens. Knows how to set a climate to receive frank communication.
4. Government. Understands, can deal with and knows how to influence at all levels—local, state, and federal. Can see the business implications in trends of public policy and attitudes.
5. Information technology. Understands concepts and limitations of computer "modeling." Is familiar with and knows when to apply or use advanced information techniques.
6. International business. Knows advantages and pitfalls in foreign sourcing, manufacturing, and acquisitions; trends in and strengths of foreign competition.
7. Market. Understands the forces, relationships, and competitive leverage in the market place. Knows what makes it grow, contract, and how suppliers, technology, distribution, service, affect it.
8. People selection and growth. Knows how to do a thorough job. Has interviewing skills. Knows what to look for and how to assess it. Has an implementable philosophy of people growth.
9. Values. Understands social trends and changes. Current on the values and attitudes of the younger as well as older generations. Can perceive and interpret the business implications.

C. Work experience

He would be best prepared for general management, by having *managed*—

1. In line or operating positions.
2. Small *and* large (numbers of people) components.
3. In more than one function.
4. In more than one business or family of businesses.
5. For more than one manager or in more than one management culture.
6. An important assignment in which he was top man with total responsibility for the success of a venture—such as a business section, program, or project, or other polyfunctional component.
7. In a business that was growing and in one that was contracting.
8. Successively more complex assignments with a strong pattern of achievement and success.

appendix D

Accomplishment analysis program

The Accomplishment Analysis Program has evolved over the last decade.

The purpose and procedures were covered in chapter 4. We have included the following material in the Appendix to further illustrate what is involved in this process:
1. A partial list of questions.
2. An example of a short report.
3. An example of a long report.
4. A follow-up study.

1. PARTIAL LIST OF
SUBORDINATE INTERVIEW QUESTIONS

I. Preliminary

Beginning with your move into your first supervisor job, would you tell me *why each change was made.*

II. Accomplishments—current job

--Refer to most recent position. What would you say are some of your more important accomplishments? I would be interested in operating results and any other accomplishments you consider important.

Probe for four or five accomplishments.

--Considering these accomplishments, what are some of the reasons for your success?

--Were there any unusual difficulties you had to overcome in getting these accomplishments?

--What two or three things do you feel you have learned on this job?

--What did you particularly like about the position?

--There are always a few negatives about a position. What would you say you liked least about the position?

--What responsibilities or results have not come up to your expectations? I would be interested in things you had hoped and planned to accomplish which were not done. I sometimes call them disappointments. (Push for several answers.)

--What are some of the reasons for this?

III. Planning, decisions

--Some managers over-plan, some under-plan. What do you think makes for effective planning?

--I am interested in how you do your planning. What planning processes have you found useful and how do you go about them?

--In what way do you feel you have improved in your planning in the last few years?

--What are some examples of important types of decisions or recommendations you are called upon to make?

--Would you describe how you went about making these types of decisions? With whom did you talk, what factors did you consider, and so on?

--What decisions are easiest for you to make and which ones more difficult?

--Where do you feel your superior has the most confidence in your decisions or recommendations, and where the least?

--What has been the biggest difference of opinion between you and your boss? Probe: Has he rejected or criticized any decision of yours?

--Most of us can think of an important decision which we would make quite differently if we made it again. Any examples from your experience?

--Most of us improve in our decision-making ability as we get greater experience. In what respects do you feel you have improved in your decision making?

2. EXAMPLE OF A SHORT
ACCOMPLISHMENT ANALYSIS REPORT
John Smith

I. Summary: personal history
Smith has been Operations Manager at #1 Plant for four years.
4 years—Plant Manager at #3 Plant
2 years—Assistant Plant Manager at #2 Plant
3 years—Rolling Mill Superintendent at #2 Plant
6 years—Assistant Rolling Mill Superintendent at #3 Plant

5 years—Moved from Apprentice Engineer to Staff Engineer in several plants.

Smith is now 46 years of age.

He has a Civil Engineering degree from University of Illinois and an M.S. in Structural Engineering from Purdue.

II. Accomplishments

A. #1 Plant Operations Manager

Smith brought the new fab mill into production fairly well. Productivity of the mill has been pushed up steadily (although we will note later this was not done entirely on his own initiative). He has introduced improved cost control methods and data. He has prepared a good five year plan. His plan has served as a model for other plants.

Smith relates well with the community. He is active in local planning groups and state business groups. He represents #1 plant well.

Smith has been faced with a tough lack of business situation. His responses have not been aggressive to this situation.

B. #3 Plant

During Smith's four years at #3 Plant the work load was low. This required aggressive action on cost reduction, reorganization, and staffing. John moved slowly on these problems and only after prodding.

He pushed the development of specialty items to increase sales volumes.

When faced with the necessity of improving quality and service and, also, reducing costs, John was reluctant in striving to do all three at the same time.

III. Strong points

Smith knows the sheet business. He does a sound job of long range planning and setting of objectives, demonstrating good analytical ability and good judgment on operating problems. John relates well with others. He coordinates well under pressure. He has had an active part in sales to major customers.

He currently serves effectively on a variety of community and industrial association committees.

IV. Limitations

John is not the demanding type. He has to be pushed to get optimum results. He avoids unpleasant tasks of discipline and removal. His decision making, while sound, is slow and deliberate. He has not developed many capable "comers."

John is not the enthusiastic type that sparks an entire organization to greater accomplishments.

V. Conclusions

A. Placement

John Smith should not be considered as a candidate for Manufacturing Manager position. While he has some of the strong points needed, his limitations are too critical.

John can continue to serve effectively where he is.

Consideration should be given to shifting him to a Product Manager type job in marketing. His analytical and planning ability are assets here. His limitations would not be critical.

B. Development

John will need periodic prodding to get optimum results. If he stays in his present position for several more years, he may well get discouraged about advancement and level off in his performance. At this point he might well devote too much time to community efforts.

It will be a challenge, not to develop John further, but to get the optimum contribution of an individual with many strengths and few weaknesses.

3. EXAMPLE OF A LONG
ACCOMPLISHMENT ANALYSIS REPORT
George Jones

I. Most recent accomplishment

George took over as "X" Project Director about a year ago. A crisis existed in Air Force training due to lack of equipment. He assessed problems in maintenance and failure rate of parts. He then sold the program to Air Force by frankly admitting mistakes and coming up with a sound program. George then pushed through the program to a successful conclusion by direct action.

As a Project Manager, George had to pressure the functional organization to produce. This he did rather forcefully.

George very early began to "trouble shoot" on difficult product design problems. He got his product through 50-hour tests, 2 months late, but overcame severe technical problems, one of which required a quick redesign of a major component.

By exerting heavy pressure on vendors he got parts needed to keep the production line moving.

George has had over 20 task-force assignments in the last seven years. On these assignments he has demonstrated the ability to work under extreme pressure, to assess a situation well, to be sensitive to customer needs and to get a plan of action carried out.

II. Brief summary of earlier experience

George received a B. A. from Harvard in physics. After three years in the Navy, he returned to Harvard for three years of graduate work in aerodynamics and applied mechanics.

George worked at another company for three years, then joined his current department as an engineer in preliminary design. He then became supervisor of component design for two years and manager of component design and evaluation for three years (group size: 115). He then managed an engineering design section for two years and then became Manager of Design Engineering. (350) people).

III. Planning and decision-making

Planning is one of George's long suits. He does a very thorough job of planning. He has repeatedly evidenced sound technical judgment. His time and dollar estimates have proven to be realistic. He is decisive. He has a strong desire to see engineering monies used in an effective manner.

George has developed an ability to "read" customers, to be sensitive to their needs in his planning.

The evidence suggests that he may "overplan" for his subordinates. He is in on all decisions of any consequence.

In some of his decisions, he may not recognize the impact on others nor on investments.

It is also sometimes difficult for him to stay within restrictions when they interfere with his getting a result.

IV. Organizing

George has taken over numerous engineering design groups. He likes to see clean-cut assignment of responsibility.

He has experienced a constant series of organization experiments within the "matrix" approach to organization of functional engineering and project engineering. His experience with organizational problems of functions other than engineering is limited.

V. Selection, development, and motivation of personnel

George has had considerable experience in recruiting, selecting and building a group of engineers. To date, he has picked men with technical background and experience to do a technical job.

As he gets larger groups, assessing managerial ability and motivation will require additional experience on his part.

Recently, George has begun to see the value of getting involvement of others in order to get them enthusiastic about an objective. He is encouraging contact between functional engineers and his customers for this reason.

In his current position George has had occasions when good men refused to join his organization. He has lost some good men too. George is basically a results-oriented fellow with little interest or concern for subordinates.

In shifting from group to group, George has learned the necessity of getting the best possible out of the people available.

To some extent this seems to have carried over to a pattern whereby he does all the planning, and decision-making, giving his subordinates periodic assignments. This pattern is not likely to develop personnel. It also means some weak men may be retained when they should be removed.

VI. Controlling

George has set up a record, report, and chart system to keep him up to date on vital aspects of the project, including a modification of the current system. He uses personal contact frequently to keep in touch with situations. He makes sure the support groups are under control.

George has developed a judicious skepticism on inputs of subordinates and supporting groups.

On some occasions he does not keep as close check on developments as is necessary. He has learned that project-type work is much more complex to control than engineering-design work.

VII. Relationships

Subordinates consider George to be tough and demanding and disinterested in them. The men who tend to either join him or stay with him are the more capable ones.

George's relations with customers are effective. He has proven to be a sound and persuasive negotiator in dealing with key men in customer organizations.

He relates well with his peers, with an occasional exception. He perfers clean-cut relationships and grants of authority.

VIII. Other characteristics

George has demonstrated the ability to get a group to design components that work. The results of his designs have been good. Until his current assignment, George had concentrated on design engineering. He has not had to have a depth or breadth of knowledge in finance, personnel, or manufacturing.

He had demonstrated the ability to work under heavy pressure, against tight deadlines.

IX. Career preferences

George prefers to have a position with heavy responsibility and cross-functional responsibility. He would prefer not to direct a functional engineering group.

He aspires to be a General Manager five years from now.

George feels his progress has been satisfactory. (Nine level increases in ten years.) Sometimes he has felt it was too slow. Several years ago he got disgusted and looked around seriously.

X. Placement action

George is a worthy candidate for an engineering manager position or for managing a large project. He will be best used in managing a project in the early stages of production.

He can benefit from another year on his current assignment. This will be particularly true as overseas markets open up for his equipment.

After that, a bigger project job would be appropriate. He is strong enough technically to move into project work in other divisions. He would be a worthy candidate for a position like Smith's.

Even though he does not prefer it, an assignment to manage a large group would also be appropriate.

George has to overcome several critical handicaps (delegation, supervision, relationship with subordinates) before he can be considered seriously for promotion to a general manager position.

XI. Development action

In retrospect, George could have benefitted by having been shifted from functional to project work several years sooner.

He could also benefit from working for a different boss. He has worked for or under his current boss for seven years.

George will have to learn how to lead, to inspire a large organization. He will have to begin to understand the needs of his subordinates and take these into account in striving for results. If he does not do this, he will be handicapped in getting and keeping good men.

George will also have to discipline himself to delegate more effectively both the planning and the execution of work. (This is probably the most critical need George has at the present time.) He will also have to learn when and how to get resource groups such as Finance, Personnel, and Legal to make needed contributions.

In his current job, George could benefit by being expected to take on higher level business negotiations as time goes on.

4. A FOLLOW UP STUDY

The Uniroyal organization has been using the Accomplishment Analysis process for quite a few years. Initially, the analyses were done by Bill Wrightnour. In the first year Wrightnour prepared analyses on twenty individuals who were deemed by line management to be potential General Managers. This study reports on the actual progress of these twenty individuals over the course of the next ten years.

Let us first look at Wrightnour's initial predictions. Predictions were made as to the likelihood of an individual becoming a general manager. Three categories were used; Above Average, Average, Below Average. Admittedly, these are not very precise. However, the main dynamic is to contrast the judgments on potential made by line managers with an independent judgment.

TABLE 1
Initial predictions

Category	Number
Above average likelihood of becoming a General Manager	12
Average likelihood	5
Below average likelihood.	3

While the number of executives is too small to permit meaningful generalization, Wrightnour could be credited with having 8 of the 12 to whom he gave Above Average ratings move up two or three levels or become a General Manager. Of the remaining four, two were definitely "misses," one appears likely to also be a miss, and one might still become a General Manager.

Those rated "Average or Below Average" numbered eight. One became a General Manager and failed. The others moved up one level but that was all.

The important contrast is that line managers felt that all 20 individuals could become General Managers. This study, even though it is limited by small numbers, does illustrate the value to top management of having replacement recommendations "validated" by an independent individual or group.

TABLE 2
Predictions versus subsequent promotion

Initial prediction	Became a general manager	Became a general manager but was removed	Moved up 3 levels but not a general manager	Moved up 2 levels but not a general manager	Moved up 1 level but not a general manager
Above average	5	2	1	2	2
Average	–	–	–	–	5
Below average	–	1	–	–	2

appendix E

Promotability forecasts

The traditional approach to thinking about future successors is to prepare a replacement chart. Usually the basis for the replacement chart is the current organizational chart. The first such replacement chart was recommended in the literature in 1948. Many companies are still using the same style. As often as not a colorful code system is required to reflect current performance, potential rating and readiness for promotion.

As we stated in chapter 4, we consider such charts to be limited. Attention is focused upon the wrong question. We call it the truck question. Who would be your successor if you got run over by a truck? The question needs to be answered. But let us not stop there. The primary result we want is "people flow," which adds up to executive continuity. There are two approaches which we feel do avoid the truck pitfall of most replacement charts. One is the promotability forecasts as done by DuPont. The other is the replacement planning for a ten-year span as done by Exxon. We will use material from these two organizations to illustrate alternatives we feel deserve serious consideration.

DuPont promotability forecast

Each vice president and general manager of an operating division prepares a Promotability Forecast annually. Four categories of potential have been established:

1. Middle management employees and above thought qualified to become division head within a 10-year period.
2. Lower middle management employees and higher thought qualified to attain at least a major Department Head (a top functional or product head position) within a 10-year period.
3. Lower middle management employees thought qualified to advance to a specified organization level within a 10-year period.
4. Young employees at lower organizational levels thought to possess the potential for very substantial managerial advancement.

A special report is prepared for each individual included in categories 1 and 2.

Provision is made for indicating for each individual the:
--Specific outstanding achievements and contributions, particularly during the past year, which are indicative of the forecast potential.
--Positions to which the individual is ready for promotion within one year.
--Positions to which the individual will be ready for promotion within one–three years.
--Whether the individual should be considered for transfer from a line to a staff position.
--Plans for the next three years for further development beyond the experience on his current position.

For Groups III and IV, only the first two of the above four items are required. This brief description does not do justice to the numerous additional follow-on steps of analysis, comparison, and planning carried out upon completion of the promotability forecasts.

Each division in the company submits an annual forecast. This data is then summarized for corporate management, after which reviews are held with the managements of each division. Through analyses, comparison, charts, etc., the divisions are encouraged to plan to insure the effective development and advancement of those individuals forecast as having substantial management potential. An example of the Promotability Forecast report form follows.

PROMOTABILITY FORECAST

Department_____Date_____Category_____

Name_____Present Position _____Level_____

1. Promotability

TIMING	Positions to which promotable in one or more fields of present division		If an employee is considered a candidate for transfer to another division, indicate below
	POSITIONS	LEVELS	POSITIONS RECOMMENDED
READY WITHIN 1 YEAR			
READY WITHIN 1-3 YEARS			

2. Highlight specific outstanding achievements and contributions, particularly during the past year, which are indicative of the forecast potential.

3. Please indicate what additional experience would expedite attainment of the potential projected and any plans you have to provide such experience.

4. Other comments:

EXXON's dual approach to replacement planning

Exxon's approach to replacement planning has evolved over several decades. As noted in chapter two the process is given regular, intensive interest by top officers. We have selected the Exxon planning process because they have gone far beyond the old chart approach. Most significantly they have two types of replacement plans. One for key executives and one for key executive positions. The position plan pictures planned movement out ahead for five years. In addition, an indication is given of movement which can reasonably be forecast for an ensuing five years.

Four documents are utilized by Exxon in doing their replacement planning. They are:

Replacement Plans—Key Executives

Plans for Key Executive Positions

Executive Resources

Individual Development Plan

This latter document summarizes the depth of executive resources deemed to have potential for a given level of management.

Sample documents follow.

| BNJ-INR-606-3A | REPLACEMENT PLANS KEY EXECUTIVES | | | | CONFIDENTIAL EXD - 12 | | |

ORGANIZATION: (Define) BOARD & MANAGEMENT COMMITTEE REGIONAL AND OPERATING ORGANIZATION "A"   **DATE:** NOVEMBER, 1970

POSITION INCUMBENT (AGE)	RATING		REPLACEMENT (AGE)	1- READY NOW 2- 1-2 YRS. 3- 3-5 YRS.	RATING	
	PERF.	POT.			PERF.	POT.
PRESIDENT * A. C. Smith (61)			C. A. Bond (49) F. H. Gordon (43) H. L. Brooks (38)	1 3 3	2 2 1	A A A
EXECUTIVE VICE PRESIDENT * C. A. Bond (49)	2	A	F. H. Gordon (43) E. G. Hall (43)	2 2	2 1	A A
VICE PRESIDENT - FINANCE * B. C. Brown (64)	3	L	F. H. Gordon (43) H. L. Brooks (38) D. O. Grant (35)	1 3 3	2 1 1	A A A
VICE PRESIDENT - LOGISTICS * F. H. Gordon (43)	2	A	H. L. Brooks (38) A. B. Davidson (42) T. L. Meyer (3)	1 1 3	1 1 1	A B A
DIRECTOR (PRODUCING) * E. G. Hall (43)	1		ro (38) ac	1 3	1 1	A A
DIRECTOR (MARKETING) G. I. Daniel (5)			. Spencer (36)	3	2	B
DIRECTOR (PLANN) A. A. Fox (56)	4	L	A. B. Davidson (42)	1	1	B
* Management Committee						

PERFORMANCE ON PRESENT POSITION	POTENTIAL FOR ADVANCEMENT
1 Outstanding or exceptional performance (usually less than 10% of the total).	A Can advance to: CHIEF EXECUTIVE
2 Performance which is definitely better than normally expected, producing results which exceed the requirements of the position (usually no more than 25% of the group).	B Can advance to: MANAGEMENT COMMITTEE
3 Performance which consistently meets the requirements of the position (typical of a majority of personnel).	C Can advance to: ---
4 Performance which on the basis of comparative effectiveness requires certain improvement in one or more basic aspects of the work.	D While not having advancement capabilities within this organization, has promising possibilities for advancement to a position in another organization. (Furnish information on FORM EXD-11 – PLANS FOR KEY EXECUTIVE POSITIONS.)
5 Inadequate performance.	
N Performance not appraised due to newness in position or other factors.	L It does not appear likely, at this time, that this man will advance beyond his present position level.

PLANS FOR KEY EXECUTIVE POSITIONS

(DEFINE) ____BOARD AND MANAGEMENT COMMITTEE_____   ORGANIZATION:

POSITION	REPLACEMENT PLAN				
INCUMBENT (AGE) IN POSITION SINCE: (MONTH/YEAR)	IN THIS SECTION SHOW PLAN FOR POSITION, INDICATING WHEN CHANGE WILL TAKE PLACE AND THE ANTICIPATED REPLACEMENT. INDICATE NEXT ASSIGNMENT FOR OUTGOING INCUMBENT.				
	19_71_	19_72_	19_73_	19_74_	19_75_
PRESIDENT A. C. Smith (61) 8/65				C.A. Bond (53) Retire 9/74	
EXECUTIVE VICE PRESIDENT C. A. Bond (49) 2/70				F.H. Gordon (47) To President	
VICE PRESIDENT-FINANCE B. C. Brown (64) 6/63		F. H. Gordon (44) To Retire		H.L. Brooks (42) To Exec. V.P.	
VICE PRESIDENT-LOGISTICS F. H. Gordon (43) 11/68	Jersey H.L. Brooks (39) To V.P.-Finance				
DIRECTOR (PRODUCING) E. G. Hall (43) 10/70			H. L. Brooks (4) H. E. Black Tra er Out		
DIRECTOR (MARKETING) G. I. Daniel (57) 2/67					
DIRECTOR (PLANNING) A. A. Fox (56) 10/69		A. B. Davidson (44) Transfer Out or Retire Early			

SNJ-INR-606-2A

CONFIDENTIAL

REGIONAL & OPERATING ORG."A"   DATE: NOVEMBER, 1970   EXD-11

IN THIS SECTION SHOW ANY DEVELOPMENTS AND PLANS WHICH CAN BE PREDICTED WITH REASONABLE CERTAINTY.					COMMENTS IN THIS SECTION EXPAND, AS NECESSARY, ON THE SKETCHED PLANS.
19 76	19 77	19 78	19 79	19 80	
					Bond is a fully qualified replacement.
					Gordon is the only internal candidate for the Executive Vice President opening, and is highly qualified for the position.
					When Brown retires in March 1971, Gordon will be moved to V.P.-Finance and given broader and varied duties in preparation for his next move to Executive Vice President.
					When Gordon moves to V.P.-Finance in March 1971, a Jersey candidate can be considered as replacement. While Brooks and Davidson are both ready replacements, Brooks could benefit from two more years as Ch. Exec.-Operating Affiliate "A", and Davidson's background fits better functionally if he is brought on Board to replace Fox.
		Retire 10/78			Hall is one of this affiliate's highest potential executives, and while he would be a strong contender for advancement in this organization, his geographical experience needs to be varied to accelerate his development for a broader Jersey role.
					Fox should be replaced no later than mid-1972 when the current reorganization is completed. While he was a strong country manager, he has not proven to be as strong as a Director. He enjoys and excels in the day-to-day management of an operation, particularly where there is a heavy marketing involvement. If a suitable position cannot be found where his particular strengths can be used, then an early retirement will be arranged.

EXECUTIVE RESOURCES

EMPLOYEES WITH POTENTIAL FOR: MANAGEMENT COMMITTEE, OR HIGHER

NAME	BIRTH DATE MO.	YR.	PRESENT POSITION (SALARY CODE)
AGE 30 - 34			
T. J. Lee	4/36		Div. Mgr. Op. Affil. "B" (A)
W. J. Rice	12/35		Treas. Op. Affil. "A" (C1.)
G. R. Wall	3/36		Mgr. Dist. B, Op. Affil."D" (C1.)
AGE 35 - 39			
H. L. Brooks	6/32		Pres. Op. Affil. "A" (E)
H. F. Black	5/35		Gen. Mgr. Div. "A" (D)
T. J. Meyer	8/33		Dir. Op. Affil. "B" (C-)
D. O. Grant	7/35		Treas. Reg. & Op.Org. "A" (D)
B. A. Davis	10/31		Pres. Op. Affil. "C" (D)
N. R. Jones	3/32		Pres. Op. Affil. "E" (D)
G. H. Spencer	7/34		Mktg. Mgr. Op. Affil. "G" (B)
B. C. Taylor	4/31		Mgr. Corp. Plng., R&O "A" (D)
H. H. Thomas	3/34		Ref. Mgr., Op. Affil. "H" (A)
G. B. Wolf	10/33		Dist. Mgr. Prod., Op.Aff."G"(C1.)
B. F. Stein	11/31		Mktg. Op. Mgr., Op. Aff. "F"(C1.)
AGE 40 - 44			
P. J. Dean	8/30		Mng. Dir. Op. Affil. "D"
A. B. Davidson	6/28		Mgr. Mfg., R&O "A"
W. C. Lloyd	10/29		Pres. Op. Affil. (E)
J. L. Stark	8/28		Dir., Op. Affil. "A" (C)
L. M. West	6/27		Asst. Gen. Mgr., D "B" (C-)
AGE 45 - 49			
T. A. White	5/21		V.P., Op. Affil. "F" (C)

ORGANIZATION REGIONAL & OPERATING ORG. "A"   DATE: NOVEMBER, 1970   EXD- 14

DATE ASSIGNED		NEXT ASSIGNMENT PLANNED		DATE		FURNISH TITLE OF HIGHEST POSITION INDIVIDUAL CAN REASONABLY BE EXPECTED TO ATTAIN.
MO.	YR.	POSITION TITLE (SALARY CODE)		MO.	YR.	
2/69		Mgr. S&T Op. Affil. "A"	(B)	11/70		Jersey Director or higher
10/70		Treas. Op. Affil. "B"	(A)	6/71		Mgt. Comm. this company
11/69		Mgr. Div. "C", Op. Affil."D"	(B-)	9/71		Mgt. Comm. this company
10/69		Dir. Reg. & Op.Org. "A"	(F)	6/73		Jersey Director or higher
8/70		Pres. Op. Affil. "A"	(E)	6/73		Ch. Exec. this company
4/70		Pres. Op. Affil. "E"	(D)	7/72		Ch. Exec. this company
8/70		Gen. Mgr. Div. "A"	(D)	6/73		Ch. Exec. this company
9/68		To Reg. & Op.Org. "C"	(E)	5/71		V.P. this company
6/70		Mgr. S&T, Reg. _ Org."A"	(D)	7/72		Mgt. Comm. this company
4/69		Dir. Op. _ffil.	(C)	8/71		Mgt. Comm. this company
2/68		Dir. Op. _il.	(C-)	3/71		Mgt. Comm. this company
10/70		A_ _n. _r D_v. "A"	(C)	8/72		Mgt. Comm. this company
3/68		D_ _., _ffil. "G"	(A)	2/71		Mgt. Comm. this company
7_		Di_ _gr. Op. Affil. "D"	(A)	1/71		Mgt. Comm. this company
_2/68		Pres. Op. Affil. "B"	(E)	3/74		Mgt. Comm. this company
10/67		Dir., Reg.& Op.Org. "A"	(F)	6/72		Mgt. Comm. this company
12/70		Pres. Op. Affil. "G"	(E)	4/74		Mgt. Comm. this company
9/69		Mgr. Mfg., R&O Org."A"	(E)	6/72		Mgt. Comm. this company
11/68		Dir., Op. Affil. "A"	(C)	6/72		Mgt. Comm. this company
10/68		Could become President, Op. Affil. "F" and could later be a Director, Reg. & Op.Org. but competition will probably remove him from contention.	(D)	6/71		Mgt. Comm. this company

CONFIDENTIAL
EXD-9

INDIVIDUAL DEVELOPMENT PLAN SNJ-SEC-166

NOTE: WHENEVER POSSIBLE, A CURRENT PERSONAL HISTORY RECORD FORM SNJ-INR-41 SHOULD BE ATTACHED TO THIS DEVELOPMENT PLAN.

POSITION (TITLE)	NAME (FIRST)	(MIDDLE)	(LAST)
President	Henry	L.	Brooks

COMPANY	DEPARTMENT	LOCATION
Operating Affiliate "A"		Country "A"

PERFORMANCE ANALYSIS (COMMENT ON THE MAN'S FUNCTIONAL AND MANAGEMENT STRENGTHS INCLUDING AREAS IN WHICH HE EXCELS AS EVIDENCED BY SPECIFIC EXAMPLES.)

Highly effective manager. Motivated by strong desire for personal accomplishment. Clear understanding of technical aspects of the business. Imaginative; sound business judgment. High order of analysis and planning.

PERFORMANCE APPRAISAL CODE

POSSIBLE ULTIMATE POTENTIAL (INDICATE SPECIFIC POSITIONS)

Director of SONJ or higher.

DEVELOPMENT NEEDS

DEVELOPMENT OBJECTIVES/EXPLANATION (SPECIFY POSITIONS OR WORK ASSIGNMENTS THAT WILL HELP PREPARE HIM FOR HIS HIGHEST ULTIMATE POTENTIAL.)

Has had just one year as Chief Executive in Country "A" an __ __ greatly benefit from another 2-3 years managing this major affiliat__ Foll__ __ng this experience, he is ready for the Management Committee an__ __ o__ __ tha__ __rience to advance in this or any other regional and oper__ __ing __ __ __ __zat__ __

SAMPLE

TRAINING (INDICATE EDUCATIONAL OR TRAINING PROGRAMS THAT WILL ALSO HELP PREPARE HIM FOR HIS ULTIMATE POTENTIAL.)

No formal training required.

DEVELOPMENT PLANS

19 71	19 72	19 73	19 74	19 75
			Director (Producing) - R&O Org. "A"	
President Operating Affiliate "A"				

TIME IN PRESENT POSITION	AGE
1 YRS. 1 MOS.	38

PREPARED BY	DATE
Management Development Committee, Regional & Operating Org. "A"	November, 1970

appendix F

A career planning program

Purpose

Most large organizations have difficulty getting useful information about their professional, technical, and managerial talent. This is particularly true of the younger employee. Therefore, one purpose of the Career Planning Program is to insure that an organization has certain basic uniform data on all college recruits who have been with the organization three years. This basic data should assist in more skillfully planning career moves, making placements, and planning developmental actions.

Most young exempt employees are acutely concerned about themselves and their careers. One young man recently told us: "Frankly, I'm more interested in learning about what makes me tick or motivates my actions than the Company could ever be." The second purpose of the program is to provide such employees with basic data about themselves and to provide them with the benefit of an effective career discussion with an experienced personnel specialist.

It is important to stress what the Career Planning Program *is not*. It is not a selection program. It will not permit saying an individual should or should not become a supervisor. However, if the program becomes a regular annual event, it will be possible, in a few years, to have data which can be used as a contribution to a selection process. This will be particularly relevant to early identification efforts of the company.

How the program works

The basic steps in the program are:

1. *Selection and invitation to participate.* Those who meet the criteria are invited to learn about the program.
2. *Orientation.* All aspects of the program are discussed in a group meeting with the program coordinator. Based on a full knowledge of the program, each individual makes his decision to participate or not. Participation is strictly voluntary.
3. *Administration.* The basic data is collected through a battery of measurement instruments. The participant spends about four hours in individual effort and five hours in a group session. Administration of the 14 instruments is handled locally by trained clerical personnel. Scoring is done locally for all but two instruments.
4. *Analysis of the data.* The program coordinator analyzes the data versus the aspirations of the individual. With experience, this process takes one to two hours.
5. *Career discussion.* The participant has the benefit of a two or three hour discussion with the program coordinator. A "profile" report form is used to relate the data to the individual's aspirations. In discussing the data, the coordinator gains additional insights into the talents of the individual.
6. *Outcomes.* Following the career discussion, several important actions take place:
    a. The participant sets up his own developmental action plans. Both the coordinator and the participant's boss are likely to be consulted before these plans are finalized. Building on competitive advantages as well as removing obstacles to career progress are fundamental in these plans.
    b. The coordinator sets up his plans to use his new, in-depth knowledge of the participant to further counsel the individual and members of management who must make decisions regarding the individual.
    c. The basic data is added to the company data bank information for future research.

What is revealed by the "profiles"?

Much of the data collected through the various instruments used in the program could be obtained through intensive interviews. The instruments simplify the process and provide uniformity and organization of the data. Some of the data comes from selected standard test instruments. Norms are developed for a company on each measurement (except the interest inventory, which has national norms) so that the individual participant can compare himself to others in the organization.

Most individuals have a fairly realistic reading on where they ranked in competition with their classmates in high school and college. (Academically by their grades; socially through their school activities; and so on). The profile data helps them see how they stand compared to competition in their current situation as an employee, and on a much broader scale. This can be seen by reviewing the content of the six profiles.

Profile 1—Biographical inventory. Eleven categories include family background, educational background, social activities, personal skills, aspirations, and job satisfaction. Responses are weighted for scoring purposes, then profiled by category according to norms developed for the company.

Profile 2—Interest inventory. Basic interest scales, occupational scales, and non-occupational scales present the individual's data compared to national norms. Interests relate to job satisfaction and job persistence.

Profile 3—Dimensions of temperament. Ten dimensions are reported. The extremes on each dimension are defined. The self-portrait generated is helpful in increasing self-understanding and in planning appropriate developmental experiences.

Profile 4—Personal values. The individual's basic motivational patterns, or values that he holds, are profiled in six scales. Values likely influence what a person does, how well he performs, his immediate decisions, his life goals, and his personal satisfactions in a given work environment.

Profile 5—Intellectual functioning. Nine separate measures are profiled. Intellectual abilities, social intelligence, creativity, reading skills, and critical thinking skills are included.

Profile 6—Life goals. Ten measures endeavor to determine the strength of an individual's life goals—defined as future oriented motivating attitudes.

Each profile, and each piece of data, is looked at separately, but never used alone. Each bit of data derives meaning from other data. Home background, formal education, work experiences and all other relevant information is considered and evaluated together in the career discussion and thereafter in planning the action steps and making the decisions which must be made regarding the individual.

Reactions of participants

Typical comments from participants to the coordinator at the conclusion of the career discussion are along these lines:

"This is the first time in my life anyone has ever helped me see where I stand and what I should do about it."

"It really helps to know someone else understands what I am like so they can help me get where I want to go."

"At first I was worried my boss would find out my results. Now I want him to know because I want his help, too."

Delayed reactions to the program from the participants are used to guide the program coordinator in making improvements. In addition to the suggestions which are solicited, the participants react to the data and the career discussion. In summary this is how the participants see it:

--The data generally confirms their own assessment of their strengths and limitations.
--The data provides some surprises concerning their strengths and limitations.
--The discussion of the data helps them firm up their convictions about their careers, and helps them in making career decisions.
--The discussion is helpful in planning self-improvement activities.
--Overall, as a result of the career discussion, they say they learned something, feel encouraged, see the process as helpful, and would recommend the program to their friends.

The coordinator becomes a valuable resource

The coordinator comes out of the career discussion with an in-depth understanding of the individual participant. The participant knows the coordinator "knows." In the process, a rapport is established which makes it possible for continued coaching and counseling with the individual on matters pertaining to his career.

The in-depth understanding enables the coordinator to be effective in working with line managers or other staff groups who are concerned with using the individual's talents. He can speak with greater authority concerning the individual's career aspirations, background, interests, temperament, personal values, intellectual functioning, and life goals.

The coordinators, therefore, see themselves as, and in fact become, a valuable resource to participant and management alike.

Research studies

By gathering and storing the data from each participant in a data bank, a variety of research studies are now being undertaken and more will be conducted in the future. One obvious outcome is that the organization will know more about its talent than is known at present. It is quite possible that some of the instruments may be able to contribute to the selection process. Whatever comes out of the research will be a bonus on top of the immediate benefits springing from the program.

Conclusions

There is concensus that it is important to identify, develop, utilize and retain talent in order to assure the continuity and success of an organization. Most medium or large organizations have difficulty getting useful information about their young professional, technical and managerial talent.

Whether enough is being done now is a matter of opinion. Expecting any one program to do it all is certainly inappropriate. There appear to be merits and also limitations associated with processes such as collecting data in the recruiting process, through performance appraisals by first-level supervisors during the first years of employment, through brief encounters with top management, through formal assessment centers focusing on one segment of the total talent in an organization.

The Career Planning Program is designed to complement the above processes. It provides for the collection of basic uniform data on all young, exempt employees. The data and discussion with a coordinator helps an individual keep his aspirations realistic, make good decisions regarding his own career, and focus his developmental efforts on top priority items. The coordinator also becomes a valuable resource to management in planning career moves, making placements, and planning developmental actions. The data is put into a data bank for future research studies.

appendix G

The Uniroyal early identification program

Early identification programs have proven to be one of the more difficult programs to initiate. Once initiated they also prove to be difficult to sustain generation after generation. The Uniroyal program has been in existence for more than 15 years. Considerable changes have taken place in the program and further changes are expected in the future. In this Appendix we will report on the:

--Evolution of the program
--Annual procedure
--Developmental assignments
--Program policies
--"Cross pollination" program—an expansion of the early identification program

The evolution of the program

Since 1949 Uniroyal has been planning for replacements. It has made appraisals of performance and estimates of potential. Replacement charts have been prepared to list the incumbents of key positions and the one or two candidates who could be considered possible replacement for each job.

About 1957 the company took a close look at its replacement planning efforts. The charts began to disturb company officials. Very often the individual named as possible replacements were as old, or even older, than those they were supposed to replace. The information on the charts was useful if for any reason someone had to be replaced immediately. But it did not serve much purpose in planning the long-term development of the organization or of the people who would make it up.

To correct this situation, the company directed that any person named as the first replacement for a general management position had to be at least ten years younger than the incumbent and that the second candidate named had to be under 35.

This created some unexpected problems. Division managers had always claimed that they had plenty of promising young people coming up. But now, when they were pinned down to picking out the best of them, they could not do so. "All of our young people are promising," they said.

While that may be true, the company wanted to be sure that it could spot those few comers who seemed most likely to live up to their promise. That led to the creation of the company's program for spotting young general management talent.

Company officials admit that it is hard to gauge an individual's potential at the start of his or her career. But they feel that this should not be used as an excuse for not trying to do so. They felt that if supervisors observe the young individual working under them closely and carefully for a couple of years, indications of managerial talent can be seen. Some of the signs of exceptional ability that the company has instructed its supervisors to look for are rapid learning and superior performance on new assignments, improvements made in operations beyond assigned responsibilities, and recognizing and working on problems without being directed by the supervisor. Further the talented young employees often stretch themselves to learn, on their own, more about other jobs and will have the broad perspective to appreciate the relationship of their own job to the total operation.

These signs of potential managerial ability should show up even within the rather narrow scope that is typical of the jobs held by the very young in business. Indeed, the company says, if supervisors give the attention they should to the development of subordinates, many talented young people will probably come to their attention. Then it becomes a matter of providing opportunities for them to develop their abilities and of testing them in increasingly demanding assignments.

Annual procedure

Annually, supervisors within the operating divisions are asked to nominate their most promising young people. The only stipulations are that nominees must be under 35 years old and must have been employed by the company for at least two years, so that their superiors will have had enough time to observe their performance.

There is no limit placed on the number of nominations that may be made, but each must be backed with concrete observations of performance that justify the judgments of outstanding management potential. These nominations, including a personal history form and a work record for each nominee, are sent to the division general manager's review board which screens the nominees to identify the best.

The review board consists of the general manager, the managers of production, sales, or whatever functional unit is under consideration, and the staff man within the division who is responsible for following up the program. For very large units, lower-level managers are included on the board at early stages in the screening, so that they can contribute their personal knowledge of the nominees.

In screening nominees, the boards are instructed to concentrate on finding those persons showing potential for general management positions. These are the jobs, the company believes, for which special emphasis on broadening is needed. Normal career progression and development opportunities are expected to provide the training needed by men headed toward top functional positions.

It is the job of the board to review the nominations and to select the individuals who are to be included, for the following year, in one of four program groups. The groups are divided on the basis of age, as follows:

Group I: Under 28 years of age
Group II: Over 28 but under 30
Group III: Over 30 but under 32
Group IV: Over 32 but under 35

Rigid limits have been established for the number of candidates that the board may qualify for three of the four groups. The suggested formula is that, for each 1,000 employees on a division's salary payroll, an unlimited number may be qualified for Group I, 1 percent for Group II, 0.5 percent for Group III, and only 0.3 percent for Group IV.

Thus, if a division has 2,000 employees on its salary roll, the board may select an unlimited number for Group I but only 20 for inclusion in Group II. For Groups III and IV the numbers drop to ten and six, respectively. The screen gets progressively finer with age. It is this feature of the program that has forced managers to go beyond saying "All of our young people are promising," to add, "But these are the best."

This rigorous screening process, while not the whole of the program, certainly is a most important factor.

Developmental assignments

However, screening the nominees and selecting those to be included in the program is only the start of the review board's annual job. The purpose of the program is to test and enlarge the capacities of individuals selected. Therefore, the board has the further responsibility of planning development programs for the individuals selected.

Job rotation is the principal method by which the company provides the special development which it believes these talented individuals need and deserve. But while rotation through various assignments occurs normally in most business careers, it often does not provide development for general management, unless it is specially guided. More often, because the rotation is confined to jobs within a single function, it results in an experienced and competent, but narrow, specialist. Further, opportunities for rotating seldom occur naturally at the most advantageous time from a development standpoint. Therefore, the company plans its job rotation for development purposes, even creating openings when suitable ones are not available.

The top managers from all the major functions within a division sit on the review board. They are in a strategic position to decide upon the job shifts that will be needed to broaden the perspectives of the successful candidates. Not only does the board designate the positions to which the candidates are assigned, it also specifies the responsibilities of department managers for reviewing and guiding the work.

Jobs in all major functions are used at times, but primarily they are found in sales, production, and product development. They are not "made work," even when they have been especially created for development, for the company believes that development comes only from facing and solving real problems. The candidates are held accountable for results in their new jobs. To make this possible, they remain in the jobs long enough to produce real results.

Company officials say that rotation not only gives the young manager a broad background in various phases of the business, but that it also forces them to learn to work effectively with widely different personalities in constantly different situations.

Program policies

The whole process of nominating, screening, and selecting candidates and planning their development opportunities is repeated annually. And it starts from scratch each year. Department heads may nominate any individual who, in their opinion, meets the requirements, whether or not they have ever been named before. An individual who begins to show signs of general management potential after several years of routine work may still be included among the nominees. No one is "frozen out" of the program merely because he was not selected when he first became eligible in terms of age and length of employment.

The fact that new candidates may be included in the program each year, coupled with the decreasing number of people who may be selected for Groups II, III, and IV, make it inevitable that some men will not be continued in the program. This is by design. The experience is intended to test these young people and to identify those best qualified for general management. But the company stresses that the persons eliminated from these groups should not be considered unfit. While they may not seem destined for general management, in the course of the program some of them show signs of rising to the top within a particular function. Their careers can then be guided along the lines of their greatest abilities.

In fact, because of the experience they have gained while a part of the program, these individuals often appear on promotional lists for executive management positions within a function.

When individuals selected for participation reach the age of 35, they are no longer eligible for any of the early identification groups. But by then, if not before, their name will probably have appeared on one or more replacement charts as someone to be watched. Thus, if they continue to develop, they will not drop out of sight when they drop out of the program.

It is not company policy to publicize either the program, the nominees, or the individuals finally selected. One reason for this is that the program is only a small, specialized part of the company's total management development effort. Many other training courses, rotation programs, and development opportunities are also available. Too much publicity concerning this program might pull it out of perspective.

Another reason for not publicizing the program is that the company wants to avoid the impression that it has created a favored group. That has not been the case. In fact, most of those who have been selected for inclusion in the groups do not know of the program or that their performance is being closely watched for evidences of growing management ability. This may seem surprising. But rotation to a new assignment is the normal experience of young people in this firm. The only difference here is that the new job may be in a completely different function.

On the other hand, this program is not a closely guarded secret. The company knows that intelligent individuals will discover that the program exists. Therefore, when and if a question arises, a frank but careful discussion is held with the person, explaining just what the program can mean for him or her. It is emphasized that they will be given opportunities to develop whatever abilities they may have, but they will not be given a guarantee of success. Continued annual selection, they are told, will depend upon continued superior performance.

Even among those successful candidates who have learned about the program, the fact of selection has not led to a change in attitude. The company points out that the people are bright enough to know that their chances of remaining in the program would be forfeited at the first show of arrogance, for by acting so they would be demonstrating a lack of maturity.

As for the feelings of those who have not been part of the program, the director of management development says that the individuals selected so far have been so superior that their rotation to more demanding assignments has been accepted by their fellow employees.

The company emphasizes, too, that every manager still has a chance to rise to the top. Previous membership in an early identification group is not a prerequisite for any top management position. Promotions are made on the basis of demonstrated superior performance.

The company considers that its program is the only logical approach to a real promotion-from-within policy. If a company wants to strengthen its total organization as well as develop its individual employees, it must build people for the positions that they will have to fill. And, if the top managers of the future are really working somewhere in the company now, today is none too soon to find them and begin training them to carry the broad responsibilities that will one day be theirs.

Cross pollination program—an expansion of the early identification program

The Early Identification Program was expanded to include "cross pollination." This made possible the rotation of high potential candidates between divisions of the company.

Based on review of all Early Identification Program groupings, the Group II candidates appear to be best suited for rotation between divisions of the company. Group II candidates are candidates under 30 years of age with four years company work experience. Therefore, Group II participants in the Early Identification Program (EIPs) have not moved into key assignments as have many of the more seasoned and experienced EIPs. The timing for a job change would be excellent for this group, since this is a critical period in an EIPs career.

1. Criteria for Selection. Development training for young potential general managers should be conceived of as a process by which individuals who demonstrate potential for general managerships are provided with accelerated opportunities to obtain knowledge and experience in a number of different functions of the business. This experience should not be thought of as either indoctrination or exposure. Rather, assignments should be to positions of real responsibility.

Implicit in this statement is the assumption that many, if not the largest part, of the skills and abilities required of a potential general manager can only be developed and tested on the job.

Another aspect of the development training which is important, particularly where selection risks are to be minimized, is that each person should be carefully evaluated on each position to which he or she is assigned. This careful evaluation should stress both results achieved as well as methods utilized.

Translated into procedures, the selection process for development training calls for the division to nominate four of the Group II candidates. The critieria were an extension of those already referred to earlier.

--Superior performance of assignment.
--Demonstrated leadership.
--Group effectiveness and desire for team development.
--Problem solving ability without direct supervision.
--Desire for responsibility, power, and chance to accomplish.
--Ability to withstand pressure.
--Good judgment and sound planning.
--Suggests unusual or imaginative approaches.
--Balance emotional stability.
--High energy potential, drive, and personal zest.

It is recognized that candidates selected for this program may not satisfy all the above; however, choice of the four top candidates should be based on these criteria.

In addition to all available sources of records, personal history information, performance appraisals, and so on, a written opinion from each candidate's immediate superior is requested.

2. *Divisional selection of candidates.* Each division is asked to submit the names of the four best Group II candidates who satisfy the criteria.

3. *Cross pollination selection committee.* A selection committee functions to screen and select a final candidate from each division for the rotation program. Divisional personnel appointed to the selection committee are familiar with the EIP program and management development in their divisions. The cross pollination selection committee:

--Screens and selects from the total group of nominated candidates, *one* Group II EIP for each division.
--Jointly determines the best rotation assignment within the divisions for the first two years.
--Meets periodically to review and discuss progress of the rotation program.

4. *Cross pollination.* Each Group II EIP candidate selected for the program is to be rotated to a new assignment and a new division every

two years. After a four-year period the EIP candidate is to return to his original division.

5. Follow-up—evaluation interview. The organization planning department follows the progress of all candidates in the rotation program. Evaluations of individual progress is determined before completion of the training assignment by the department.

Responsibility for EIP development plan

1. Division. The divisions of the company are responsible for implementing the training and rotation of EIP candidates under the plan. They:

--Determine a suitable assignment that will represent an increase in responsibility and salary for the incoming candidate.

--Pay relocation costs.

--Plan for return of EIP to the original division after the four year period, unless EIP has been promoted to a permanent position.

2. Organization planning department. The organization planning department is responsible for the administration and follow-up. They assist the divisions:

--In screening the best candidates from each division for the EIP rotation program.

--In evaluation of candidates.

--In coordination and follow-up.

appendix H

Advanced management skills program

The Advanced Management Skills Program was designed by Mahler Associates to overcome two difficulties often encountered by organizations utilizing advanced management educational programs. First, organizations find it extremely difficult, once the high-potential young executives have been selected, to free them up for four weeks or longer. The longer the course, the more difficult it is. As a result, the prime candidate is often passed over and a secondary choice attends.

Second, there is general consensus that an advanced educational course broadens the executive. The student agrees, his boss agrees, management development staff agrees, professors agree. Increasingly, there is also a high level of agreement on the absence of any demonstrable change in subsequent behavior as an executive. The managers gained certain theoretical knowledge but they did not gain skills appropriate to their level.

We, therefore, designed an advanced management skills program with specific objectives to develop skills, to get the skills applied, and have an impact on job performance.

PROGRAM STRUCTURE

The program consists of eight one-week units. The schedule calls for one week a quarter for a two year period. This schedule has a distinct educational advantage. Participants not only learn a skill, they are encouraged to apply the skill and report back on it at the next session.

The schedule also permits timely preparatory assignments for each unit.

Each unit is designed to fit into an integrated overall management process. Participants do not get a random assortment of inputs which they must sort out and adapt for their own use.

PROGRAM METHOD

The primary stress is upon learning skills. The skills are advanced ones relevant to a general manager. Methods and techniques are mastered, primarily by actual practice. Necessary supporting background knowledge or theory is provided.

Participants devote very little time to listening to lectures or discussing standard cases. They devote considerable time to analyzing data from their own organization. Discussion and practice leading to skill predominates.

All units have proven themselves as learning experiences over a period of years in several large enterprises. A description of the outcomes and content of each unit follows. A unit includes one week of the program.

PROGRAM CONTENT

Unit 1—The process of management

Outcomes. Program participants will:
1. Recognize that management is a process.
2. Identify their initial convictions about five basic processes: planning, organizing, leading, controlling, and innovating.
3. See the interrelationship of the five basic processes.
4. Acquire common terminology about management.
5. Achieve a foundation upon which to build management skills.

Content. A day is devoted to each of the five basic management processes of planning, organizing, leading, controlling, and innovating.

Little use is made of lecture. Discussion of back-home situations, case discussions, simulated exercises, and role playing are the primary methods used. Participants are expected to have read several assigned books prior to this initial week.

Unit 2—Business planning skills

Outcomes. Program participants will develop skill and experience in:
1. Long-range conceptual thinking.

2. Relating conceptual thinking to short-term planning.
3. Developing long-term objectives.
4. Developing short-term objectives.
5. Designing their own management-by-objectives program.
6. Installing an objectives program in their own organization.

Content. As the unit title suggests, emphasis is given to developing skill in preparing and using long-term and short-term objectives.

Prior to this unit, participants are asked to read a volume of selected readings pertaining to the future. Stress is placed upon preparation of objective documents which participants use on the job. Again, little use is made of lectures. Actual experience in preparation of planning documents is the key process. As an example of integration, both long-term and short-term objectives are used in Unit 3.

Unit 3—Organization planning skills

Outcomes. Participants will:
1. Recognize there are four basic aspects to organizational planning: structure, power, job design and staffing.
2. Develop skill in processes of analyzing the current structure and in planning a future one. They should be able to anticipate how any proposed organization will actually perform.
3. Develop skill in analyzing power problems and in managing power. Power is a broader and more useful concept than authority.
4. The job design is directly related to short-term objective processes covered in Unit 2. Finally, participants will develop skill in making improved staffing decisions.

Content. Attention is given to four basic aspects of organization planning: structure, power, job design, and staffing. Processes are suggested for first analyzing the current situation on each of the four organizational aspects and planning future changes in one or more of these aspects.

Limited use is made of lectures. Stress is placed upon working through an analysis of an actual back-home situation and planning future changes. Selected references for advanced reading have been prepared for this unit.

Units 4 and 5—Team-building skills

Outcomes. Program participants will develop skill and experience in:
1. Understanding forces affecting group behavior.
2. Managing conflict.
3. Achieving effective team effort.

4. Analyzing factors influencing organizational effectiveness.
5. Programming remedial action to increase organization effectiveness.

Content. This unit requires two weeks. They are separated by three months. The units are an adaptation by Robert Morton to fit the need of this program. He refers to his basic program as Organization Development Laboratory.

Considerable use is made of data from participants' own organizations. Participants explore alternative approaches to practical problems using small group exercises and assignments, with some lectures.

Unit 6—Management dialogue skills

Outcomes. Program participants will develop skill in:
1. Conducting a selection interview.
2. Discussing performance results with a subordinate.
3. Discussing behavioral problems with a subordinate.
4. Conducting career discussions.
5. Analyzing their coaching practices and planning improvements.

Content. As in previous units, stress is placed upon developing skills. A day is devoted to analyzing results of a coaching practices survey which subordinates of the program participants will have completed. Appropriate improvements will be planned.

A day is devoted to the mechanics and dynamics of four types of dialogues or interviews:
--the selection interview,
--the performance discussion,
--the behavioral problem interview,
--the career discussion.

Unit 7—Controlling skills

Outcomes. Participants will develop skill in:
1. Analyzing the current control system in their own organization.
2. Planning improvements in control systems.
3. Really putting the exception principle to work. This is facilitated by the objectives developed in Unit 2.
4. Thinking through to new tactics of control based on behavioral theory.

Content. Skill is still the primary outcome. A process for analyzing the assumptions underlying the current control practices in each enterprise is provided. In addition, the process leads to identification of inappropriate redundancy and to significant gaps.

This unit ties back to previous units to assist the participants to achieve needed integration across the processes of management with particular emphasis on the motivation complexities of controlling.

Unit 8—Innovation skills

Outcomes. Participants will develop skill in:
1. Analyzing ways to innovate more effectively.
2. Analyzing impediments to innovation in their own organization.
3. Planning personal innovative efforts.
4. Encouraging innovating efforts in their own organization.

Content. Use is made of the latest knowledge on innovation. Analytical processes are carried out for both an individual and a group.

Use is made of data collected in participant's own organization.

Again, reliance is placed on processes of stimulating innovation. Use is made of relevant theory but this is done primarily by incorporation of theory into the processes.

PARTICIPANTS

Enrollment in the program is relatively small in number, about 20, to facilitate skill acquisition.

The program is designed for participants who meet the following critieria:

--Currently hold a general manager position or have a strong likelihood of being appointed to a general manager position in the next two or three years.

--Generally, come within the 32–45 age bracket.

--Have a strong interest in acquiring management process skills.

appendix I

A check list for individual coaching practices

1. **Establishing goals**
   a. Have specific goals been established for each individual reporting to you?
   b. Have established goals been kept up-to-date?
   c. Have goals been set which require "stretching" to reach?
2. **Delegating effectively**
   a. Have you been willing to "take risks" in permitting subordinates to perform on their own?
   b. Have you avoided having your subordinates bring their "problems" to you rather than their recommendations?
   c. Have you delegated without "abdicating"? Do you put the proper balance on the amount of supervision provided?
3. **Providing knowledge of how subordinates are doing**
   a. Have you provided timely praise and recognition for "jobs well done"?
   b. Can your subordinates be sure of receiving timely and appropriate criticism when it is deserved?
   c. Are discussions of performance with subordinates carried out in a matter-of-fact, business-like manner? Are you specific in expressing your opinions?
4. **Providing assistance when and as needed**
   a. Do you provide timely assistance by reviewing plans and strategies employed by your subordinates?

    b. Have you provided encouragement on difficult undertakings of subordinates?

    c. Have you provided suggestions and other assistance when needed by your subordinates?

5. **Rewarding on results**

    a. Have financial rewards gone to those subordinates who have produced results—without exception?

    b. Have promotions gone to the best qualified subordinates—without exception?

    c. Is there a procedure and a policy, known to your subordinates, for relating rewards to results?

6. **Understanding of subordinates**

    a. Do you know the aspirations and ambitions of each of your immediate subordinates?

    b. Do you know the more important motivations of each of your subordinates?

    c. Have you demonstrated a genuine concern for each of your subordinates?

7. **Making contacts developmental**

    a. Think of your contacts during the last two weeks with each of your subordinates. Did you consciously endeavor to teach the subordinate at any time?

    b. Do you have a minimum schedule for developmental contacts with your subordinates, or do you let contacts occur at random?

    c. Do you take advantage of contacts with individuals several levels below you to make them developmental, to manifest an interest in the individual?

8. **Providing an atmosphere of two-way confidence**

    a. Have you developed an effective working relationship with each subordinate—no exceptions?

    b. Can serious differences of opinion be expressed without any residue of hostility or anxiety?

    c. Do your subordinates believe that you have confidence in them?

9. **Planning a sequence of developmental experiences**

    a. Do you have in mind, for each subordinate, the next one or two developmental experiences you want him to have?

    b. Have you deliberately provided for at least two developmental experiences for each of your subordinates in the last six months?

    c. Do you have some mutually agreed upon plan of action for the development of each of your subordinates, either on the present job or for a future job?

10. **Making effective use of both day-to-day and annual coaching methods**
    a. Do you find that, as a part of your day-to-day coaching, you are making notes, making plans and anticipating the next annual coaching interview?
    b. Do you find that, as a part of your annual coaching interview, you and your subordinates plan follow-up action of an informal nature?
    c. Can you recall at least one instance, for each subordinate, where some effective day-to-day coaching paid off later in your annual interviews, and vice versa?

11. **Using group coaching sessions**
    a. Have you a regularly scheduled group meeting with your subordinates which you use, at least in part, for development or coaching of your men?
    b. Have you had your immediate subordinates report their goals to each other in a group meeting?
    c. Have you had your immediate subordinates report on their progress in achieving goals in a group meeting?

12. **Improving your interviewing skills**
    a. Have you found yourself making a conscious effort to improve upon one or more of the fundamentals of coaching interviewing?
    b. Do you keep up-to-date on new techniques of interviewing as one way of getting ready for your more difficult interviews?
    c. Can you say that your interviewing has improved in the last 12 months?

appendix J

Suggestions for effecting change in individual performance by coaching

Although it is not possible to give suggestions on dealing with specific problems, several general suggestions which can be adapted to individual situations are as follows:

1. *Do not try to change personality: Concentrate on changing performance.*

An executive recently expressed strong dissatisfaction with a subordinate. After listening for some time, I asked if the subordinate failed to maintain scheduled production. "No, he was on schedule." Quality? "That was O.K." Costs? "Not too bad." Employee relations? "Excellent."

"Well, then," I asked, "why aren't you satisfied?" Sheepishly, he replied, "Well, he just isn't my type of manager." What he meant was: "He doesn't do the job the same way I would!"

There are several reasons to support the suggestion to concentrate on performance rather than personality:

1. Personal characteristics are difficult to change.
2. Dictating ways and means of obtaining results is poor managing.
3. Individuals resent such efforts.
4. Often, it is not necessary.

Some may complain, "But personal traits are responsible for failure to get results!" Fine, but concentrate upon getting *the* improved result. Do not limit yourself to one type of action. Most important: Do not think of the subordinate as having an unsatisfactory personality. Instead, think of him as an individual who fails to get results you expect. It will open up many new ways of coaching him.

2. *Improve your own personal coaching skills.*

Stimulating individuals to change requires skill—in fact, a variety of skills. Yet, how many executives have invested any time in increasing their own skills of observation, listening, appraising, discussing, and counseling? One of the most important reasons for doing nothing is fear on the part of the executive. One top executive recently admitted: "I do appraise and interview my men, but I dread it." Ask a local management development staff man or a practical professor from a nearby university to help you and others in your group to get this increased skill. Do not assume you can read a book or watch a movie or listen to a lecture. This skill must be *practiced* under the observation of a competent critic.

3. *Determine the extent of agreement between you and your subordinate on what is expected of him.*

A new general manager and a research director recently came to a parting of the ways in what was explained as a personality clash. The real problem, however, lay in failure on both sides to discuss, and come to agreement on, what was actually expected. Disagreements often develop, not about major responsibilities, but about the priority to be assigned to each.

Do not assume agreement exists. Discuss it thoroughly. Reduce the understanding to writing. One good technique is that of having the subordinate prepare specific objectives.

4. *Determine the extent of agreement between you and your subordinate on how well he is doing.*

One executive was well satisfied with a subordinate's productivity, but extremely dissatisfied with his relationships with others. In an interview with his subordinate he found that the latter held exactly the opposite opinion of his performance.

Have a thorough discussion of the objectives or responsibilities established by the subordinate. Listening to the subordinate's own views first will give you a better basis for determining the extent of agreement.

The earlier suggestion on improving your skill is particularly appropriate here and for the following three suggestions.

5. *Establish a need for changed performance and secure understanding and acceptance of this need.*

"Theirs not to reason why" may be an old quotation, but it is quite prevalent in current supervisor-subordinate relationships. Overcoming resistance to change requires that the individual both "see and feel" a need to change. This may be done verbally or by letting a subordinate stub his toe on a tough problem. Often, an executive is so concerned about getting results that he overlooks this suggestion.

6. *Explore causes before planning action.*

Deciding that performance improvement is necessary is a good step, but it is not the only decision that must be made before you jump into action. Discuss your subordinate's performance with him first. He may lack knowledge, skill, experience, or the proper attitude. Perhaps you, as his supervisor, are hindering his performance. Other individuals or groups may also need to change. Once the causes have been established, the action can follow readily.

7. *Consider changing the situation as well as the individual.*

This is usually the last thing to be considered. Often, it is ignored altogether. One plant manager recently deplored his foreman's performance. A thorough study revealed the key change needed was additional foremen to reduce the overload of work. But this change occurred after several years of fruitless training activity.

Another manager tried every technique in the book to improve a subordinate's performance. Finally, in desperation, the manager transferred him to another type of work, and he is doing very well in his new position.

A general manager was about ready to conclude that his chief engineer would never become an administrator; he would never really delegate. Somewhat inadvertently, a change in the organization structure was arranged. Since this change, decided improvement has become apparent in the administrative ability of the chief engineer.

8. *Use special help when you have done your best.*

Assisting subordinates to change can be difficult. You may try all of the suggestions mentioned above and still not be successful. If you have done your best and still have not succeeded in getting the desired changes, you may need to get the help of a skilled specialist. More and more companies have such a specialist on their management development staffs or on their staff of industrial physicians. Local universities also have specialists who may be of assistance.

appendix K

Uniroyal policy on company-wide selection

POLICY

When an opening occurs or a new position is created at a key management level, it is one of the management's most important responsibilities to see that the position is filled promptly with an individual who has demonstrated a capacity for greater responsibility and has the qualifications of experience, ability, and training that the job requires. Any position, such as factory manager's or sales manager's staff and above in operating divisions, or its equivalent in staff departments, is defined as a key management position for the purposes of this policy.

To provide for breadth of experience for individuals who have potential for more responsible management assignments, it shall be company policy when filling any such position, for the divisional general manager or corporate staff department director involved to nominate for the position no less than five candidates, in order of preference. At least three candidates *must be* from another division or department of the company. Promotions at a key management level are subject to the following conditions:

a. *Middle management positions* (as reflected by specified salary grades).

The order of preference and final selection must be endorsed by the director, management development and the vice president–administration, finance, or personnel, depending upon the functional area of the promotion. If there is agreement on nominations, approval is granted. If agreement cannot be reached, the recommendation must be submitted to the president's office by the vice president–personnel for resolution and decision. Requests for approval should be submitted in accordance with the promotion procedure.

b. *Top management positions* (as specified by salary grades). Recommendations for promotion to these positions must be approved by the President. Requests for such approval must be forwarded by the divisional general managers and corporate staff department directors, with the order of preference endorsed by the director, management development and the vice president–administration, finance, or personnel, depending upon the functional area of promotion. Requests for approval should be submitted in accordance with the promotion procedure.

c. To assist in the development of future candidates for Corporate positions, the Corporate Staff Department Director should give his endorsement when the promotion as outlined above involves a key job within a division in a functional area which falls within the responsibility of a major corporate staff department, i.e., industrial relations, purchasing, traffic, engineering.

PROMOTION PROCEDURE

A Management Promotion form must be completed in duplicate by the Divisional General Manager or Corporate Staff Department Director, and must be accompanied by a personal history form for each of the candidates nominated and, if it is a new job, a Management Function Analysis for the job concerned.

Upon approval by all concerned, the original copy should be returned to the Management Development Department, where it will be placed in a master corporate file of all management promotions.

A. When making recommendations, the following should be considered:
1. The major specifications in terms of experience, education and special abilities needed for the position.
2. Comparison of the past experience and demonstrated performance of all candidates with the job specifications.
3. The effect of the proposed moves on long range organization plans.
4. The potential of each individual for advancement beyond the position for which he is being considered.
5. The development opportunities that might exist in the position.

B. Careful application of the above policy will help:
1. Make sure that all possible candidates are being considered.

2. Avoid emergency appointments.
3. Avoid premature advancement.
4. Avoid potential loss of promising individuals.
5. Further the development of a promising individual for top management positions.

appendix L

Uniroyal policy on international assignments

Preface

The world grows smaller with regard to time of travel and ease of communication. Likewise, our Company is becoming more global in character as evidenced by our world-wide name change. Hence, these trends are putting a growing importance on international activities.

In view of this, it would appear that as time goes on the transfer of employees between countries will become increasingly desirable to transmit technical and managerial know-how and to develop candidates for division, departmental, and corporate managerial positions requiring multi-national decision making.

Policy

In order to expedite international experience, personnel given an International Assignment must be assured that their career opportunities will continue, assuming satisfactory performance, after a period of experience offshore.

Procedure

1. It will be Company procedure in the future to interview all individuals who may be considered as possible candidates for foreign assignments to determine their personal situation as it relates to an International Assignment. Interviews may be requested by individuals who have such an interest, as well as by management.

2. The opportunity to learn a foreign language will be made available at Company expense to any management employee and spouse who is in a position to consider an offshore assignment.
3. When an opening occurs in a position (above a given salary grade) candidates from all offshore locations as well as from domestic divisions will be considered—as currently required by the Company's Management Promotion Policy.
4. A specific time period for the assignment will be agreed upon by the individual, the requesting division, the originating management, and the corporate office. When individuals return at the end of this period, they will be reassigned to their original division in a position of at least equal importance to the one held offshore, or preferably one which represents a promotion, contingent upon their performance and accomplishments.
5. When an individual is selected and approved for an assignment as outlined above, a record of the specific job, dates, and so forth, must be sent to the Management Development and Training Department for inclusion in the individual's personal file and for follow-up.
6. General Managers will receive a quarterly report listing all Uniroyal personnel on International Assignments. This report will contain current information which will assist in maintaining continuity of career planning and progress for individual employees.

appendix M

The selection decision process*

The selection decision process can be used for an internal promotion or for a selection from outside. The process involves three steps:
1. Identifying five important results to be expected of the newly appointed manager.
2. Determining five important specifications.
3. Analyzing two or more candidates against the specifications.
A brief discussion of each step follows:

1. Identifying results

It is suggested that five important results be identified. The number five is arbitrary. We find that many managers have only one or, at most, two results in mind when making a selection decision. We also find that the definition of a position will change. In some cases the priority shifts, in other cases new results emerge. It helps to state the results as precisely as possible. Once a list of results has been prepared, the five most important can be selected.

The identification of results to be accomplished should be done by the hiring manager.

---

* This illustration is adapted with permission from a book by Walter R. Mahler, entitled *Diagnostic Studies*, published by Addison-Wesley, Reading, Mass., 1973c.

2.   Determining specifications

Managers quite often have difficulty in thinking through what they consider to be the most essential specifications to a given position. It is helpful to identify numerous ones so a final selection of five important ones can be made. The specifications selected should be ones on which potential candidates will differ. If a technical degree is absolutely essential and all candidates are likely to have such a degree, then this important requirement would be eliminated because it does not help to differentiate among candidates.

Getting independent judgments on specifications is helpful. This is particularly true when a manager's superior wants to review and approve the final choice. The choice of five important specifications is, admittedly, an arbitrary number. We prefer to keep the process a simple one; one which is carried out rigorously on every selection decision.

3.   Analyzing candidates

It is helpful to have two or more candidates to match against the specifications. Some organizations encourage consideration of several individuals who are not in the immediate organization as well as insiders. It is advisable to have the manager and his superior each complete independent analyses. An example of a completed worksheet is provided.

CANDIDATE ANALYSIS SHEET

POSITION: ___X___ ANALYSIS BY: ___WST___ DATE: ___7/11___

I. Results: List the five more important results he will be expected to achieve.

1. Provide a sensitive and effective "second avenue of communications" between customers and the top management of the group
2. Develop sufficient stature to personally represent the company at major conferences with customers
3. Upgrade the caliber of field personnel
4. Direct effort aimed at identification of new business opportunities for the company
5. Secure and maintain confidence of operating managers

II. Requirements: List the five more important requirements for success on the job.

III. Candidates versus Requirements°

	A	B	C	D	E
1. Three or more years experience as an operating manager with a record of accomplishment	1	1	3	2	5
2. Personally compatible with president and operating managers	2	1	3	3	4
3. Skillful in communications, in influencing, in persuading, in establishing rapport with customers and influential men	2	2	2	4	1
4. Capable in administering a diverse group	1	2	2	2	5
5. Sound judgment on business, political and technical problems (across spectrum of business)	1	3	3	3	3
Overall Rating	1−	2+	3−	3+	5
Ranking	1	2	3	4	5

° Rating:
1. Fully meets, no reservation
2. Generally meets, minor reservation
3. Generally meets, moderate reservation
4. Generally meets, major reservation
5. Fails to meet

appendix N

Ten/ten program*

Introduction

It is generally recognized that the way an organization metes out rewards and penalties sets a tone or climate. This tone or climate may be a stimulating one or just the opposite. It is not likely to be seen as a stimulating climate if there is little or no differentiation between top performers and bottom performers.

The Ten/Ten Program is designed to assist a top manager to achieve effective differentiation between top and bottom performers. It is also designed for periodic use as a substitute for the "meat axe" approach to a reduction in force.

A given group of employees is identified for study. All functional managers might be studied. All general managers in a large company might be studied. The diagnostic part of the program involves identifying the ten percent of the group considered to be top performers and the ten percent considered to be bottom performers. Each individual case is then subjected to special analysis and an appropriate action plan established and implemented.

Program administration

Program administration involves the following steps:
1. Decision on persons or groups to be included.

* Adapted with permission from a book by Walter R. Mahler, entitled *Diagnostic Studies,* published by Addison-Wesley in 1973.

2. Instructing the managers who are to identify high and low perform-
    ers.
3. Identification of top ten percent and bottom ten percent.
4. Completion of data sheets, including plans of action.
5. Implementation action.
6. Follow-up report.

Instructions

An example of a set of instructions follows. It is illustrative of the type
of instructions which the top executive will need to issue.

INSTRUCTIONS

I would like for each of you to review the effectiveness of our utilization of division manpower. While times like these suggest that particular emphasis be given to eliminating unproductive manpower, I feel
that such an analysis should be viewed more broadly. I, therefore, want
your review to also cover our best performers. People, as individuals
and collectively, are by far our greatest asset. We must develop this
asset more wisely. We can accomplish this by a thorough review of our
personnel resources and a program for action.

I would like to have you complete a thorough review of your exempt
salaried people in terms of performance. Following this review, please
list the ten percent of your people who are the most effective and the
ten percent who are least effective contributors.

When these groups have been identified, you should consider and
recommend desirable action programs for each of the individuals
within these two groups. For the top group, programs may include
management development programs, expanded job responsibilities,
tougher objectives, promotion, salary increases. Such a program for the
bottom group should include, where necessary accelerated training for
improved performance, closer supervision, probation, demotion, reduction in salary, early retirement.

Criteria which might be taken into consideration in selecting the top
performers include:

--Those technical people with less than seven years of service who
are giving evidence of being promotable three or more levels.
--Those individuals between 30–40 years of age whose performance
and potential are both consistently excellent.
--People past 40 years of age who are key performers now and need
special consideration in terms of development and promotion
within the next 5–10 years.
--Those beyond 50 years of age who are indispensable and who must
be rewarded in other ways than anticipation of promotion.

Criteria which might be taken into consideration in selecting the bottom group include:

--People whose contribution has slipped as they have grown older and/or who have lost the drive necessary to grow with the job.

--People who, because of long service, are being paid larger salaries than the contribution of the job warrants.

--Those who were deemed inadequate at some previous job, but who now occupy jobs created for them to avoid termination.

--Younger people whose performance is at best only adequate and who are not considered capable for training, upgrading or promotion.

--People in the age group 55-65 who are special problems due to the impairment of physical abilities, obsolescence of skills, or reduced energy output.

The determination of the departmental subunits within which the analysis is to be made has to be yours. It is obvious, however, that groupings of 20 or more are necessary to offer a sufficient base for objective discrimination. When the evaluation has been made in your subunits and you are ready to recommend individual programs of action, I will review the program with you.

Report form

An example of a report form follows.

TEN/TEN PROGRAM								
____ Top 10%						Division: ____		
____ Bottom 10%						Prepared by: ____		
NAME	5-YEAR PERF. TREND	PRESENT SALARY	SALARY GRADE	5-YEAR ANNUAL SALARY INCREASE PERCENT	AGE	YEARS OF SERVICE	YEARS ON PRESENT JOB	PLANNED ACTION

appendix O

The executive manpower
status report

The Executive Continuity effort consists of six major programs. They are:
--Promotability forecast
--Individual development plans
--Annual manpower reviews
--Selection process
--Early identification program
--Calibre of general manager

The Status Report endeavored to measure the extent to which a given program or procedure was implemented, the quality of the implementation and, insofar as possible, some of the final outcomes.

A scoring system was devised to permit getting a score of 100 on each of the six major programs and on the overall results. It was expected that the numbers would permit ready determination of weak areas, of basic trends, and of comparative situations.

For each of the six programs a brief statement of purpose is given. This is followed by a series of questions which have to be answered. A scale is provided to facilitate arriving at an overall score.

The quarterly analysis is prepared by the top staff man in each operating division. The annual report is prepared cooperatively by a corporate analyst and the divisional staff man.

A special scoring system is set for each of the six major programs.

Quarterly reports are prepared for major operating divisions. An annual report is prepared for the entire organization for the president.

While the precision of the numbers is admittedly on the crude side, the attention generated by the data is distinctly on the positive side.

An example of the Executive Manpower Status Report is included in this Appendix.

Promotability forecast

Purpose. To encourage managers to accurately identify men under their supervision who have the potential for promotion, and to identify immediate back-ups. In addition, men in other components deemed to have potential are identified.

Measures of effectiveness of processes or promotability forecasting (to be answered for each general manager)

	A	B	C	D	E
1. How many promotables from "own" component on forecast? (Hereafter, called "own" promotables.)	10 or more	8–9	5–7	3–4	2 or less
2. How many "own" promotables were questioned in manpower reviews?	10 or more	8–9	5–7	3–4	2 or less
3. Any "own" promotables names on forecast for previous year who were removed this year?	none	1	2	3	4 or more
4. How many key promotions made within a component were made of men whose names did not appear on promotability forecasts?	none	1	2	3	4 or more
5. What percentage of names on "own" list have been covered by an accomplishment analysis?	75 or more	50 to 75	30 to 50	10 to 30	10 or

Scoring

	A	B	C	D	E
1. Number	☐	☐	☐	☐	☐
2. Multiply by	20	14	10	6	0
3. Product of lines 1. and 2.	☐	☐	☐	☐	☐
4. Summary rating (Add numbers on line 3.)	☐				

Individual development plans

Purpose. To encourage managers to plan and implement specific and practical developmental actions which will have "own" promotables "standing taller" at the end of the year.

Measures of effectiveness of individual development plans (to be answered for "own" promotables for general manager)

	A	B	C	D	E
1. How many of the individual development plans for "own" promotables were specific, practical, and scheduled?	all	$^4/_5$	$^3/_5$	$^2/_5$	less than $^2/_5$
2. How many of the plans were implemented on schedule?	75% or more	40%	30%	20%	10% or less
3. How many "own" candidates had some type of educational experience? (Two days or more in duration during the year.)	75%	60%	50%	40%	less than 40%
4. What percent of "own" candidates have had experience in more than one major function?	50%	40%	30%	20	10% or less
5. How many job moves of "own" candidates were made *primarily* for developmental reasons? (Report $^1/_2$, 1 for number of development moves, 2 for total number of moves.)	$^1/_4$	$^1/_6$	$^1/_8$	$^1/_{10}$	less than $^1/_{10}$

Scoring

	A	B	C	D	E
1. Number	☐	☐	☐	☐	☐
2. Multiply by	20	14	10	6	0
3. Product of lines 1. and 2.	☐	☐	☐	☐	☐
4. Summary Rating (Add numbers on line 3.)			☐		

Management manpower reviews

Purpose. To permit both supervisor and subordinate to have a thorough discussion of the management manpower situation in the component.

Measures of effectiveness of reviews

	A	B	C	D	E
1. Thoroughness of review preparation.	very thorough		thorough		thoroughness lacking
2. Thoroughness of review discussion.	very thorough		thorough		thoroughness lacking
3. Candor of both supervisor and subordinate in review discussion.	very thorough		thorough		thoroughness lacking
4. Review discussion reveals positive attitude toward management manpower responsibilities.	very thorough		thorough		thoroughness lacking

Scoring

	A	B	C	D	E
1. Number	☐	☐	☐	☐	☐
2. Multiply by	25	20	15	10	0
3. Product of lines 1 and 2.	☐	☐	☐	☐	☐
4. Summary Rating (Add numbers on line 3.)	☐				

Selection process

Purpose. The selection process should give consideration to best qualified candidates. The process should be an efficient one. Those selected should be successful.

Measures of effectiveness of selection process

	A	B	C	D	E
1. How many general managers have been removed for performance reasons in last year?	none	1	2	3	4 or more
2. How many general manager positions were filled expeditiously. (Within one month?)	all	1 exception	2 exceptions	3 exceptions	4 or more exceptions

		A	B	C	D	E
3.	How many occasions were three qualified candidates available for consideration in general manager appointments?	all	1 exception	2 exceptions	3 exceptions	4 or more exceptions?
4.	Were decisions on general manager appointments based on matching candidates with specifications?	In all cases	1 exception	2 exceptions	3 exceptions	4 or more exceptions
5.	How often was a general manager appointed from within the component? ($\frac{1}{2}$ = one out of two appointments.)	$\frac{1}{2}$	$\frac{1}{3}$	$\frac{1}{4}$	$\frac{1}{5}$	Less than 1 in 5

Scoring

		A	B	C	D	E
1.	Number	☐	☐	☐	☐	☐
2.	Multiply by	20	15	10	5	0
3.	Product of lines 1. and 2.	☐	☐	☐	☐	☐
4.	Summary Rating (Add numbers on line 3.)	☐				

Early identification program

Purpose. To identify high potential young men early and accelerate their development.

Measures of early identification program

		A	B	C	D	E
1.	Has each operating group identified high potential young men?	all	1 exception	2 exceptions	3 exceptions	4 or more exceptions
2.	Have cross functional moves been scheduled for the high potential men?	For 50%	For 40%	For 30%	For 20%	For less than 20%
3.	Have cross functional moves been implemented on schedule?	In all cases	1–2 exceptions	3–4 exceptions	5–6 exceptions	7 or more exceptions
4.	Have other developmental moves been planned and implemented on schedule?	In all cases	1–2 exceptions	3–4 exceptions	5–6 exceptions	7 or more exceptions

	A	B	C	D	E
5. How many high potentials have been promoted in last year?	3/4 or more	2/4	1/4	1/5	less than 1/5

Scoring	A	B	C	D	E
1. Number	☐	☐	☐	☐	☐
2. Multiply by	20	15	10	5	0
3. Products of lines 1 and 2	☐	☐	☐	☐	☐
4. Summary Rating (add number on line 3).	☐				

Calibre of general manager

Purpose. To secure an adequate number of general managers for future needs, to improve upon current effectiveness of general management and keep down losses of general managers and potential general managers.

Measures of general managers calibre

	A	B	C	D	E
1. How many general managers quit the company during the year?	none	1	2	3	4 or more
2. How many potential general managers (men on promotability forecasts) quit the company during the year?	none	1	2	3	4 or more
3. How many individuals in operating divisions were promoted to general manager level position in other divisions?	4 or more	3	2	1	0
4. How many promotions to general manager position were made from within the division?	all	1 exception	2 exceptions	3 exceptions	4 exceptions
5. How many general managers in division are not fully satisfactory?	none	1	2	3	4 or more

Scoring	A	B	C	D	E
1. Number (Add from above five questions.)	☐	☐	☐	☐	☐
2. Multiply by	20	15	10	5	0
3. Number	☐	☐	☐	☐	☐
4. Summary Rating	☐				

Overall summary rating

1. Promotability forecast

2. Individual development plans

3. Manpower reviews

4. Selection process

5. Early identification program

6. Calibre of general managers

Sum of six

Overall summary
rating divided
by six

appendix P

Executive continuity questionnaire

Organization Component	Completed by	Date

EXECUTIVE CONTINUITY QUESTIONNAIRE

INSTRUCTIONS

Over a period of years Mahler Associates has identified ten requirements which are basic to executive continuity. The Executive Continuity Questionnaire is designed to "mirror" the current status of these ten requirements in an organization.

The term "top management" refers to the chief executive of the component to be studied. In some instances, there are several executives, in an office of the Chief Executive.

The term "key manager" applies to those men who report to "top management." They are usually general managers with profit responsibility. However, they may be functional managers.

The term "executive position" refers to positions at the top three levels of the organization under study. The term "executive" applies to men in such positions.

For analysis purposes, five questions have been asked pertaining to each of the requirements. Provision has been made for five possible answers. Circle the one which most closely reflects your own answer.

	Answer				
REQUIREMENT 1. *Top management interest and action*	*Definitely yes*	*More yes than no*	*More no than yes*	*Definitely no*	*?*
1. Is top management concerned about selecting competent key managers?	DY	Y	N	DN	?
2. Has the responsibility for developing future key managers been placed on successive levels of management?	DY	Y	N	DN	?
3. Does top management personally set the example by taking appropriate action at periodic intervals?	DY	Y	N	DN	?
4. Has top management spent any time in conferences on the subject of future key managers?	DY	Y	N	DN	?
5. Is there any sustained interest and support for a development program on part of top management? Is this sustained during periodic shifts in top leaders?	DY	Y	N	DN	?

	Answer				
REQUIREMENT 2. *An effective staff contribution specific to executive personnel*	*Definitely yes*	*More yes than no*	*More no than yes*	*Definitely no*	*?*
1. Has the responsibility for providing an effective staff contribution been specifically assigned? (The amount of staff effort would vary by size of organization.)	DY	Y	N	DN	?
2. Does the staff report to or have ready access to top management?	DY	Y	N	DN	?
3. Has the staff worked out a comprehensive approach to be implemented over the next five years?	DY	Y	N	DN	?
4. Has the staff avoided becoming a "kingmaker," a "clerical function," or "theoretical analyzers"?	DY	Y	N	DN	?
5. Does the staff command the respect and confidence of top management?	DY	Y	N	DN	?
REQUIREMENT 3. *Identification of kind and number of executives needed in the future*					
1. Has top management discussed and established position specifications for the key manager type positions?	DY	Y	N	DN	?
2. Has thought been given to the type of key managers which will be needed ten years from now?	DY	Y	N	DN	?
3. Is replacement planning a sincere effort to think through future problems and future actions? Are specific actions planned and implemented?	DY	Y	N	DN	?
4. Has an estimate of future needs been prepared? Is it updated regularly?	DY	Y	N	DN	?
5. Has an effort been made to identify young men, under 30, deemed to have potential as top level managers?	DY	Y	N	DN	?

	Answer				
REQUIREMENT 4. *Objective, descriptive information about candidates for executive positions*	*Definitely yes*	*More yes than no*	*More no than yes*	*Definitely no*	*?*
1. Is an effort made to get objective, comprehensive descriptive information about key executives? Are several sources used?	DY	Y	N	DN	?
2. Are the records maintained for candidates comprehensive and up to date?	DY	Y	N	DN	?
3. Does top management avoid relying primarily on personal knowledge about key personnel?	DY	Y	N	DN	?
4. Is an effort made to record actual accomplishments of key personnel with thoroughness and uniformity?	DY	Y	N	DN	?
5. Have provisions been made to have managers use "good" information as it becomes available?	DY	Y	N	DN	?

	Answer				
REQUIREMENT 5. *Accelera-tion of the development of high potential candidates*	*Definitely yes*	*More yes than no*	*More no than yes*	*Definitely no*	*?*
1. Has recruiting effort been specifically designed, at least in part, to provide appropriate raw material for general managers of the future?	DY	Y	N	DN	?
2. Are capable young men given risk-taking experiences early in their career?	DY	Y	N	DN	?
3. Has provision been made to select and train managers who are to supervise high potential individuals?	DY	Y	N	DN	?
4. Are cross-functional moves made for high-potential candidates?	DY	Y	N	DN	?
5. Are cross-divisional (businesses) moves encouraged? Are both line and staff positions used?	DY	Y	N	DN	?

REQUIREMENT 6. *A corporate-wide approach to the selection of general managers*	Answer				
	Definitely yes	*More yes than no*	*More no than yes*	*Definitely no*	*?*
1. Does top management get involved in appointments two and three levels down, when they have implications for development of future general managers?	DY	Y	N	DN	?
2. Are key managers required to consider "outsiders" as well as candidates from their own component? Do "outsiders" get selected at least half the time?	DY	Y	N	DN	?
3. Are key managers expected to make use of the staff when filling key positions?	DY	Y	N	DN	?
4. Does top management personally review the replacement plans of key executives to insure corporate-wide placements?	DY	Y	N	DN	?
5. Has "parochialism" in filling key positions been avoided?	DY	Y	N	DN	?

REQUIREMENT 7. *Educational programs*

	Definitely yes	*More yes than no*	*More no than yes*	*Definitely no*	*?*
1. Do individuals have a regular opportunity to take courses at major stages in their career?	DY	Y	N	DN	?
2. Does top management make judicious use of outside courses?	DY	Y	N	DN	?
3. Does top management avoid expecting too much of their educational activities?	DY	Y	N	DN	?
4. Are higher level managers used regularly to provide formal instruction to other managers?	DY	Y	N	DN	?
5. Has stress been placed on courses which actually develop managerial skills?	DY	Y	N	DN	?

REQUIREMENT 8. *Integration of personnel and management functions into a continuity approach*	Answer				
	Definitely yes	*More yes than no*	*More no than yes*	*Definitely no*	*?*
1. Do compensation policies and salary administration help stimulate development and retention of key personnel?	DY	Y	N	DN	?
2. Has a management by objectives program been established? Does it stress both business results and development of personnel?	DY	Y	N	DN	?
3. Have any special organization structural arrangements been made to help development of general managers?	DY	Y	N	DN	?
4. Do company-wide placement and promotional policies help get right developmental decisions?	DY	Y	N	DN	?
5. Do management controls help? Do executives get credit for successful development efforts?	DY	Y	N	DN	?

	Answer				
REQUIREMENT 9. *Increased effectiveness in coaching high-potential personnel*	*Definitely yes*	*More yes than no*	*More no than yes*	*Definitely no*	*?*
1. Are high potential personnel likely to get effective coaching by their superiors?	DY	Y	N	DN	?
2. Is there a performance appraisal process in existence? Does it stress results? Does it stress self-appraisal?	DY	Y	N	DN	?
3. Have executives, from top level on down, been given any instructions to help them develop their coaching skills?	DY	Y	N	DN	?
4. Do executives talk with their subordinates about their future, their ambitions, their development plans, and similar matters?	DY	Y	N	DN	?
5. Have the current coaching practices of executives been measured or surveyed?	DY	Y	N	DN	?

	Answer				

REQUIREMENT 10. *Design of a "systems" approach to meet the unique needs of a given organization*	*Definitely yes*	*More yes than no*	*More no than yes*	*Definitely no*	*?*
1. Have specific end results or objectives been established by top management for the executive development program?	DY	Y	N	DN	?
2. Have plans been made for programs to be initiated over the next five years to produce a comprehensive program?	DY	Y	N	DN	?
3. Have specific actions to be taken by "line" executives been established for the overall approach?	DY	Y	N	DN	?
4. Have the specific contributions expected of the staff been established for the overall approach?	DY	Y	N	DN	?
5. Have measurements been started on a modest scale? Are future measurements programme'd?	DY	Y	N	DN	?

appendix Q

Exxon management development program guide for new companies

This appendix presents an example of Exxon's management development program guides for new companies.

General

In some cases an already staffed company may be acquired; in other cases where a new company or division is established an initial staff must be assembled. In either case, top management is likely to be preoccupied in the early stages with meeting immediate rather than longer-term needs. However, it is desirable to move, in due course, toward a mature management development effort designed to meet the long-term needs of the organization for key personnel, and, ultimately, to become a contributor to Exxon's executive supply. Our purpose here is to set forth a series of measures designed to launch a management development effort in a manner compatible with the Exxon philosophy in this area.

Accordingly, for the guidance of a new company or a new division management we have identified and defined in this section the essential components of management development work and have recommended specific measures for getting started. However, it should be kept in mind in reviewing this material that management development is not simply a set of static procedures, nor is it a settled, unchanging doctrine.

Management development is, broadly stated, a way of managing. It represents an attitude toward how people develop as managers. It also represents an organized method for judging and improving the quality of the organization in terms of its key employees. Specific measures for carrying out management development may be grouped under three headings, as follows:

1. *Climate.*—A variety of measures designed to instill and maintain a favorable climate for the development of managers and to secure the involvement of all levels of management in the process.

2. *Administration.*—Suitable arrangements for establishing authority and accountability for management development as well as the provision of staff services.

3. *Procedures.*—A series of recommended management development tools and methods.

These are described briefly in the three sections which follow. In Section IV there is set forth a recommended sequence of actions for initiating a management development effort.

SECTION I
THE CLIMATE FOR MANAGEMENT DEVELOPMENT

Progress in management development is likely to become a reality where the following conditions exist:

--Where there is a regular supply of quality professional and technical employees with drive for improvement and a conviction that the company represents an opportunity.

--Where the various intermediate levels of management recognize that their own success as managers is significantly affected by their capacity to develop promising employees.

--Where top management regularly demonstrates as a company objective the maintenance of high standards of performance and promotion and a disposition to recognize and reward merit as well as deal with ineffectiveness.

Obviously, such a climate can only be generated over a period of time. We recommend the following specific measures at an early stage in order to begin building a favorable climate:

1. The adoption and promulgation of a management development policy that communicates to the organization the company's philosophy in this area. The sample policy statement is presented for consideration. It may be adapted for use in new companies or divisions.

2. Acceptance by the chief executive of a personal leadership role in the program. This can best be demonstrated by his serving as Chairman of the company's Management Development Committee.

3. The establishment of periodic management development reviews which fix accountability for management development on the same plane as reviews of operating results. This is particularly valuable in placing the management development effort in perspective. Such reviews will represent a principal means by which the chief executive secures understanding on the part of department and division managers of the company's management development philosophy.

4. The commitment of considerable top management time to the identification of developing managers, to the selection process, and to development planning.

5. Attention by top management to the quality of the recruiting effort which provides the managerial candidates.

COMPANY MANAGEMENT DEVELOPMENT POLICY

Policy

Systematic and organized efforts must be made to insure that the development of tomorrow's managers is not left to chance.

The development of adequate management replacements is a responsibility of each supervisor and is equally as important as efficiency, costs, and productivity.

Objectives

The objectives of this company in its management development effort are to:
1. Seek out and identify prospective management talent as early in the employment career as possible.
2. Provide opportunity and encouragement for present and prospective management members to develop themselves in all the management skills, and to acquire broad business understanding and judgment so that the full management potential of each individual may be realized.
3. Build an adequate reserve of qualified personnel for key management positions, both in this company and affiliated companies.
4. Fill key management positions with the best qualified individuals.

Administration

It is expected that Contact Directors and the chief executive officers and managers of Regions, Divisions, Subsidiaries, and Headquarters departments will take steps to achieve these objectives.

While it may be desirable for each Region, Division, Subsidiary, and Headquarters department to establish committees for reviewing the progress of its organizational elements, it is important that the line management not be relieved of its responsibility in this effort. Where such committees are established, the ranking manager or supervisor in any specific organization or locality should be the chairman of the committee.

The Compensation and Executive Development Committee has the responsibility of reviewing the progress of the Regions, Divisions, Subsidiaries, and Headquarters departments in attaining the objectives.

The Secretary's Department has the responsibility for advising all segments of the organization on the latest research, techniques, and methods in the field of management development and for issuing the necessary administrative procedures to insure uniform reporting of results.

Confidential nature of data

Since data collected and recorded in the reporting of progress in this effort involves individuals and their future with the Company, strictest confidence is to be exercised in the handling of all such material.

SECTION II
ADMINISTRATIVE ARRANGEMENTS

The following measures are recommended:

1. Establishment of a central Management Development Committee, as follows:

    Chairman——Chief Executive

    Members——2 or 3 Executive Officers or Directors

    (In case of small boards, it may be desirable to include all directors.)

    Secretary——Management Development Advisor

    Normally, the Committee's responsibility will include:

    --review and approval of changes in the organization structure;

    --review and approval of key appointments;

    --review and approval of executive compensation matters;

    --review of performance and potential appraisals, review and approval of development plans of key personnel and promising younger employees, review and approval of replacement plans.

    In the larger multi-unit companies subordinate management development committees will be desirable.

2. Provision for staff service. It is recommended that staff service for management development be assigned to the Secretary's Department. A qualified individual, either the Secretary or a senior member of the department, undertakes responsibility for:

    --advisory service to the Chief Executive and other members of management on management development;

    --provision of staff service to the Management Development Committee;

    --the development of suitable procedures and tools for conducting management development work.

SECTION III
MANAGEMENT DEVELOPMENT PROCEDURES

A variety of tools and methods are used in management development work. These tools and methods aim at carrying out successfully four processes which are fundamental to management development work:

1. *Performance Appraisal.* The appraisal of individual performance is undertaken as a means of considering how performance may be improved as well as an aid in judging the employee's probable further progress.

2. *Estimate of Ultimate Potential.* These estimates establish targets against which to plan individual employee development and provide the means for accelerating development.

3. *Development Planning.* By this means we consider the steps designed to assist an employee in realizing his full potential in a manner consistent with the needs of the organization.

4. *Replacement Planning.* By these means we consider the relative strength of the organization in terms of ready and forward replacement candidates for key positions.

It is recommended that a plan be drawn to install each of these processes and that the management development advisor arrange for training managerial employees in their use.

SECTION IV
LAUNCHING MANAGEMENT DEVELOPMENT
IN A NEW COMPANY

Up to this point, we have identified the essential components of a management development effort and defined their purposes. What, then, is the best approach to getting started in a new company or division? It is obvious that a management development effort must evolve over a period of time. The precise timetable for getting under way will vary from one company to another. The sequence of actions necessary to lead toward a mature effort may also vary. However, the following outline suggests a sequence which should meet most needs. In setting forth this outline, it is assumed that the organization structure has been established and defined and that organization charts have been prepared.

1. Assign an individual the responsibility for staff management development services.
2. Adopt and promulgate a company policy on management development.
3. Appoint a Management Development Committee and arrange for defining its functions.
4. Develop a schedule for the initial cycle of management development reviews to be presented to the Management Development Committee by the head of each department and division.
5. Following the completion of this cycle, arrange for a consolidated review to be presented to parent company representatives.
6. In each successive cycle, progressively broaden the program by adding features designed to meet the longer-term needs of the organization for key personnel.

The nature of periodic management development reviews presented to the Exxon Compensation and Executive Development Committee is set forth in the section of this Guide entitled "Affiliate Management Development Reviews." (See Appendix E for explanation.) This material will be useful to the new company management in establishing the pattern of internal reviews to be carried out within the company as well as in preparing for the parent company review. It is desirable to establish promptly a schedule of internal reviews to be presented by department and division managers. This will provide an early occasion for the chief executive to underline each manager's responsibility for management development and to achieve full understanding of company objectives in this area.

At the same time, it may frequently be desirable to move step-wise with the various elements of management development. The choice of starting point and sequence will normally turn on the nature of the more urgent problems. For example, in the first round of reviews it may be desirable to confine attention to performance appraisal and replacement plans— deferring potential appraisal and development planning until the second round. Similarly, it may be desirable to restrict coverage in early rounds to relatively senior levels in the company—moving to broader coverage in succeeding rounds. The ultimate goal, of course, should be a mature and complete effort which becomes a basic part of the manager's job at all levels.

appendix R

A case study of a diagnostic study approach

This particular organization is a manufacturing company with more than a billion dollars in sales. The top level consists of a chairman and president. The next level has three group vice presidents. Each has four or five general managers (referred to as Divisional General Managers). An outside consultant interviewed each of the above mentioned executives. His findings identified conditions which were deemed to have an important positive impact on executive continuity in the company, and conditions having a negative impact.

A special Task Force of key executives met with the consultant to work out a systems design. The Task Force discussed the factors identified by the consultant. They combined and clarified some of the items and then each Task Force member allocated 100 points to the positive factors and 100 points to the negative factors. This provided a way to rank the factors based upon the Task Force's judgment as to their importance.

The following factors are ranked in order of importance as determined by the Task Force. Several low ranked factors have been omitted.

A. POSITIVE CONDITIONS
Rank   *Importance Weight**

1. Dissatisfaction on part of top management with limited general manager resources in the corporation.

   22

2. Ambition of younger managers to become general managers and their perception of future opportunities in the company.   19
3. Some key managers have keen interest in general manager development and continuity.   17
4. Availability of a number of younger managers with high potential.   12
5. Some key managers are willing to push cross-functional moves.   11
6. Availability of in-house training and development resources in management processes, management skills, etc.   9
7. Existence of competitive compensation and benefit programs to attract and retain high talent employees.   9

B. NEGATIVE CONDITIONS
Rank   *Importance Weight**

1. Management climate sometimes interferes with development of general manager instincts. (Close review, second guessing, intolerance for error, over concern about mannerisms.)   18
2. Many managers do not regard personnel planning and development as essential to achieving profit and growth objectives.   15
3. Lack of sufficient cross-functional promotional movement.   14
4. Lack of uniform understanding of knowledge, skills, characteristics, and work experiences required for success as general manager.   13
5. Top management's deep concern with respect to general manager development and continuity has not been adequately communicated to all managerial levels in the corporation.   11
6. Lack of adequate individual coaching by superiors.   11
7. Insufficient objective criteria for evaluating individual performance and assessing general management potential.   9

---

* Average of the 100 points each Task Force member allocated to each "Negative Condition"

8. High potential young employees not given early opportunities to manage.   9

The design document, representing the combined efforts of the consultant and the Task Force, is presented below.

EXECUTIVE CONTINUITY PROGRAM
FOR THE CORPORATION

As a result of management concern over the limited general manager resources of the Corporation and the lack of management continuity through the Company, a Task Force of key executives representing varied interests and responsibilities was established to examine the problem, attempt to determine causes and suggest possible solutions.

The Task Force discussions identified a number of factors regarded as having a negative effect on our ability to develop competent general managers and ensure a continuous flow through the organization as well as several factors which were considered positive influences. The factors were weighted in order of their importance by the Task Force members.

As a result of these discussions and survey findings, the following objective was established.

"It is the objective of the Corporation to develop a continuous flow of general managers such that top management will have a difficult choice to make from two or three qualified internal candidates when making appointments to any general manager position."

In order to achieve this objective, it must be recognized that:

1. The identification, growth and selection of general managers is a complex and difficult undertaking and requires a "systems" approach. The elements of the System are important in and of themselves, but more important is the interrelationship among them.

2. A sustained effort is required. Results will not be achieved by on-off, start-stop approaches and periodic bursts of enthusiasm. Continuity of effort requires that the System become a part of the Corporation's regular way of managing. In other words, it must become "institutionalized."

3. Implementation must be seen as a *line management responsibility*, extending directly from the Chief Executive Officer to each executive. A staff contribution is built into the System's design, but this is secondary to the processes involving direct action by top management and each line executive.

The following major elements of the System are proposed as essential to achievement of the foregoing objective and the establishment of a system of management continuity.

1. Manpower Review.
2. Establishment of Specifications for General Manager Development.
3. Accelerated Recruitment/Development—Policy & Program.
4. Management Seminar.
5. Management-by-Objectives—Policy & Program.

MANPOWER REVIEW

The Manpower Review Process is the most potent tool in the entire general management continuity effort. It ties together many related elements, promotes diagnostic thinking, and stimulates planning and commitment for the future. Basically, it is an in-line review by one manager of a subordinate manager's status of and plans for his organization and manpower.

The purposes of the Review are:

1. To demonstrate top management's interest in and concern for the development and utilization of key manpower resources;

2. To stimulate timely attention to *organization* forms and needs;

3. To direct corporate and divisional attention to critical manpower problems and opportunities;

4. To develop a common understanding of the quality and depth of management resources throughout the company;

5. To secure commitment to the development and execution of plans for individuals and organizational units.

Division President Manpower Reviews will be held annually with the Corporate President, the appropriate Group Vice President, and the Vice President-Corporate Relations being present.

The Reviews should follow a format. However, they are intended to be informal to permit thorough discussion of the current status of management power. The reviews also provide an opportunity for higher level management to push for commitments on timely action.

SPECIFICATIONS FOR GENERAL MANAGER DEVELOPMENT

The Task Force survey revealed that one of the chief barriers to achieving general management continuity was the lack of uniform agreement and understanding of the knowledge, skills, characteristics, and work experience required for success as a general manager. The Task Force prepared the following specifications representing a "model" of background and developmental experience for general management:

1. *Education Background*
   The general manager of the future will have more than a technical degree and will likely be a graduate of a 5-year program which stresses liberal arts as well as technical education. He may be a B.S. with an M.B.A.

2. *Sales and Marketing Experience*
   He will have had considerable experience (minimum 3–5 years) in selling and marketing industrial products, either as an individual contributor or a manager, or both.

3. *Manufacturing Experience*
   He will have had experience (minimum of 3 years) in a manufacturing organization, including management of fairly large groups of employees.

4. *Administrative Experience*

He will have had experience (minimum of 3 years) in administrative or staff functions such as finance, employee relations, planning, etc.

5. *Mini-Business Experience*

He will have had experience in managing a mini-business. This may be a small subsidiary, a new venture project, or a small business group within a Division. A minimum of 3 years is required.

6. *Opportunity to Manage*

He will have an opportunity to supervise early in his career and should have had a significant supervisory job at least by the age of 30.

7. *Track Record*

The general manager of the future will have demonstrated a strong pattern of achievement and success in progressively more complex managerial assignments and will have consistently exhibited high skills in:

--selecting and developing competent subordinates,

--business acumen (sound business judgment, willingness to take risks, anticipate industry trends),

--leadership (ability to inspire, motivate, challenge).

ACCELERATED RECRUITMENT AND DEVELOPMENT—POLICY & PROGRAM

The recognized limited general manager resources and lack of management continuity throughout the Company require two approaches:

1. We must promptly recruit 5 or 6 outstanding young general managers (age 30–40) and bring them into the organization as assistants to top operating executives or as general managers of relatively small or medium-size business areas. This is necessary not only because many of our top functional managers have not had the variety of work experience required for a general management assignment, but also because our organization suffers from an insular or provincial history and needs an infusion of new ideas, new managerial techniques and new perspectives.

2. In order to ensure a continuous resource of general management talent in the organization, it is apparent that potential general managers must be identified early in their careers and their development accelerated in terms of the specifications set forth above.

Guiding principles are:

--a small number of individuals in each Division and Corporate Department will be identified who are deemed to have high potential for general management;

--stress will be placed upon early identification (about twenty-five to thirty years of age);

--individuals will be given accelerated opportunities to develop between the ages of 25–35;

--the program must have the interest and direct attention of each Division President or Corporate Department Head;

--the program will not be publicized.

MANAGEMENT SEMINAR

A Management Seminar will be designed to deal directly with those factors identified in the survey as impacting negatively on the development of general management continuity. Since the majority of these factors appear to involve inadequate communications or lack of common understanding as to Corporate management philosophy and objectives, it is proposed to give the top 200 executives in the Corporation an opportunity to meet and discuss management problems with the Chairman, President, and Group Vice Presidents.

A series of five such meetings will be planned for the fall. Where appropriate, prominent resource persons from leading educational institutions and management consulting organizations would also be invited to participate.

It is expected that this series will better enable senior management to communicate its management philosophy, expectations, and standards to a wider range of key executives throughout the Company and at the same time achieve a clearer understanding of how this philosophy is viewed several levels below the point of traditional contact.

MANAGEMENT-BY-OBJECTIVES—POLICY & PROGRAM

An effective Management-by-Objectives Program is of real value to the development of general managers.

Such a program requires that executives be results-oriented. Regular dialogues between superiors and subordinates about accomplishments contribute to accelerate self-development.

It should therefore be Corporate policy that executives be required to set and meet three types of objectives:

--Operating (Profit Center effectiveness),

--Relationships (Interpersonal effectiveness),

--Self-improvement (Individual effectiveness).

Effective objectives setting and measurement is difficult at best and the state of the art varies widely throughout the Company. For this reason, it is planned to initiate this effort at the Director level and above and so introduce it to lower levels in the organization on a gradual basis.

References

These references are designed to help the reader who wants to refer to the original sources.

Chapter 1

1. Holden, Paul E., Pederson, Carlton A., and Germane, Gayton E. *Top Management.* New York: McGraw-Hill Book Company, 1968, pp. 203–204.
2. Steiner, George A. *Top Management Planning.* London: The Macmillan Company, 1969, p. 256.
3. Drucker, Peter F. "The Need for Executive Development." *Advanced Management,* January, 1953, pp. 5–7.
4. Smith, H. Gordon. An unpublished paper entitled "Selection and Development of Top Managers," August 18, 1959.
5. Greenwalt, Crawford H. Speech before the New York Society of Security Analysts, September 7, 1961, an unpublished paper.
6. National Industrial Conference Board. *The Chief Executive and His Job,* Personnel Policy No. 214, pp. 9–12, 28, 30–31.
7. Holden, Paul, and others. *Top Management,* pp. 207–208.

Chapter 2

1. Holden, Paul E., Pederson, Carlton A., and Germane, Gayton, E., *Top Management.* New York: McGraw-Hill Book Company, 1968, pp. 203–204.
2. "Jersey Standards' Executive

Stockpile," *Dun's Review*, December, 1970.
3. Drucker, Peter. *The Practice of Management*. New York: Harper & Row, 1954, p. 114.
4. Sloan, Alfred P. *My Years with General Motors*. Garden City, New York: Doubleday and Company, 1964.
5. McGovern, J. W. Unpublished memorandum, dated December 26, 1957.

6. Mace, Myles A. "The President and the Board of Directors," *Harvard Business Review*, March–April, 1972, pp. 37–49.
7. Estes, Robert M. "Outside Directors More Vulnerable than Ever," *Harvard Business Review*, January–February, 1973, pp. 107–114.
8. Drucker, Peter. "What We Can Learn from Japanese Management," *Harvard Business Review*, March–April, 1971, pp. 110–112.

Chapter 3

1. LeVino, Theodore. *Managerial Manpower Planning and Placement*, an unpublished manual prepared for use within General Electric, pp. vi–1.

Chapter 4

1. Heidrick and Struggles. *Profile of a President*, private publications for years of 1962, 1967, and 1972.
2. Miner, John B. *Studies in Management Education*, New York: Springer Publishing Co., 1965, pp. 41–46.

Chapter 6

1. Drucker, Peter. *Technology, Management and Society*. New York: Harper & Row, 1970, p. 176.
2. Livingston, J. Sterling. "The Myth of the Well-educated Manager," *Harvard Business Review*, January–February 1971, pp. 79–89.

3. Berlew, David E. and Hall, Douglas T. "The Management of Tension in Organization: Some Preliminary Findings", *Industrial Management Review*, Fall, 1964, p. 36.

Chapter 7

1. Mace, Myles L. *The Growth and Development of Executives*. Boston: Graduate School of Business Administration, Harvard University, 1950.

2. Livingston, J. Sterling. "Pygmalion in Management", *Harvard Business Review*, July–August, 1969, pp. 81–89.

Chapter 8

1. Livingston, J. Sterling. "The Myth of the Well-educated Manager", *Harvard Business Review*, January-February 1971, pp. 79–89.
2. *Bricker's Directory of University-Sponsored Executive Development Programs*. South Chatham, Massachusetts: Bricker Publications, annually.
3. Andrews, Kenneth R. *The Effectiveness of University Management Development Programs*. Boston: Division of Research, Harvard Business School, 1966.

Chapter 9

1. Alfred, Theodore. "Checkers or Choice in Manpower Management," *Harvard Business Review*, January–February, 1967, pp. 157–169.
2. Glickman, Albert S. and others. *Top Management Development and Succession*, Supplementary Paper No. 27, Committee for Economic Development, November 1968.

Chapter 10

1. Kahn, Herman and Wilner, Anthony J. *The Year 2000*. New York: MacMillan Company, 1967.
2. "The 88 Ventures of Johnson and Johnson," *Forbes Magazine*, June 1, 1972, pp. 24–28.
3. Feinberg, Mortimer. *Effective Psychology for Managers*. Englewood Cliffs, N.J.: Prentice-Hall, 1965, pp. 375.

Index